Red
November
Black
November

SUNY Series in American Labor History
Robert Asher, editor

RED NOVEMBER

BLACK NOVEMBER

Culture and Community in the
Industrial Workers of the World

*Salvatore
Salerno*

STATE UNIVERSITY OF NEW YORK PRESS

*The Tie Vapauteen cartoons and graphics reprinted
here are courtesy of IHRC, University of Minnesota.*

*Published by
State University of New York Press, Albany
© 1989 State University of New York*

*For information, address State University of New York
Press, State University Plaza, Albany, N.Y., 12246*

Library of Congress Cataloging-in-Publication Data

Salerno, Salvatore, 1949-
      Red November, black November: culture and community in the
   Industrial Workers of the World/Salvatore Salerno.
           p. cm.—(SUNY series in American labor history)
      Bibliography: p.
      Includes index.
      ISBN 0-7914-0088-3.—ISBN 0-7914-0089-1 (pbk.)
      1. Industrial Workers of the World—History. 2. Syndicalism—
   United States—History. 3. Trade-unions—United States—History.
   I. Title. II. Series.
   HD8055.I4S25   1989
   331.88 '6'09—dc19   88-39378
                                                                         CIP

10 9 8 7 6 5 4 3 2 1

For my father,
Ben Salerno

Contents

Illustrations   ix

Acknowledgements   xi

Introduction   1

1. Historians and the I.W.W.   19

2. The Myth of Frontier Origins   45

3. Anarchists at the Founding Convention   69

4. The I.W.W. and the C.G.T.   93

5. Art and Politics: Anarcho-Syndicalist
   Tactics in I.W.W. Art Forms   119

6. Wobbly Sensibility:
   Conclusions and Implications   143

Notes   153

Bibliography   183

Index   213

Illustrations

1. The Battering-Ram of Industrial Union—
   "Yo, Heave Her"   6

2. The Masters Do Not Want the Workers to Organize
   Industrially   11

3. They Can't Keep It from Ringing!   14

4. The Sphinx: "How Little You Look To Me
   Mr. Exploiter."   23

5. Hell-Fire and Brimstone! They Are All Leaders and
   Editors   27

6. Viatonta Agiteerausta [Innocent Agitation]   31

7. Direct Action Makes Capitalism See Stars   40

8. Lavoratori! Diamo Ancor Forza al Braccio!
   [Workers! Give Me More Strength in My Arm!]   44

9. Sopimusten Kahleissa [Chained by Contracts]   49

10. Our Toast: "Let Preachers Have Their Heaven, Give
    the Employers Hell, and Take the World for the
    Workers"   59

11. One Ray of Thy Light, O Sun! One Stroke of Thy Arm,
    O Labor!   68

12. Oikeuden Lopullinen Uhri [Final Sacrifice to Justice]   84

13. The French Unions Are Infecting the Army
with Anti-Militarist Propaganda 92

14. Ford and Suhr Information 114

15. Silent Agitators 116

16. Wowie! 117

17. Parliamentarianism [Which?] Direct Action 118

18. You Are Robbed on the Job. Fight There. 121

19. The I.W.W. Will Fight to Uphold the Rights of
the Working Class 128

20. The I.W.W. Will Make It Hot for the Employment
Sharks. 133

21. Industrial Organization, Using These Two Balls,
Will Make a Clean Sweep Every Time. 136

22. When Will They Grab the Spiked Club? 138

23. Workers of the World Unite! [untitled graphic] 141

24. The Brighter Day 142

25. No Real Cause for Disbelief—Just I.W.W. Agitation 148

26. Preacher, Politician, Labor Leader [untitled graphic] 149

27. Mr. Block: He Shows the "Damned Foreigners" 150

Acknowledgements

The research and writing of this book was made possible only by the cooperation and support of many people. Their assistance, enthusiasm, and encouragement sustained me in difficult moments and guided me through the countless impasses I encountered in researching and recovering the I.W.W.'s past.

I would like to begin by thanking Robert Asher and SUNY Press for their belief in the potential of my manuscript and for their efforts in its publication. Special thanks to Peggy Gifford and Elizabeth Moore for their editorial work turning the manuscript into a book. The following persons gave graciously of their time and energy: Paul Avrich, Marty Blatt, Paul Buhle, Peter Carlson, George Carey, Robert D'Attilio, Ronald Creag, Sam and Esther Dolgoff, Charley Fisher, Archie Green, Jim Green, Anne Kaplan, Larry Kaye, Nancy and Steve Kellerman, Denise Mayotte, Eugene Povirk, John McGuigan, William Preston, Harvey O'Connor, Peter Rachleff, Timo Riippa, Dave Roediger, George Ross, Richard Schmitt, Willa and Esther Schneberg, Charley Shively, Barie Stavis, Fred W. Thompson, Arne Thorn, Dave Tucker, June and Diane Wiley, Joel Wurl, and Meridel Le Sueur. I greatly benefited from their knowledge and experience and their suggestions about source materials and people to contact. I especially want to thank all those with whom I corresponded—particularly: Chet Brant, Rey Devis, Bob Halstead, Joyce Kornbluh, Henry J. Pfaff, W. Dirk Raat, Franklin Rosemont, and Virgil J. Vogel—for the thoughtful letters and important manuscript materials they made available to me.

I appreciated the archival assistance I received during my visits to Wayne State and Labadie. My deepest appreciations go to Dione Miles and Ed Weber. I thank Candace Falk, editor, Emma Goldman Papers Project, for helping to find material on Emma Goldman. I especially thank Pietro Ferrua, Archie Green, Franklin Rosemont, and Fred W. Thompson for opening their personal collections and their homes to me during my stay in their cities.

Of the many people who took an interest in my research, several need to be singled out for their special contributions. Without the political and moral support of Steve Kellerman, my study would have never got off the ground. I thank him for his friendship, knowledge of labor history, grasp of the I.W.W.'s complexities, enthusiasm and insight into my work. Eugene Povirk provided me with many I.W.W. materials that I was otherwise unable to uncover. My understanding of the labor radicalism of the period was deepened through our friendship and his unparalleled knowledge of the literature and history of the labor movement. My long time friend, Larry Kaye, provided crucial intellectual and emotional support through the entire project. He read many of my drafts and tirelessly discussed the complexities of cultural theory and its relevance to historical and sociological inquiry. His insights into working-class culture and knowledge of sociological theory helped shape the contours of my study. My friend, Richard Schmitt, continually affirmed the importance of my work and gave generously of his time and energy. I greatly benefited from Archie Green, whose reading of my early draft gave my study direction and scope. I thank him for his sustained interest in my work and the generosity with which he shared his knowledge and expertise of labor lore. I also thank Esther Schneberg for her sensitive reading of an earlier draft of my manuscript and for her invaluable editorial suggestions. To Jim Green, whose patience and ability to convey the intricacies of theory and history are unequaled, I owe a special debt of gratitude. I am grateful for the care, support, and criticism he showed throughout the years of my research on the I.W.W. Maury Stein, friend and mentor, I wholeheartedly thank. Without his guidance and broad knowledge of culture and society, my project on the I.W.W. would never have been completed. Finally I give my deepest appreciations to Denise Mayotte, Franklin Rosemont and Peter Rachleff for their friendship, support, and interpretative and editorial suggestions.

Introduction

Although the historical experience of the Industrial Workers of the World (I.W.W.) has been examined by a great many writers, there is a need for a synthesis that examines the dialectic between indigenous and foreign (European) influences on the I.W.W. Such a synthesis requires particular attention to the role of immigrant-worker intellectuals, artists, and other rank-and-file elements associated with the I.W.W. during its formative period. This book offers an analysis of the cultural influences affecting the emergence and development of the I.W.W.'s labor radicalism and provides an assessment of the nature and extent of the impact of European syndicalism on the I.W.W. before the outbreak of World War I.

Concerned chiefly with establishing the indigenous character of the I.W.W., historians have uniformly argued that the I.W.W. owed its birth to an interaction between exceptional economic and political conditions in the United States and the responses of American labor activists. Such explanations of the I.W.W.'s origins fall into two distinct yet related theories. The first, developed by Paul F. Brissenden, countered popular misconceptions that sought to reduce the I.W.W.'s labor radicalism to a product of bad economic conditions unique to a particular period. Brissenden elaborated on the I.W.W.'s forerunners, stressing continuities in labor's struggles against capital. Melvyn Dubofsky, who developed the second theory, credits the responses of miners to changes in economic conditions in the western United States for the I.W.W.'s appearance on the labor scene.

Brissenden's indigenous forerunner theory acknowledged the European prototypes of the industrial form of labor organization in the United States. He argued that the so called new unionism, which the I.W.W. was said to represent, had complex antecedents originating in the British trade union movement in the early part of the nineteenth century. The I.W.W., however, was heir to European precursors only in the sense that the new movement shared similar goals. The main inspiration for the formation of the I.W.W. came from distinctly American sources. Brissenden traced a trajectory of influences within the American labor movement that began with the ideas of industrial unionism, articulated by the Knights of Labor, and ended with the Western Federation of Miners and its offspring, the American Labor Union, the I.W.W.'s most proximate and significant precursors. He argued that the I.W.W.'s appearance signified a continuity with prior attempts by American labor to build industrial unionism rather than the emergence of a new revolutionary code suddenly borrowed or invented in the first decade of the twentieth century. Brissenden also held that the I.W.W. represented a departure from past attempts at industrial unionism to the extent that elements from these diverse organizational forms and political sensibilities had come to exist within the same organization.[1]

Brissenden's theory is essentially correct in explaining the I.W.W.'s emergence as the product of a half century of struggle between labor and capital. His theory, however, is seriously flawed for its lack of analysis and underestimation of the role played by immigrant rank-and-file activists who carried European traditions of revolutionary unionism into the American labor movement. This omission stems from the many misconceptions surrounding the role and impact of European syndicalism on the American industrial union movement.

The beliefs, principles and tactics of revolutionary syndicalism were carried into the American industrial union movement not only by immigrant laborers who had contact with the European movement, but also through native worker intellectuals influenced by European syndicalist ideology. The basic weakness in Brissenden's explanation of the I.W.W. emergence, therefore, revolves around his lack of attention to the significance of the convergence between American and European traditions of labor radicalism. This neglect has broader consequences than the misinterpretations of the I.W.W.'s formative influences and has affected historical perceptions of how European syndicalism ideas were later expressed and their degree of incorporation into the I.W.W. principles and practices.

Historical studies of the I.W.W following Brissenden did not depart from his fundamental finding concerning the I.W.W.'s indigenous character; rather, subsequent studies elaborated on the relative importance of the I.W.W.'s American forerunners.[2] Of these studies, Melvyn Dubofsky presents the fullest attempt at a definitive theory to account for the birth of the I.W.W. Dubofsky reduced Brissenden's complex interaction of forerunners to a single source of influence. Dubofsky argues that the I.W.W. emerged out of a frontier activism indigenous to the hard rock miners in the western part of the United States. Their activism, which first formed the Western Federation of Miners, emerged not from ideas but grew out of their confrontations with changing social and economic conditions of the western mining industry at the turn of the twentieth century.[3]

Like Brissenden, Dubofsky also fails to come to terms with the contribution of immigrant labor activists as well as the impact of ideas derived from European sources by native worker intellectuals. Both historians make subtle assumptions that prevent them from seeing these influences as factors in the I.W.W.'s formation. Both perspectives—whether they locate the I.W.W.'s emergence in a continuity between past and present elements originating within diverse regional sources or in responses of workers to specific regional conditions— assume that the I.W.W.'s formation occurred within a closed system, autonomous within geographic, political, and historical boundaries. Nationalist or regionalist interpretations of the I.W.W.'s emergence are at odds with anthropological and sociological findings concerning the modern phase of America's cultural development. Theories resulting from research in these fields view the development of American culture as neither original nor indigenous but as configurations in which original native formations were modified and fused with elements borrowed from Europe, Asia and Africa.[4]

The autochthonic perspective on the development of social formations within the modern phase of America's cultural development was formed in reaction against cosmopolitan rationalism.[5] Rooted in complex attitudes regarding the effects of the "new" immigration on American culture, reactions to cosmopolitan rationalism indicated not only widespread perceptions of foreign influences as threats to the nation's identity but a desire to create a preserve in which the fidelity of American culture could be defended.[6] Reflecting a combination of nativist and isolationist strands within American politics, the auto-chthonic perspective has been consistently invoked to de-legitimate the penetration of European culture into American institutions and social life during peak periods of immigration and especially during and after World War I.[7] In arguing that the I.W.W.'s emergence was rooted in elements of the national culture, i.e. earlier American form of union-ism, Brissenden initiated a shift in the application of the perspective. In emphasizing the aspects of the new movement that developed independently of European influences, Brissenden counter-ed prevailing popular interpretations that sought to discredit the I.W.W. by equating its emergence with the work of foreign agitators and the movement's later anti-war activities with a German plot to sabotage the Allied powers. Such sentiments fueled the passage of criminal syndi-calist laws which led to the arrest and imprisonment of I.W.W. organiz-ers throughout the United States.[8] What began as a defense to create legitimacy for a movement under attack has ended in the complicated denial of the European influences connected to the formation and development of the I.W.W. in Dubofsky's attempt at a definitive history.

The I.W.W. cannot be considered simply as a foreign import or conspiracy nor understood as a spontaneous response to class struggle. Immigrants activists did play an instrumental role in the birth and development of the movement, and native activists self–consciously drew on the experiences of European syndicalists in developing the principles and clarifying the goals of the form of industrial unionism that the I.W.W. came to represent. Drawing from unskilled immigrant workers, disfranchised trade unionists, and a variety of conflicting political groups, the I.W.W. began essentially as a countermovement. The found-ers opposed the principles and practices of the American Federation of Labor (A.F.L.) and the reformist strategy of parliamentary socialism. Instead, they articulated a revolutionary form of class consciousness in a series of labor principles based on working-class solidarity.[9] Underlying the I.W.W.'s activities in the pre-World War I period were efforts to derive, from the diverse patterns of activity and sources of political and cultural influence emerging out of the international labor community, an associational context that would augment concerted action among workers excluded from or in conflict with existing political and labor formations and contain the potential for alliance. The I.W.W.'s early years were, therefore, characterized by a constant interplay between activism and theoretical development in which the movement's original principles were tested, modified, and redefined.

The problem of cultural interaction and influence in the formation of the political ideology of twentieth–century countermovements is virtually an uncharted domain within the literature on social movements, labor history, and left-wing political theory.[10] Lack of attention to this aspect of the I.W.W.'s formation and development, therefore, pervades the narratives reconstructions of the I.W.W.'s past. Rather than retreating from the ways in which countermovements attempt to make the complexity of cultural traditions usable in favor of current theory that locates the I.W.W.'s labor radicalism in responses to economic conditions alone, labor historiography and left-wing social theory need to be directed toward the ways cultural traditions, ideas, and expressions provide the integral dynamics enabling movements to develop.

In the period before the outbreak of World War I, the I.W.W. sought to occupy a terrain encompassing the revolutionary tendencies arising from the activities of fluctuating networks of labor, cultural, and political activists. Proto-syndicalist tactics gained through contact with unorganized workers and anarchist and left-wing socialist ideologies articulated by rank-and-file members were modified and integrated into the I.W.W.'s developing philosophy of industrial unionism during the period I define as its movement stage. During this formative period, roughly from 1908 to 1914, the I.W.W. drew from but did not imitate the proto-syndicalist tactics and ideology encountered in its contact with unorganized immigrant and native workers. Syndicalist ideology and tactics, derived in part from this contact but also initiated by the I.W.W.'s rank-and-file membership, entered the I.W.W. through the art forms and unofficial literature of its membership.

Continually in the process of formulation and reformulation, the I.W.W. did not aim or achieve a formal position on ideology, tactics, or organizational form. During this critical stage of the I.W.W.'s devel-

THE BATTERING-RAM OF INDUSTRIAL UNION---"YO, HEAVE HER"

Inspired by George Yvetot's influential pamphlet on direct action, the above cartoon appeared in the *Industrial Worker,* May 20, 1909, p. 1.

opment, new meanings and symbols, derived from the amalgam of anarchism, syndicalism, and Marxism, became attached to the I.W.W. philosophy of industrial unionism and were expressed through the movement's art forms rather than through official policy or literature. The revolutionary pluralism that emerged formed an associational context rather than a single ideology, a sensibility based on the emotion of working-class solidarity rather than doctrine, and a concern with agency rather than fixed organizational formation.

Few historical studies, however, have indicated the importance of the I.W.W.'s social and cultural presence.[11] The attention of historians has been directed almost exclusively at identifying stable, formal elements of the I.W.W.'s political philosophy and toward the institutional features of its organizational form. Overly concerned with identifying the I.W.W.'s indigenous characteristics, the predominant historical perspective abandoned the I.W.W.'s internationalism[12] and the overwhelming diversity of its activities for an arid formalism that merely catalogued strikes and debated the I.W.W.'s status as a labor union.

Analyses of the I.W.W.'s relationship to the European syndicalist movement have been equally myopic. The debate regarding the ideological sources of the I.W.W.'s radicalism began in the early teens yet continues to occupy the attention of contemporary historians. The debate, however, has been confined either to a search for the definite syndicalist text or to whether enough transatlantic ties can be established with France to warrant the attachment of a syndicalist label on the principles and tactics of the I.W.W. in this period.[13] The debate has ignored many of the principal carriers of European syndicalism into the American labor movement as well as the manner in which the I.W.W. expressed its affinities with the European syndicalism movement, that of the art forms improvised by I.W.W. rank-and-file members. The debate has, therefore, ended in a stalemate on the question of the meaning of the I.W.W.'s relationship to the European syndicalist movement and has generated confusion and disagreement as to the type of labor unionism the I.W.W. represented or whether the I.W.W. acted primarily as a labor union in the period before the outbreak of World War I.[14]

Although the I.W.W. ardently advocated the industrial form of union structure, it is inaccurate to regard the I.W.W. as primarily a labor union in this period.[15] Prior to 1915, the unit of organization and focal point of the I.W.W.'s activities were in the locals,[16] which in many instances were a far cry from labor unions. Scattered throughout the United States, the locals differed from region to region in form and activity. The range of activity varied from organizing workers into the I.W.W. to serving as contact points for I.W.W.'s and Magónistas fighting in the Mexican revolution.[17]

Though diversity characterized the forms and activities of the locals, a type came to predominate in the period before World War I. This type was the mixed local not tied to a particular shop or industry. In addition to representing a variety of occupations, the mixed local's members included seasonal and unemployed workers. Typically, the energies of the mixed local were divided among employment problems, issues relating to the status of the movement, and concerns of community and region. At times the mixed locals acted as propoganda clubs, opening their halls to speakers touring the region or providing a platform for Socialist candidates in local elections. The greatest concentration of these locals was found in the midwestern and western states.[18]

In addition to and as part of agitational, educational, and recruitment activities, the mixed local provided social and cultural support to itinerant fellow workers and community members. John Reed, the radical journalist who wrote for *The Masses* and *The Liberator* and helped to organize a pageant to promote the I.W.W.'s 1913 strike against Paterson, New Jersey silk manufacturers,[19] made the following observations on the social and cultural role of the mixed local in the West:

> Wherever, in the West, there is an I.W.W. local, you will find an intellectual center — a place where men read philosophy, economics, the latest plays, novels; where art and poetry are discussed, and international politics.... In Portland the I.W.W. local was the liveliest intellectual center in town.... There are playwrights in the I.W.W. who write about life in the 'jungle' and the 'Wobblies' produce the plays for audiences of 'Wobblies.'[20]

Reed's observations underscore the importance of the mixed locals as cultural and intellectual centers of the movement.

The mixed local, however, was not the only catalyst and base of support from which the movement drew its political, cultural, and social identity. En route to a job, strike, or free-speech fight, footloose Wobblies would congregate in the "jungles," camps improvised by hobos or I.W.W.'s, scattered through the United States. Some were continuously inhabited while others only intermittently. Typically located on the outskirts of towns and cities, jungles were set up in close proximity to railroad lines, near the intersection of railroad lines, "tank towns" where trains would stop for water or fuel, and along highways in the southern states and on the West Coast.[21] The size of the jungle varied with the locality and time of the year. In the Midwest and the West, jungles swelled during harvest time from camps of a few score to hundreds of floaters. In the winter months, jungles in the South and along the West Coast were set up by migrants escaping the rigors of the northern climate. Usually all who arrived were welcome, regardless of race or nationality; however, in permanent I.W.W. jungles those not holding red cards (I.W.W. membership cards) were excluded.[22]

The jungle not only provided a point of contact for footloose Wobblies, but also served as a social space where a variety of native and immigrant seasonal workers and unemployed workers intermingled. Some of these workers were indigenous to the region; others had left jobs in eastern factories, crossed the Mexican or Canadian border, or were part of a globe-trotting proletariat that had been following seasonal work from continent to continent.[23] In these settings I.W.W. members were recruited; information exchanged on job conditions, police, "employment sharks," and town officials; and strategies invented before venturing into the "slave market" to find employment hewing forests, harvesting crops, laying track, tunneling mountains or building ravines.

Commenting on the importance of the mobility of the floater in the jungle, a writer in *Solidarity*, the I.W.W.'s eastern organ states:

> The nomadic worker of the West embodies the very spirit of the I.W.W. His cheerful cynicism, his frank and outspoken contempt for most of the conventions of bourgeois society, including the more stringent conventions which masquerade under the name of morality, make him an admirable exemplar of the iconoclastic doctrine of revolutionary unionism....
>
> Nowhere else can a section of the working class be found so admirable fitted to serve as the scouts and advanced guards of the labor army. Rather they may become the guerrillas of the revolution — the francs-tireurs of the class struggle.[24]

James B. Gilbert in his study of literary radicalism concludes that in drawing from and intervening in the lives of the tramp, migratory and immigrant worker, the I.W.W. provided a context for the development of a type of social revolutionary who became the creator of a new culture contained in song books and expressed through poems, graphics, and short stories that appeared in the I.W.W.'s newspapers.[25] The art forms that emerged through the I.W.W.'s contact with unskilled native and immigrant workers and rebel tramps celebrated and politicized the marginality that came from living on the fringes of society. The celebration and politicization of the migratory workers' culture can be seen in anonymous cartoons, graphics, and hobo ballads such as "The Bum on the Rods and the Bum on the Plush"; as well as in many of the I.W.W.'s early songs, such as "Hallelujah on the Bum" (also known as "Hallelujah, I'm a Bum") or Joe Hill's famous "Preacher and the Slave."[26]

The diversity and mixture of native and immigrant workers that represented the I.W.W.'s western membership is supported by available statistics. These statistics suggest that the ethnic and native composition of the I.W.W. western membership was not markedly different from its membership drawn from eastern cities, where a higher concentration of immigrant workers prevailed. In the West, composition was divided between native-born workers constituting 58 percent of the membership, and foreign-born, comprising 42 percent.[27] Taken together with Reed's observations and available statistical information on the I.W.W.'s membership, it is apparent that the I.W.W. drew its radical sensibility from a mixture of cosmopolitan and rural experience. Therefore, attempts to locate the I.W.W.'s labor radicalism in a native incarnation of class struggle or as an exotic manifestation of a European revolutionary tendency merely simplify and dichotomize the complexity of the cultural sources influencing the I.W.W.'s development.

Although this fragmentary information testifies to the richness and complexity of the culture out of which the I.W.W. developed, an anti-tramp bias pervades the serious attempts by scholars and journalists to document the way of life of the I.W.W. migratory workers.[28] In studies and journalistic accounts that appeared between 1918 and 1920, the casual worker who joined the I.W.W. was pictured as a "rather pathetic figure . . . racked with strange diseases and tortured by unrealized dreams that haunt his soul."[29] Although the accounts by Rexford Tugwell and Carlton Parker reflect complex biases and testify to the authors' paucity of knowledge regarding the migratory workers' way of life, these studies continue to be uncritically cited to provide a false sense of the cultural dimension of the I.W.W.'s labor radicalism.

Elaborating on the findings of these researchers, Dubofsky, for example, simply embellishes these biases connecting migratory workers to the "culture of poverty," a theory based on even more controversial

The Masters Do Not Want the Workers to Organize Industrially.

Anonymous cartoonist satirizes state and local opposition to footloose I.W.W.. soapboxers. *Industrial Worker*, February 12, 1910, p. 1.

evidence.[30] Using the data to conclude that the I.W.W.'s membership was drawn from the "flotsam and jetsam of industrial capitalism's frequent shipwrecks," Dubofsky then draws a picture of the footloose Wobbly as a homeless drifter, brutalized and degraded by character-debasing employment patterns and lacking the benefits of normal sex. Uprooted, feeling impotent and alienated, they showed a "high susceptibility to unrest and to radical movements aimed at destroying society." The I.W.W. appealed to the disinherited, he argues, primarily because it offered a way out of this "culture of poverty."[31] In adding the notion of a culture of poverty to the unprovable assumptions and implied relationships derived from insufficient data on the casual laborer, Dubofsky increased the scholarly misrepresentation of the Wobblies by confusing poverty with culture and thereby denying the importance of the I.W.W.'s contribution to the politicization of the migratory workers' culture.

Dubofsky's flawed analysis of the culture from which the I.W.W. drew its membership is symptomatic of larger issues within the interpretative framework that has guided analyses of the I.W.W. The concern with mapping events on a national level to lend an institutional semblance and formality to the I.W.W.'s ideology and activities has overshadowed the links forged by the I.W.W. among working-class culture, politics, and social formation. The I.W.W.'s agency and activity on the local level showed fluidity of form and function, and the movement's reliance on oral tradition and art formed a diffuse iconoclastic ideology. These important dimensions of the I.W.W.'s pre-World War I presence have, however, fallen outside the pale of organizational history. In organizational accounts, the mixed local is tacitly acknowledged as a troublesome feature of the I.W.W.'s structural and organizational presence; the jungle, when not seen as a liability, is used as a romantic and colorful source of anecdote to fill out the dry details of strikes and convention proceedings.

A number of consequences result from the neglect of these sources of cultural influence on the movement. Many of the foreign language newspapers that emerged out of the I.W.W.'s contact with immigrant activists can no longer be found or exist only in fragmentary form in archives and private collections scattered throughout the world. Biographical information on immigrant worker intellectuals and artists who wrote for these papers is equally difficult to come by. The difficulty of obtaining biographical information on I.W.W. artists and essayists is further complicated by the circumstances of their existence. In a letter to Joyce Kornbluh, Richard Brazier writes of the pre-World War I artists he had contact with:

> We Wobblies were very restless men and as we were mostly migratory workers, were on the move continually....
>
> Most of us were only concerned with the present and our origins and pasts were seldom talked about. Not that there was anything shameful about them but it's just that we were more concerned with the things of the moment, the conditions of the day, and how best to change them if we could.[32]

Little effort was made to interview I.W.W. artists or essayists; most did not leave any remembrances of their activities. In short, there is an overwhelming lack of information regarding the activities and way of life of the I.W.W.'s artists and worker intellectuals, the floaters and rebel tramps in the jungle, and the activities of the mixed locals when its members were not engaged in strikes or related conflicts. The more insidious consequences of this neglect is the difficulty of recovering from this culture elements that acted as catalysts and sources of influence shaping I.W.W. pre-World War I identity.

A poem by Sterling Bowen, "To an Unknown Proletarian," underscores the problems encountered in documenting the culture and lived experience of the migratory worker:

> Where is the headstone that with wind and sleet
> Is scarred through having humbly born his name?
> Does nothing mark the end of the way he came?
> Nothing to tell us down what lonely street
> He went to die? Too tractless were his feet!
>
> From Fargo past the prairies, heart half-tame,
> He sang and toiled with reapers, not for fame,
> And there's no wake upon the billowing wheat,
> No; there's no wake upon a sea of grain:
> And he has vanished as the fires expired

Many Wobbly artists signed only with their I.W.W. numbers; others failed to sign their work at all. This artist signed his/her cartoons "A. Slave." *Industrial Worker,* November 21, 1912, p. 1.

Where last he camped, a harvester of pain.
So all I know is that a man they hired

For meager wages and a full distain
Gave, singing, all that life and death require.[33]

In this poem Bowen reminds us that the culture of the migratory worker lives primarily in the objects of their tasks—whether it is harvesting grain, mining ore, digging ravines, or raising beams—and therefore has little visibility within society. Bowen's poem carries no specific agitational or formal polemical content; its historicity cannot be established through reference to a specific strike action or formal political event.[34] Rather, the significance of the poem lies in its articulation of the workers' anonymity within the dominant culture, and in Bowen's appeal to the class feeling and experience of his fellow workers.

Appeals to class feeling rather than formal ideology is characteristic of many of the art forms that defined the I.W.W.'s form of industrial solidarity. This emphasis and appeal to class feeling is also evidenced in the poetry and songs which emerged from hobo culture and were appropriated by the I.W.W. An important part of this poetry as well as other I.W.W. art forms concerns the expression of a class consciousness that lies outside of formal political ideology. These art forms become political because of their opposition to the nonproletarian elements of the dominant culture and imply syndicalist beliefs. Sharper syndicalist expressions that incorporate elements of French syndicalism also appear early on in the I.W.W.'s development. French syndicalist beliefs and symbols were grafted on to I.W.W. poems and graphic art in much the same way that the music of popular tunes were used to carry the class feeling and experience contained in the words of I.W.W. songs.

Joe Hill, a Swedish immigrant and itinerant worker whose poems and songs came to be known internationally, frequently employed the symbols of French syndicalist beliefs in his work.[35] "The Rebel's Toast" provides an interesting example of the incorporation of French syndicalism while reflecting the language of the Midwestern floater:

If Freedom's road seems rough and hard,
    And Strewn with rocks and thorns
Then put your wooden shoes on, pard,

And you won't hurt your corns.
To organize and teach, no doubt,
Is very good — that's true,
But still we can't succeed without
The Good Old Wooden Shoe.[36]

Hill uses the symbol of the wooden shoe to refer to the tactic of sabotage popularized by French syndicalists. The term was used by French artisans ". . . to describe the clumsiness of scabs brought in from rural areas where wooden shoes (sabots) continued to be worn after they had passed out of use in the city." It came to denote the clumsy work of the sabot-clad-scab as an alternative to the walkout.[37]

Wobblies typically incorporated forms of symbolism, whether derived from French sources or popular tunes, to illustrate the lived experience of their struggle. The use and mixture of derived and inherent forms of knowledge and symbols by Wobbly artists indicate the complex nature of the penetration of European syndicalist beliefs into the I.W.W.'s political culture. These examples also demonstrate the important role played by art forms in politicizing the work and life conditions of the migratory and immigrant laborer.

I am not concerned, however, with showing how poetry or other art forms can be used to reconstruct the migratory or immigrant laborer's way of life or motivations for joining the I.W.W. Rather, my interest is in locating the importance of these creative expressions within the political, social, and cultural context of the I.W.W.'s development. Since it is beyond the scope of this project, as well as the availability of documentation, to consider the role and impact of artistic formations on all aspects of the I.W.W.'s development in the pre-World War I period, my study will focus on the aspects that involve the earliest phase of the I.W.W.'s cultural expressions and their relationship to the I.W.W.'s principles of industrial solidarity. The bulk of my study will be concerned with establishing the importance of the I.W.W. as a countermovement that drew from diverse political and cultural groups and will emphasize the role and contribution of immigrant intellectuals and other rank-and-file elements. After I have established the political and cultural context out of which the I.W.W. emerged, I will limit my discussion of the significance of the I.W.W.'s art forms to their importance as vehicles for expressing affinities with European syndicalists and to the meaning of their penetration into the early phase of the I.W.W.'s development.

CHAPTER ONE

Historians and the I.W.W.

The I.W.W. has been a subject of investigation and debate among historians, and labor and political activists, since its inception in the summer of 1905. In spite of all this attention, the meaning of the I.W.W. labor radicalism is by no means clearer or any less controversial today than it was in the early teens when the first major studies began to appear. The controversies that resulted from the early debates and research into the I.W.W. continue to occupy the attention of contemporary historians. Current interpretative studies and narrative reconstructions have not, however, resolved the early issues that surround the meaning of the I.W.W.'s ideological synthesis, its relationship to the I.W.W.'s activities, and the social formation that came to define the I.W.W. presence prior to the outbreak of World War I.

In spite of serious inaccuracies, current interpretative studies and narrative reconstructions persist in relying on an organizational perspective inherited from earlier historians of the I.W.W. This perspective, which dominates I.W.W. historiography, has resulted in the unfortunate consequence of attributing an institutional presence to the I.W.W. frequently at odds with its activities and philosophy in this period. Important aspects of the I.W.W.'s social, cultural, and political activity have therefore been occluded by this emphasis on a structural interpretation of the I.W.W.'s labor radicalism.

Early historians confronting the task of analyzing the I.W.W.'s labor radicalism encountered critical gaps in the documentation of the I.W.W.'s formative period. These gaps were left in the wake of an internal schism that immediately followed the I.W.W.'s inaugural convention. In the confrontations between hostile factions, materials and documents that had been preserved and collected over a ten-year period were stolen in October, 1906.[1] Since the documents were never recovered, the history of the I.W.W.'s emergence and first year of existence became a controversial matter, particularly the I.W.W.'s relationship to the native and European anarcho-syndicalist movements.

Unable to substantiate transatlantic ties between the movements and reflecting complex biases against the immigrant anarchist movement in America, early historians discounted the strength of European anarcho-syndicalist influences as a formative factor in the I.W.W.'s emergence. Early accounts were further flawed in limiting their search and analysis of these influences to formal affiliation and organizational duplication, a limitation which not only discounted the role of immigrant activists who carried syndicalist beliefs into the American labor community, but also denied the significance of the penetration of European syndicalist beliefs into the native anarchist and left-wing socialist community. Historians therefore advanced inadequate theories to account for the nature of the pre-World War I syndicalist movement while evading the complexities involved in documenting the I.W.W.'s formative influences. Paul F. Brissenden, for example, presented a contradictory and ambiguous explanation of the impact of the Confederation Generale du Travail's (C.G.T.) syndicalism on the I.W.W. He dismissed the significance of French syndicalist influences on the founders by arguing that such influences did not enter the I.W.W. until sometime after 1908. He labeled the I.W.W. syndicalist, however, and considered it to be the American counterpart of French Syndical-

ism, although he failed to account adequately for the factors precipitat-
ing such a sudden manifestation or to explain their meaning.[2] The
subject, therefore, continues to be debated among contemporary historians of the I.W.W. and will be dealt with in a separate chapter.

For the most part, historians of the I.W.W. drew heavily from the
then dominant perspective on labor historiography initiated by the
Wisconsin school of labor economics and trade union history.[3] Using
the school's method of institutional analysis, Brissenden and John G.
Brooks confined their attentions to events in which formal ideological
and organizational expressions could be inferred. These early historical
accounts analyzed the I.W.W.'s labor radicalism primarily through the
I.W.W.'s convention proceedings, strike activity, pamphlet literature
and official organs, considering their significance to outweigh the more
objectionable and controversial counterinstitutional and revolutionary
nature of the I.W.W.'s presence. Little effort was made to document the
cultural dimensions of the movement's activities nor were attempts
made to interview the less visible rank-and-file worker intellectuals and
artists who formed the backbone of the movement and from whom the
movement's earliest syndicalist tendencies developed. Attention was
directed away from the I.W.W. as a social movement that mobilized
oppositional political and cultural groups as a means of creating counterinstitutional formations that would serve the revolutionary end of
social reconstruction. Along with the shift toward institutional analysis
went the concern for the significance of the I.W.W.'s introduction of
artistic and cultural activity into its labor radicalism as well as the
significance of the I.W.W.'s contributions to the emergence of a proletarian cultural movement in the United States.

The earliest accounts of the I.W.W. written by journalists, labor
and political activists were equally incomplete and, to a large extent,
polemical. For the most part, they reflected concerns over the meaning
of the I.W.W.'s emergence and what it suggested about the new movement's relationship to anarchism and the European syndicalist movement.[4] In the liberal and conservative press, cursory notices of the
I.W.W. convention appeared as column fillers. Beginning with the
I.W.W.'s free-speech fights and early strikes, coverage varied from
accounts that discredited the I.W.W. as a foreign threat to the American
way of life to those that dismissed the I.W.W. as an essentially ephe-

meral and trivial social sore of industrial condition that would disappear with the next change in the economy.[5] Reformist and doctrinate socialists, threatened by the I.W.W.'s mass appeal and critical of the I.W.W.'s tactics of direct action, tirelessly admonished the I.W.W. for confusing socialist principles with anarchy.[6] Those sympathetic to the I.W.W. sought to rescue the I.W.W. from factional attacks and public misconception.[7] In the I.W.W.'s official literature, worker intellectuals criticized attempts to reduce I.W.W. labor principles to a single ideological source and emphasized the importance of working-class solidarity over particular theories or rigid prescriptions for action.[8]

These problems of interpretation and documentation grew in complexity and magnitude following the 1908 split and reached a peak when America entered World War I. In 1917, state and federal agents began raiding I.W.W. halls throughout the country in an all out effort to suppress the movement. Many I.W.W. halls, their contents confiscated or destroyed, were left in shambles. Hundreds of I.W.W.'s were arrested, many of whom were later imprisoned under criminal syndicalist laws.[9] Following the passage of these hastily enacted laws, the I.W.W. developed a defensive posture toward association with the European syndicalist movement. Yet references to and support for the movement continue to appear in the I.W.W. press in news articles and art forms such as songs, graphics and cartoons.[10]

A concern with reexamining the I.W.W.'s labor radicalism began in the 1950s. This interest peaked in the late sixties with the publication of a dozen books, ranging from biographies of the I.W.W.'s most prominent figures to an attempt at a definitive history.[11] With the exception of Joyce Kornbluh's anthology which provides materials documenting the importance of the I.W.W.'s movement culture, the bulk of this new literature merely reexamined the narrative content of the early accounts for factual flaws, embellishing and extending the interpretation of early accounts. These studies, therefore, did not challenge the formal economic and institutional perspective which dominated the early and official histories of the I.W.W. This failure to locate the I.W.W.'s labor radicalism within a social and cultural perspective not only resulted in a deadlock of contradictory definitions of the I.W.W.'s radicalism but also compounded many of the misjudgments concerning the I.W.W.'s impact in the period before the outbreak of World War I.

THE SPHINX: "HOW LITTLE YOU LOOK TO ME MR. EXPLOITER."

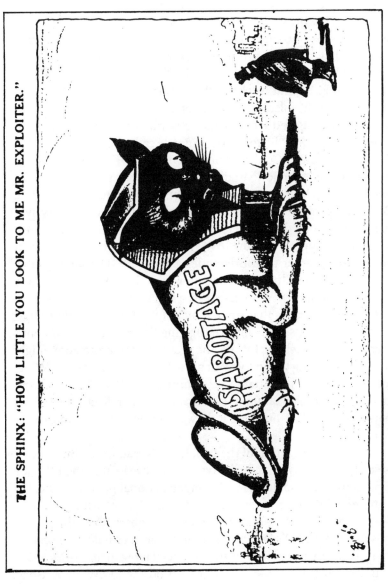

Solidarity, May 26, 1917, p. 1. The Sab Cat mixed French syndicalism with Wobbly humor. Its meaning ranged from the conscious withdrawal of efficiency on the job to more militant forms of direct action. The cartoonist suggests that the tactic is as old as exploitation but remains as vexing as the riddle of the sphinx to the capitalist class.

The problem inherent in using a strictly organizational perspective to interpret the social formation that contained the I.W.W.'s labor radicalism can readily be seen in this literature. Fred Thompson, in his revised official history, suggests that the I.W.W. did not really begin to function as a labor union until sometime after 1909.[12] Robert Tyler, in his study of I.W.W. activities in the Pacific Northwest, found that "only once . . . during the first weeks of the lumber strike of 1917, did the revolutionary I.W.W. [also] become an operating labor union, and this success...was fleeting and accidental."[13] Joseph Conlin, in his interpretative study, insists that "history has too neatly categorized the I.W.W. as 'revolutionary studies." Conlin argues that the I.W.W. "...was founded as a labor union and functioned rather well as a labor union during the years before World War I."[14] Philip Foner, on the other hand, claims that the I.W.W.'s organizational presence resembled the revolutionary syndicalism of the Confederation Generale du Travail (C.G.T.) and presents evidence to suggest that the I.W.W.'s relationship to French syndicalism occurred earlier than Brissenden believed.[15] The only notable exception to the prevailing preoccupation with the I.W.W.'s status as a labor union is found in William Preston's perceptive review of these accounts. Preston argues that since much of the I.W.W.'s early energy, leadership, and funds were spent struggling against the government's legal campaign to crush the I.W.W., the problem of interpretation might be settled by referring to the I.W.W. as a defense organization.[16] While Preston's point is an important one, limiting the I.W.W.'s activities to that of a defense organization does not adequately reflect the I.W.W.'s diversity in this period, nor does it draw attention to the complexity of its social formation.

A close examination of the conclusions reached by Brissenden in his study of the I.W.W.'s formative period reveals that the I.W.W.'s labor radicalism did not lend itself to organizational patterns typical of labor unions before the outbreak of World War I. The statistical information he compiled on the organization and membership of the I.W.W. demonstrate that the I.W.W. exhibited turnover rates reflecting organizational characteristics more common to social movements. Brissenden found that during the pre-World War I period the I.W.W. established approximately 2,000 locals and issued 200,000 membership cards. By 1915, the I.W.W.'s formal organization had dwindled to 15,000 members distributed among 150 locals. These figures indicate that 7.5 percent of the locals chartered and individuals enrolled in the I.W.W. remained at the end of this ten-year period. According to his computations, the average turnover (of both individuals and locals) was 133 percent.[17]

When the turnover rates of members and locals are combined, they indicate that the I.W.W.'s formal organizational presence amounted to a mere .02 percent of all those gainfully employed and .4 percent of all trade unions.[18] While these statistics do little more than confirm the insignificance of the I.W.W.'s formal organizational presence as a labor union in the pre-World War I period, they have also been interpreted to suggest a lack of consensus and theoretical clarity. Brooks, for example, in his early account of the I.W.W. blamed the fluctuating numerical strength of the I.W.W.'s formal membership on an "inherent dislike of organic restraint" among the membership and concluded, "No one uses the word 'organization' oftener or practices it less."[19] Others have blamed the transient characteristics of the I.W.W.'s formal organizational presence on contradictions between organizational and tactical theory.[20]

While these statistics underscore the transient and noninstitutional nature of the I.W.W. in this period, they do not reflect a lack of theoretical clarity or design on the part of the I.W.W. as is often assumed. They point to a long-standing neglect of a significant portion of the working class by craft unions, indicating a more widespread problem whose historical roots run deep and are of a more complex nature than the organizational failures attributed to the I.W.W. Since the I.W.W's major objective was recruitment of the unemployed and unskilled workers in job categories over which existing craft unions had declined jurisdiction, the fluctuating numerical strength and transient nature of the I.W.W.'s membership and organizational forms must be understood differently.

While these figures reflect the I.W.W.'s tenuous presence in industries abandoned by craft unions, they are not correlated with the high turnover rates in industries in which the I.W.W. struggled to gain a toe hold.[21] Moreover, the figures provide no information on those members who, as a result of unemployment or economic austerity, were forced to allow their dues to lapse but remained committed to the

I.W.W. Textile workers in Paterson, New Jersey, for example, were so close to economic catastrophe that they did not join in order to save the thirty cents a month dues; yet they were totally sympathetic to the I.W.W.[22] Paul Sebestyen, a Hungarian immigrant who became an I.W.W. organizer, presents another facet of the problem in assessing the I.W.W.'s membership in formal organizational terms. Sebestyen, known for his oratorical skills which included an ability to speak several languages, played a significant role as an I.W.W. organizer, most notably in the Akron, Ohio rubber strike of 1912-13, without becoming a formal dues-paying member. In an oral history interview Sebestyen explained:

> In Chicago [at the time] Haywood was secretary. And . . . there was a strike in Buffalo, and he says, 'Paul, you better go out there,' And I became an organizer. But as for being a dues-paying member, I never believed in dues-paying members, it don't mean anything. . . I never was a bona fide member, and I never left it [I.W.W.].[23]

These examples demonstrate that the I.W.W.'s membership was larger and less formal, its philosophy of industrial solidarity broader and more complex than the concern with formal organizational criteria or available statistical information indicates.

Irving Abrams, who helped to organize the first I.W.W. local in Rochester, New York, explains that the I.W.W.'s counterinstitutional emphasis was strategic and aimed at building the base for a revolutionary movement. Abrams described the I.W.W.'s priorities in the period before the outbreak of W.W.1 as follows:

> The priority...was agitation. That's what it was. The priority was let's bring the storm. ...The idea was as long as you had the footloose rebel traveling from one place to another, go to jail, and you could make a big noise. That was the theory that was underlying at the time, more than anything else. It wasn't the idea to build a labor organization as such, per se. The organization was into general membership. While we talked about unions, while we talked about industries, ultimately at that time, the slogan was, "Bring the revolution."[24]

HELL-FIRE AND BRIMSTONE! THEY ARE ALL LEADERS AND EDITORS

I.W.W. cartoonist shows futility of efforts by police and local officials to jail I.W.W. leadership during the Spokane free-speech fight. *Industrial Worker*, November 17, 1909, p. 1.

In contrast to the statistical information on the I.W.W.'s formal membership and organizational structure, Abrams' observations suggest that the transient nature of the membership and the movement quality of the I.W.W.'s organizational presence reflect not only a concern with mobilizing sectors of the working class excluded from the domain of craft unionism, but also with occupying a terrain for the expression of revolutionary tendencies emergent among labor activists. The I.W.W., therefore, appealed to dissidents who had rejected the community and politics advanced by political socialists and trade unionists. The I.W.W., wrote Ricardo Flores Magón, "is composed largely of men who have ceased to care for their jobs, who are rebels against business and have made up their minds to beat their way through life."[25]

The footloose rebel can not be assumed to be completely accounted for in the statistics on the I.W.W.'s membership. The footloose rebel was typically a tramp, hobo, or migratory worker who identified with the I.W.W.'s anti-evolutionary creed that opposed compromise or reconciliation with the employing class. Though these workers identified with the I.W.W., it is likely that many did not become formal members. Agitating in boxcars en route to jobs or strikes, in the jungles, or from soapboxes in the slave markets of towns and cities, footloose workers played a critical role by carrying and interpreting the I.W.W.'s message of industrial solidarity in speeches, songs and personal stories. Richard Brazier, I.W.W. songwriter and member of the committee that collected and published the I.W.W.'s first songbook in 1909, describes his initial contact with the I.W.W.:

> What first attracted me to the I.W.W. was its songs and the gusto with which its members sang them. Such singing, I thought, was good propaganda, since it had originally attracted me and many others as well; and also useful, since it held the crowd for Wobbly speakers who followed.[26]

"Hallelujah, I'm a Bum," one of the many selections from the I.W.W.'s *Little Red Song Book,* for example, gained particular popularity as an agitational tool among workers on the road.[27]

Little, however, has survived to provide a sense of the social space, context, and texture of the lived experience of the rebel tramp who created and carried much of the culture that animated the movement. Upton Sinclair's historical novel, *Jimmie Higgins,* and Charles Ashleigh's thinly veiled autobiographical novel, *Rambling Kid,* based on the author's experiences as an I.W.W., contain some of the few descriptions of life among footloose Wobblies in the decade before the outbreak of World War I. Both novels provide rare glimpses into the nature and diversity of cultural and social contact among I.W.W. organizers, hobo philosophers, poets and minstrels in the jungles, saloons, and flophouses along skid road.

In Sinclair's novel, the protagonist quits his factory job to turn to the hobo life under the guidance of his Wobbly friend Wild Bill. Hopping freight trains, they travel to the turpentine-country of the Northwest, stopping in mining camps along their way. Upon reaching their destination, the two men wander through the forest and stumble upon a jungle. Here, Jimmie Higgins, who had been leading the comparatively peaceful life of a home-guard socialist propagandist, meets another kind of worker. Higgins listens to "blanket stiffs" and rebel tramps exchange stories on the progress of the class struggle and argue over strategies and tactics. Heated discussions about the European anarcho-syndicalist tactics of sabotage and direct action intermingle with Wobbly songs that praise the unemployed and migratory workers and dignify their struggle against the masters of industry. Men around the camp fire talk about history, recalling the slave revolts in ancient Egypt and Greece. One man narrates how he managed to astound a family in a remote farm house by playing Rachmaninoff's "Prelude" on a badly out-of-tune piano. Though Sinclair's description carries romantic elements, it too is based on contact with Wobbly culture.[28]

In his study of homeless men, Nels Anderson interviewed footloose workers in Chicago's Hobohemia and in the jungles of the Midwest. Among card-carrying I.W.W. organizers and agitators struggling to form locals and organize unskilled and migratory workers, Anderson found the following pattern typical of their efforts:

Wherever he goes it is the mission of the "Wobbly" to sow the seeds of discontent and to harass the employer. Certain members go from job to job as "investigators." They usually remain long enough to start a disturbance among the regular employees, and get discharged. Agitators regard a long list of dismissals as evidence of success.

Agitators are followed by the pioneer organizer:

> Official agitators make no effort at organizing. They merely "fan the flames of discontent" and pass on. They are followed by the pioneer organizer, an aggressive individual who starts the work of forming a local. He is of the militant type and often gets no further then to arouse the men to the need of organization. Sooner or later he also gets discharged, which is to him evidence that he has "put it over."

A second organizer:

> ...follows the militant and reaps what they have sown. He works cooly and quietly in organizing the workers. He persuades and argues, but not in the open. The employer only learns of his presence when he has won over the men and is ready to make demands.[29]

While the I.W.W.'s activities did not always lead to formal membership or institutional forms of organization, the I.W.W. nevertheless had a strong presence as a movement during its formative period. Its strength lay in the movement's ability to reach a diverse population of immigrant and native unskilled laborers. The I.W.W.'s ubiquitous presence perplexed and frustrated conservative observers. Senator William E. Borah, speaking before a Congressional investigation in 1918, warned of the futility of further efforts to suppress the I.W.W.:

> You cannot destroy the organization that is an intangible proposition. It is something that you cannot get at. You do not know where it is. It is not in writing. It is not in anything else. It is a simple understanding between men, and they act upon it without any evidence of its existence.[30]

"VIATONTA AGITEERAUSTA"

Innocent Agitation. *Tie Vapauteen,* January 1924, Vol. 6, no. 1, p. 30.

Historians concerned with mapping the formal characterisitics of the I.W.W.'s pre-World War I presence, however, have been uniformly critical of the lack of stable institutional formations and have therefore disregarded the significance of the I.W.W.'s movement culture. John Crow, in his study of the relationship between the I.W.W.'s early ideology and activities, offers the following criticism of the efforts accompanying I.W.W. organizers:

Thousands of "militants" would go out on strike in a textile center
or a mining operation. I.W.W. organizers, if not already on the
scene, would rush to the area and start signing up members. The
workers would generally flock to the call and sign up with great
spirit and every sign of solidarity. The strike would run its course,
the I.W.W. usually playing a significant role. . . . When the workers
would return to the job, the union as a continuing force on that
particular job, would simply vanish. The only thing left on the
scene were some memories of the union's organizers in the minds
of the strikers of the union's organizers on the battle front in the
strike action against the employer. As an organization, however,
the I.W.W. was not to be found.[31]

Critical of Crow's analysis, Thompson has argued that the problem Crow documents is not peculiar to the I.W.W., but one faced by
labor organizers in general, particularly in situations where unions
originate out of strikes. Once the strike is resolved, the union fades from
the foreground and workers lose their enthusiasm for meetings, arguing
that they are only important in crisis situations. Thompson observed
that dues check-off, a practice the I.W.W. had never used, is a frequent
bureaucratic measure used to insure a semblance of organizational
continuity but is no substitute for solidarity. "It isn't that the I.W.W.
wandered away," he concluded, "leaving workers alone; they just quit
being members of the I.W.W."[32]
    Crow's findings are also contradicted by social historians who
have studied the culture and politics surrounding labor radicalism in
specific localities. James R. Green, in his study of the Brotherhood of
Timber Workers (B.T.W.) in the southern pine region of the United
States, found that the I.W.W.'s presence provided crucial support to the
nearly defeated Brotherhood. The B.T.W.'s appeal for affiliation brought
I.W.W. organizers into the region in 1911. Drawing on earlier indigenous forms of resistance to the policies and practices of the region's
industrialists, I.W.W. organizers worked to promote solidarity between
black and white timber workers and won a broad base of support for the
union among townspeople and farmers, thus allowing the Brotherhood
to regain lost ground and grow.[33] Local studies by social historians have
caused such staunch formalists as Conlin to admit the existence of

"many I.W.W.'s" which he now feels are "impossible to rationalize from the perspective of a labor union, or a revolutionary group, or an ideology."[34]

The organizational perspective, as exemplified by Crow, is not only faulty on its own grounds, but also fails to do justice to facts as shown by Thompson and Green, obscuring the real nature of the I.W.W. which Conlin dimly perceives. More than the enigma Conlin finds, the debate surrounding formal characterization reveals the many limitations of a strictly institutional reading of the I.W.W. Implicit to this reading of the I.W.W. and the debate it has engendered is the assumption that the consciousness of workers participating in the movement was reflected primarily through institutional forms. This is an assumption which the essence of the I.W.W. clearly contradicts.

The paucity of the I.W.W.'s institutional presence underscores a commitment to mobilizing workers in the circumstances of their existence, a concern which, given the needs and circumstances of the population the I.W.W. sought to reach, often proved antithetical to the building of formal membership. The overriding historiographic emphasis on the I.W.W.'s formal membership and organizational form, when not correlated with the foregoing, has only detracted from the importance of the I.W.W.'s presence as a social and cultural movement in this period. Moreover, such an approach fails to evaluate the extent to which the I.W.W.'s organizational presence pioneered forms designed to mobilize the unemployed, migratory, and unskilled workers abandoned by existing labor unions and the formal and alternative political parties. The organizational perspective exhibits confusion and lack of theoretical clarity by obscuring the I.W.W.'s unswerving allegiance to the large section of the proletariat condemned to relentless mobility and devastating marginality because of grueling industrial conditions. The I.W.W. unremittingly addressed the problem which craft unionism ignored and political socialists failed to ameliorate through reform efforts.

Out of the efforts of agitators and pioneer organizers, the mixed local emerged. The mixed local represented the I.W.W.'s early attempt to redress the problems encountered by organizers in their efforts to mobilize workers in industries that lacked unions or were plagued by high turnover rates. Though the Constitution made some provisions for workers who were not members of organized Industrial Locals in their place of employment, delegates at the I.W.W.'s second convention found it necessary to offer a resolution establishing this form of local. The mixed local, according to this resolution, was not intended to be "a permanent institution in the I.W.W." Instead it would act merely as the "the propaganda [body] that [would] build up the industrial union of the future. It is a recruiting station [only]." The change in the I.W.W.'s formally stated organizational structure to accommodate the mixed local acknowledged the fact that in many parts of the country I.W.W. locals were not sufficiently large or stable enought to warrant the creation of locals formed on strictly industrial lines. As the balance of the power within the I.W.W. shifted West, the mixed local became the I.W.W.'s standard organization form.[35]

Before 1916, few Industrial Union Locals or mixed locals had functioning industrial unions, though they were affiliated with the I.W.W.'s General Administration.[36] A far cry from labor unions, the mixed locals which came to predominate in this period engaged none-theless in a wide range of activities that broadened both the meaning and emphasis of the I.W.W.'s labor radicalism and combined agitation, education, and recruitment with social and cultural forms of support. Some of the mixed locals acted primarily as propaganda clubs, using their halls for meetings. At times, however, these mixed locals also provided a point of contact and refuge to hobos, rebel tramps, and itinerant fellow workers, some even contained "jungle kitchens" where meals could be cooked.[37] The mixed locals also became a base of support during labor conflicts and when authorities threatened the social and cultural activities of the labor and political community. In some parts of the United States, mixed locals developed into intellectual and cultural centers of the movement. Combining art and politics, such locals sponsored gatherings for the community: plays were performed; Wobbly poets read their work; and political debate on a broad range of topics, introduced by selections from the I.W.W.'s *Little Red Song Book,* could be heard.[38]

Between 1909 and 1916, these locals engaged in numerous free-speech fights in cities throughout the United States.[39] The early free-speech fights saw hundreds of I.W.W.'s jailed for their protest of city ordinances that prohibited soapboxing on public streets. Western locals also engaged in birth control agitation, circulating Margaret Sanger's magazine *Woman Rebel,* printing the first thousand copies of her "Family Limitation" pamphlet, and challenging the legal prohibition against its distribution. Locals eventually provided a network that sponsored rallies and meetings and generated support for the legal defense of birth control advocates.[40] Locals in California, Arizona, and Texas aided anarchist revolutionaries of the Partido Liberal Mexicana, with hundreds of I.W.W.s joining the Magónistas in the struggle against the Porfirio Diaz dictatorship.[41]

While statistics reveal the transient nature of the I.W.W.'s formal organizational presence as a labor union during the period before the outbreak of World War I, it is clear that such statistical information is limited in terms of what it can say about the I.W.W.'s identity as a countermovement. Statistical patterns and formal organizational characteristics observed, documented, and analyzed by historians do not adequately divulge the complexity of the social and cultural patterns informing the I.W.W.'s labor radicalism. The lack of analysis directed at the meaning of the I.W.W.'s turnover rates combined with the organizational assumptions and defenses regarding the I.W.W.'s formal status as a labor union amount to little more than a tendency to confuse statistics with cultural and social patterns. While available statistical information on the I.W.W. does little more than suggest phenomena that accompany the development of social movements, these phenomena have been construed to indicate problems that pertain to a different stage of the I.W.W. development.[42]

During the pre-World War I period of the I.W.W.'s development, a mixture of formal association with informal and diffuse activity defined the movement's social formation. The disparity between formal organization and numerical strength, therefore, represented a stage of development when efforts were being made to unite diverse groups into a single association. Herbert Blumer locates this phase of collective behavior as situated between the appearance of general and specific types of social movements.[43] Interpreting Blumer's distinction, Joseph Gusfield differentiates between directed and undirected segments within a movement. Gusfield characterizes the directed segment of the movement as "organized and structured groups with specific programs, definite ideology and stated objectives." While the undirected segment "is characterized by the reshaping of perspectives, norms, and values which occur in the interaction of persons apart from a specific associational context."[44] Applying Gusfield's distinction to the I.W.W., it is apparent that in its formative period, the I.W.W. was a movement divided between the achievement of industrial solidarity through a formal policy with definite aims and the provision of a terrain for the expression of broader revolutionary tendencies.

The I.W.W.'s formative energies were therefore spent in a struggle to resolve the tensions and contradictions arising out of its abandonment of the structural basis of craft unionism, while remaining open to the revolutionary tendencies issuing from the self-activity of rank-and-file activists. These efforts broaden the loci of struggle but also produced tensions and conflicts that led to frequent schisms and realignments. The I.W.W.'s formative period was an attempt to create an agency which addressed factionalism within the labor and political community while remaining equally concerned with reaching the submerged sectors of the working class. "There was no common ground," William E. Trautmann, the I.W.W.'s General Secretary and leading worker intellectual reported to the delegates attending the I.W.W.'s second convention, "upon which labor's hosts could unite for concerted action prior to the first convention of the I.W.W.; not a place where they could combine for the struggle against their common foe; and when the Industrial Union Manifesto was issued, an agency had to be found to act as this intermediary...."[45] The early I.W.W. deliberately set out to act as this intermediary. In the period before the outbreak of World War I, the I.W.W. drew its identity from its struggle to contain opposing tendencies within the anarchist and socialist movements and workers disfranchised from craft unionism. These aspects of the I.W.W.'s attempts at building an intermediary agency can clearly be seen in the movement's ideology of industrial solidarity and in the relationship of this philosophy to the I.W.W.'s methods of action.

The Preamble, the I.W.W.'s statement of its philosophy of industrial solidarity, stimulated intense debate among the participants attending the I.W.W.'s founding convention. The issue underlying the debate was summarized by Clarence Smith. Critical of the broad meaning of industrial solidarity implied by the Preamble, Delegate Smith referred to its essence as a "toadying" to the various political tendencies represented at the convention. Smith took issue with the following paragraph:

> Between these two classes (working class and employing class) a struggle must go on until all the toilers come together on the political, as well as the industrial field, and take and hold what they produce by their labor, through an economic organization of the working class without affiliation with any political party.

He then went on to say:

> It seems to me that this paragraph is intended to be such that the supporter of this movement can point to it when talking to a pure and simple trade unionist and say, "That is just what you want and expresses jut what you believe in." I believe it is intended to be such that a socialist can be pointed to this platform with the statement that "this is socialism." I believe it is intended to be such that an anarchist can be confronted with the platform and told, "This means anarchy as it is written right in this paragraph."[46]

The "toadying" to which Smith referred was in fact a compromise. Unknown to most of the delegates, this compromise was effected during a last minute meeting of Thomas J. Hagerty, the *Preamble's* author, William E. Trautmann, and Daniel DeLeon. The compromise was intended to reconcile the anarcho-syndicalism of the *Preamble's* author and supporters with the socialisms of the Socialist Party (S.P.) and the Socialist Labor Party (S.L.P.).[47] It was this inclusion of anarchist principles and tactics which differentiated the I.W.W. as a revolutionary force within the labor movement, a point to which I shall return in chapter 3.

References to which ideology best represented the I.W.W.'s form of labor radicalism, therefore, varied greatly. William D. Haywood, constantly in leadership roles, often presented contradictory versions of which ideology best represented the I.W.W.'s form of industrial solidarity. Speaking to a group of people in his small room in Greenwich Village during the Lawrence textile strike, Haywood was quoted by a reporter as praising syndicalism:

Syndicalism is just the simple, beautiful gospel of us folks that work for a living. Syndicalism is the power of all people to act in a body at one time to better their own conditions. Syndicalism is the creed of direction action by one big union of all the workers of the world. Syndicalism is the acting character of a real industrial democracy. It is socialism with its working clothes on.[48]

On another occasion, Haywood referred to the I.W.W.'s philosophy of industrial solidarity as socialist: "Industrial unionism is socialism with its working clothes on."[49]

Other I.W.W.s denounced what they perceived to be a "campaign of confusion" on the subject of the I.W.W.'s relationship to European syndicalism:

Syndicalist process denotes the logical evolution of the new social system—from below—out of the depths—building on the firm foundations of working class initiative and constructive genius and leaving behind the old spirit of dependency upon "authority" and "saving grace" of outside classes. In other words it denotes the practical fruits of working class awakening, of class consciousness, of working class action....[50]

The subject of the I.W.W. relationship to the European syndicalist movement will be more closely examined in the chapters that follow.

The I.W.W. was concerned with substantive principles and actions, not formal ideologies. "Tactics are revolutionary only as they are in accord with revolutionary ends," proclaimed the *Industrial Worker* (*I.W.*), the I.W.W.'s official western organ. "No exact formula can be set down as the proper tactic to pursue, for precisely the same action may be revolutionary in one case and reactionary in another."[51] The earliest official history, written by Vincent St. John, stresses a similar point regarding the I.W.W.'s position on tactics:

As a revolutionary organization the Industrial Workers of the World aims to use any and all tactics that will get results sought with the least expenditure of time and energy. The tactics used are determined solely by the power of the organization to make good use of them.[52]

"The I.W.W. is a collective missionary of social revolutionaries," wrote a member in a letter to the *I.W.* "As such it does not question the right of the toiler to have recourse to all means of emancipation from the fetters of capitalist industry."[53]

Beginning in 1909, the *I.W.* started a series of articles that examined the I.W.W.'s principles of industrial unionism. In the lead article of the series, "The Guiding Principle," the editor warned agitators and organizers against adopting fixed organizational formulas or rules. The I.W.W.'s success, the editor argued, did not:

> ... depend alone on the mere organizational FORM. .... Success depends on the united action of the worker, but it is not needful that the details of the FORM AND RULES of the union be always fixed or utterly alike. We must be prepared to marshal our forces and dispose of them as best suits the occasion and as will best defeat the enemy. The CLASS FEELING of the worker, and the previous experience had, together with a common knowledge of the ends to be gained must be relied on, if necessary, to take the place of any rules made before hand.[54]

The I.W.W.'s disdain for abstract doctrine, rigid methods of action, and formal organizational strategies initiated a complex departure from existing forms of labor organization and radical political sensibilities. The I.W.W.'s reliance on rank-and-file initiative, its rejection of the labor contract as a basis for its association with capital, its refusal to impose on its membership precise organizational formulas or methods of action, and its opposition to political ideology as a vehicle of working-class solidarity demonstrate the completeness of this departure. The I.W.W. pioneered new forms of strike culture and organizational strategy that extended the role and meaning of unionism. Its labor radicalism was deepened through songs, poems, and graphics that spoke directly to the alienation of the industrial worker. Through its art forms the I.W.W. was able to transcend the literalism which constrained the language of formal ideology, thereby bringing new symbols and meanings to political activity. Through these forms the I.W.W. inspired and animated working class subcultures, galvanizing and transforming them into oppositional forms of social and political activity.

DIRECT ACTION MAKES CAPITALISM SEE STARS

Industrial Worker, February 6, 1913, p. 1.

The I.W.W. built its oppositional culture through its contact with workers in the circumstances of their existence, mobilizing diverse and relatively transient loci of working-class subcultures. "There is neither measurement nor appreciation of this new movement," wrote an early observer following the Lawrence textile strike. "Year by year each isolated group gets new strength and confidence from the thrill of its wider brotherhood. Scarcely a week passes when some electric event does not furnish proof of these tidal sympathies."[55] I.W.W. agitators appealed to the class feeling of workers and community members through direct action rather than political ideology. The I.W.W. emphasized the mobilization of local radical culture and communicated tactics through direct action rather than through formal ideology or institutional structures. In one way or another, the I.W.W.'s methods aimed at subverting the wage labor system, the bureaucracy of social institutions, and the authority of the state. In *The Trial of a New Society,* Justus Ebert wrote:

> The I.W.W. is laying the foundations of a new government. This government will have for its legislative halls the mills, the workshops, and factories. Its legislators will be the men in the mills, the workshops and factories. Its legislative enactments will be those pertaining to the welfare of the worker.

The I.W.W. envisioned a new society that would be administered from the point of production by workers, ending forever the old system of government based on injustice and greed. I.W.W. members therefore struggled to expand the role of unions, seeing in them more than mere economic institutions to effect reforms of the capitalist system. The I.W.W. struck at the roots of the capitalist system, challenging the definition of American life imposed and diffused by government and business elites. The I.W.W. strove to find paths to a future society in which exploitative and authoritarian social relations would be replaced by solidarity and free access to social wealth. In this sense, the I.W.W.'s methods and organizational forms were transitional, preparing and empowering workers for eventual social revolution.

"The strength of the I.W.W. is not in its thousands of membership—," wrote the editor of the *I.W* in the summer of 1913, "it is in its revolutionary ideas as they are translated into action against the employing class and all its institutions. In fact, a large portion of the I.W.W. strength lies outside of its actual dues-paying body." The editor concluded with the following comments on the I.W.W.'s organizational presence:

> An organized body of workers is necessary to combat the organized masters, but employers do not fear mere organization by industries.... What the employers do fear, however, is revolutionary aim and revolutionary action in connection with the correct industrial formation.
>
> There is not an institution in society today that is worthy of being perpetuated in its present form. Revolution against all coercive or repressive action, no matter where it comes from, is the supreme duty of the worker.[56]

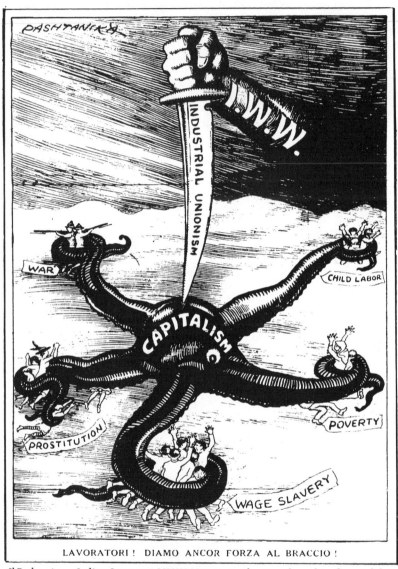

Il Proletario, an Italian-Language I.W.W. Newspaper, borrowed graphics from *Solidarity* and the *Industrial Pioneer.* The editor would usually add a caption in Italian. The above caption reads: "Workers! Give Me More Strength in my Arm!"

CHAPTER TWO

The Myth of
Frontier Origins

Historians of the I.W.W. have paid little attention to the I.W.W.'s immigrant influences.[1] Virtually every historian who has dealt extensively with the I.W.W. has located its beginnings in sources of American indigenous labor activism. It is problematic, as I have argued, to regard the I.W.W. labor radicalism as solely a product of native labor activism. The omission of immigrant influences as a contributing factor in the origins and development of the I.W.W.'s labor radicalism stems from the many misconceptions that surrounded the role and impact of European syndicalism on the American industrial union movement. This chapter examines the ascendancy of the frontier activist perspective and begins the ground work of rectifying the minimal attributions by scholars to the role played by immigrant activists and intellectuals in the formation of the I.W.W.'s pre-World War I revolutionary ideology.

The frontier activist theory of the I.W.W.'s development begins with Lewis Levine whose essay on the development of syndicalism in America represents the first scholarly attempt to deal with the subject.[2] In his essay, Levine attempted to debunk popular myths that either identified the I.W.W. as a branch of the C.G.T. or claimed that the I.W.W. owed its origins to a few individuals who suddenly decided to imitate French ideas and methods. At the time, the origins of syndicalism and its relationship to the I.W.W. were the subjects of debate in the popular and radical press. The neglect of the origins and development of syndicalism in America had led to confusion and lack of consensus on what critieria to evoke in assessing the relationship between the movements. Writings in the *International Socialist Review,* William English Walling blamed this confusion on bourgeois journalists and magazine writers. Walling elaborated on the differences between the I.W.W., French syndicalism, and the newly formed Syndicalist League of North America and expressed alarm that "the public, including a large part of the working class, [were] employing the term" in referring to the I.W.W.[3] In a short article in the *New Review,* Robert Rives La Monte criticized the differences Walling emphasized between the I.W.W. and syndicalism. La Monte argued that the revolutionary spirit of syndicalism was its cardinal feature which he felt transcended "in importance the mere organizational form" or strategy of its expression. Referring to Walling's observations as a "strange anxiety to differentiate," La Monte asked:

> If we can use the word *Socialism* in England, France, and America in spite of local differences of organization and tactics, why not syndicalism?[4]

In her essay on syndicalism, reprinted in *Solidarity,* the I.W.W.'s eastern organ, Bessy Beatty argued that the difficulties precluding an understanding of syndicalism and its relationship to the I.W.W. were not due to general ignorance, but to the nature of syndicalism itself. "Syndicalism in its form," she wrote, "is as nebulous as moon rings, in its expressions as varying as the face of a moody woman."[5]

Levine addressed the contradictory assessments of the differences and similarities between European syndicalism and industrial unionism by arguing that both movements appeared simultaneously in

America and Europe; the idea that French syndicalism directly influenced the I.W.W., he reasoned, was therefore an exaggerated claim. Levine held that the emergence of syndicalist tendencies in America could only be understood through an analysis of the responses of American workers to economic and political developments in this country. "In the labor movement of America itself," Levine wrote, "will be found the record of persistent gropings and painful efforts through which American workmen slowly arrived at the ideas and ideals known by the French name." The new type of unionism in the United States, Levine argued, occurred within western labor organizations, of which the Western Federation of Miners (W.F.M.) and its offspring the American Labor Union were the most important:

> Many circumstances combined to impart to the Western Federation of Miners that spirit which made it the bugbear of corporations and employers and the advanced guard of revolutionary unionism in America. The men were pioneers, hardy and self-assertive. They had gone into the West as independent fortune-seekers. The introduction of machine processes had reduced them to the position of wage-workers. The extractive nature of the industry helped them to crystallize their resentments; their hands were drawing directly from the earth wealth that enriched others. All these circumstances bred bitter feelings against their employer. The strikes in the mining districts of the West came nearer to real warfare than did any other contests in the history of the American labor movement. Armed bodies of strikers, fights with militia and federal troops, barricades, dead and wounded, bullpens—such has been the regular course of strikes in the mining districts of the Rockies.

Between 1902 and 1905, "the new idea of revolutionary industrial unionism, which regarded the union as the growing cell of the socialist society, was firmly established in the American labor movement."[6]

Shortly after the publication of Levine's essay, Ralph E. Souers, a sociology student at the University of Chicago, submitted a thesis that subjected the I.W.W.'s identity and sources of influence to further analysis. Building on Levine findings, Souers showed differences in the structure and infrafunctioning between the I.W.W. and the C.G.T. While admitting external similarities in ideology and tactics, he noted that the movements differed in aim. Souers went on to argue that, though external similarities existed, they were superficial, as the I.W.W. had minimal contact with immigrants from native environments where syndicalism had made headway. Though the first to suggest that the ideas and tactics of European syndicalism could have entered the I.W.W. through immigrants who had had contact with the European movement, Souers was unable to find sufficient data on immigrant groups he felt could have carried syndicalist beliefs into the American labor community to warrant further investigation of the possibility.[7]

The lack of data Souers encountered continues to present a problem. Migration studies have been overwhelmingly preoccupied with one phase of the process, that of immigration and its consequences on the receiving countries. Migration in the period between 1880 and 1914, however, was as much a transoceanic phenomenon as it was an intra-European phenomenon. Port of departure did not always guarantee port of origin. France's slow and lagging industrialization attracted many Europeans, among them Italians, Poles, Belgians and Spaniards. By 1920 France became the second most important country of immigration in the world. Between 1886 and 1910, for example, over one and a quarter million Italians migrated to France. Before World War I, between five and ten thousand Italian immigrants entered the United States from countries other than Italy each year, coming mainly from France, Argentina, and Brazil where there were strong syndicalist movements.[8]

In the nineteenth century, Germany supplied many more immigrants to the United States than any other country. In the early years of the twentieth century, Italians were the most numerous, followed by Russians and Poles. Relatively few in numbers, French immigrants were therefore not directly responsible for the diffusion of European syndicalism into the American labor movement in the period before W.W.I. Italian immigrants, working in mining and on track gangs or settling in large towns to become factory workers, constituted the most significant carriers of syndicalist politics and culture. Russians and Poles, who largely entered the needle trades, were also important in the infusion of syndicalist ideas, beliefs, and tactics into the American labor movement.[9]

Sopimusten kahleissa.

"Chained by contracts." *Tie Vapauteen,* December 1922, Vol. 4, No. 2, p. 11. Finnish militants in Duluth, Minnesota, who affiliated with the I.W.W. in 1914, carried on an active propaganda in support of anarcho-syndicalism in *Tie Vapauteen* (Road to Freedom), a monthly journal, well into the 1920s.[10]

Italian and Spanish anarchists in Paterson, New Jersey, for example, leaned toward a workers' union organizational model based on anarcho-syndicalism well in advance of the I.W.W. inaugural convention. In the pages of the "Right to Existence" group's organ, *La Questione Social* (L.Q.S.), appeared many articles reporting on the European revolutionary syndicalist movement as well as appeals to striking silk workers to adopt syndicalist tactics in their struggles against manufacturing magnates. George Carey's study of the Paterson anarchists demonstrate the group's important role in the dissemination of European syndicalist politics and culture to the western part of the United States.[11]

Under the direction of the Spanish anarchist, Pedro Esteve, the Paterson group became involved with the struggles of both soft and hard rock miners in Colorado, sending monetary support and publicizing their struggles in the pages of *L.Q.S.* "Esteve and other Paterson anarchists," Carey wrote, "spent months out West working on union forming activities" with the W.F.M. and the United Mine Workers contributing to "the thrust that saw the I.W.W. founded."[12]

In 1902, Esteve began a tour of mining communities in the western and eastern states to help in propaganda and organizational activities, hoping to develop and expand contacts of the Paterson group. By the time of the I.W.W. founding convention *L.Q.S.*'s readership reached from Colorado to New Castle, Pennsylvania. The paper regularly ran articles from western correspondents which reported on the struggles of coal and metal miners and resulted in a permanent column entitled "From the Mining World." On May Day, 1903, along with strike news from Colorado, appeared the beginnings of a two-part article on the anarcho-syndicalist idea of the general strike as a prime weapon of revolutionary struggle.[13]

In Paterson, the group formed the Universita Populare, which organized public lectures, discussions, social gatherings, and study groups. Eventually, a series entitled Libreria Sociologica was introduced to expand the group's publications. The Libreria Sociologica made available inexpensive Italian editions of works by such anarchist thinkers and activists as Elisee Reclus, Peter Kropotkin, Errico Malatesta, Saverio Merlino, Michael Bakunin, and Johann Most.[14]

Among these anarchists, Johann Most played a seminal role in the origins and development of American syndicalism. Born in Augsburg in 1846, Most's contact with revolutionary politics began in Switzerland among a group of socialist workmen. In his teens he joined the Zurich section of the International Working Men's Association and began his career as a socialist agitator. Leaving Zurich for Vienna in 1868, his agitational activities led to arrest and imprisonment. Following his release he set out on an extended propaganda tour. Banished from France following the outbreak of the Paris Commune, Most returned to Germany to take an active part in the unfolding socialist movement. During the next seven years, he worked as an organizer, edited several socialist papers, and wrote pamphlets and labor songs. Following the passage of the Bismark anti-socialist laws, he was expelled from Germany. Emigrating to London, he made contact with other fugitive radicals and launched the *Freiheit.*[15]

Between 1879 and 1880, the *Freiheit* shifted from a socialist to an anarchist perspective, becoming the most uninhibited radical newspaper of the day. In its pages, Most called for the violent destruction of capitalism, the state, and all repressive insitutions. An article on the assassination of Czar Alexander II, which not only glorified the act but encouraged others to emulate it, led to his arrest and imprisonment. Following his release, he received an invitation to undertake a lecture tour in the United States from the New York Social Revolutionary Club. Most accepted the invitation and decided to transfer the *Freiheit* to New York and resettle in America.[16]

Arriving in America, Most became involved with the social revolutionary movement and, more than any individual, was responsible for its growth. Drafting the *Pittsburg Manifesto,* which established the International Working People's Association (the Black International), Most galvanized the social revolutionary movement. Most and his followers objected to any form of compromise with existing institutions and declared their opposition to trade unions and their struggle for immediate economic gain. But under the leadership of Albert Parsons and August Spies, there emerged opposition among native, German, French, and Bohemanian sections of the movement to Most's position on the trade union question. Despite their agreement with Most and his supporters about the futility of the ballot and the need for armed insurrection to overthrow the established order, the midwestern social revolutionaries advanced the idea that unions constituted the instrument of social revolution and would eventually replace capitalism with a cooperative commonwealth in which workers would administer the economy for their own needs. Endorsed by a majority of delegates attending the Pittsburg congress, the "Chicago idea" represented an amalgam of socialist, anarchist, and other radical ideas derived from both American and European traditions.[17] Though lacking the ideas of the general strike and sabotage which had not yet achieved theoretical development, the "Chicago idea" anticipated by some twenty years the doctrine of anarcho-syndicalism.[18]

The ideas which formed the basis of anarcho-syndicalism, however, did not originate with Parsons and his supporters. In the 1860s and 1870s Michael Bakunin, Pierre-Joseph Proudhon, and other libertarians associated with the First International originally proposed the formation of workers' associations, both as a weapon of class struggle and as the structural basis of the cooperative commonwealth. Initiated by the libertarian wing of the First International, the modern revolutionary syndicalist movement superseded earlier national versions of syndicalism that had developed among the Owenites in the 1830's, making it no longer possible to connect or identify syndicalist belief systems with a specific or indigenous locality. Christian Cornelissen was the first to argue that although the French working class is credited with the organized expression of revolutionary syndicalism, the ideas which formed the basis of the movement did not originate with the worker intellectuals responsible for the birth of C.G.T. The ideas which formed the basis of revolutionary syndicalism began with the International's congress at Basel (1869), Cornelissen argued, and were later elaborated during international congresses that met in Brussels (1891), Zurich (1893) and London (1896).[19] In spite of the acknowledgment by James Guillaume, historian of the First International and colleague of Bakunin, of the importance of the First International to the birth of the revolutionary syndicalist movement ["What is the C.G.T. if not the continuation of the First International?"][20] no effort was made to generate a theory that located the origin of the syndicalist movement in the same source.[21]

A belief system that grew out of the lived experience of the international proletariat, syndicalism did not follow a straight line of development. "The movement," wrote the secretary of the C.G.T., "is characterized by much incoherence; it brims with inconsistency. It is thus because it is not the result of actions performed in accordance with specific dogmas but because it is a product of life, modified and renewed from day to day."[22] Syndicalist ideas were passed by word of mouth, occasionally appearing in newspapers, and became the inspiration for songs, speeches, poetry, and graphics. Rather than representing a closed system of ideas, a definite philosophy or theory, syndicalism was a belief that found expression in the struggles, social activity and cultural forms of the international proletariat. The ideas and expressions of syndicalist patterns of activity were not the result of national characteristics, but part of a common cultural sphere. These expressions took on different forms in different countries, due to the diversity in external living conditions and not to inborn national characteristics. The modern form of revolutionary syndicalism spread through intricate patterns of "cross fertilization" that traveled between the continents.[23]

The complexity of these patterns of "cross fertilization" can be seen in Most's later activities. In the middle nineties, when the syndicalist movement in France attracted worldwide attention following the conferences at Limoges (1895) and Tours (1896), Most made himself spokesperson of the new movement. Through the *Freiheit*, which he edited for twenty-seven years, Most introduced German and Russian immigrants in the needle, brewery, and building trades to the movement's ideas and tactics. Seeing in the European syndicalist movement "the practical form of organization for the realization of communist-anarchism," Most published all the leaflet literature available at the time. In the *Freiheit* appeared the writings of Pelloutier, Pouget, Pierrot, John Turner, S. Nacht (Arnold Roller), Victor Dave, and others making propaganda for the syndicalist movement. Johann Most expressed enthusiasm for the I.W.W., but died before the I.W.W. had gone through its first year.[24]

The manifold origins of American syndicalism and the relationship of the I.W.W. to the European revolutionary syndicalist movements continued to be ignored in the accounts that followed the work of Levine and Souers. Partisan and journalistic accounts of the I.W.W. like those of John Spargo and Andre Tridone, though suggestive of the manifold origins of American syndicalism, were riddled with inaccuracies. Neither account discussed the importance of the "Chicago idea" or the contributions of immigrant activists to the birth of the industrial union movement. Both accounts merely dichotomized the American and European movements, discussing similarities and differences between European syndicalism and the I.W.W.[25] Paul F. Brissenden's study published in the fall of 1913, was the first comprehensive scholarly account of the I.W.W.'s formative period. In it Brissenden made an oblique attempt at addressing the complexities of the I.W.W.'s immigrant influences. In this initial study, he characterized the I.W.W. as the American counterpart of the C.G.T. He argued that revolutionary industrial unionism more accurately expressed in English what was implicit in the French term. Brissenden felt that syndicalism expressed "the most modern phase of the revolutionary movement." Though he argued that the I.W.W.'s conception of industrial unionism "consist[ed] of a synthesis of the Socialist indictment of capitalism and part of the Socialist programme, the anarchist method and idea, and the unionist idea of organization," he stressed the I.W.W.'s socialist origins. He made no attempt to show or elaborate on immigrant anarchist influences in the industrial union movement. Instead, he attributed the emergence of the I.W.W.'s form of labor radicalism to earlier American labor organizations expressing a revolutionary socialist character and militant industrial form.[26] "The I.W.W.'s organization," he later concluded, "is an indigenous American product, if ever there was such a thing."[27]

Though Brissenden considered the W.F.M.'s dramatic strikes at Coeur d'Alene, Cripple Creek, Telluride, and Idaho Springs "as the birth signs of the coming industrial unionism of the I.W.W.," he failed to elaborate on the maze of influences responsible for the W.F.M.'s labor activism.[28] Stressing the W.F.M. as chief among the I.W.W.'s predecessors, Brissenden included other forerunners in his explanation of the I.W.W.'s emergence while ignoring the importance of the immigrant anarchist movement to the development of an American form of syndicalism. Considering the efforts of the Haymarket anarchists a liability,[29] Brissenden argued that other forerunners were primarily responsible for the development of the I.W.W.'s revolutionary industrial unionism. Among those antecedents named by Brissenden were the Brewery Workmen's Union (B.W.U.), for its model of "the correct thing in labor union structure"; and the Socialist Trade and Labor Alliance (S.T.&L.A.) which, in the decade before the I.W.W.'s emergence, had exhibited "a militant socialist union organization on industrial lines."[30]

Following Brissenden's study, historians continued to stress the responses of western miners to industrial conditions in their explanations of the I.W.W.'s emergence. Writing in 1934, Travers Clements and Lillian Symes asserted that the I.W.W.'s beginnings were thoroughly native. The I.W.W. grew out of:

> ...conditions—not theories—and was primarily the expression of that vague, passionate, rowdy, undisciplined spirit of protest that was beginning to make itself heard among the unskilled proletarian substratum ignored by the official labor movement, among the hard fighting Western miners, still imbued with the direct-actionist traditions of the frontier.[31]

Charles and Mary Beard, in *The Rise of American Civilization,* concluded that the I.W.W. "arose from the peculiar labor conditions of the far West." Foster Rhea Dulles argued that the radicalism of the I.W.W. came more from western workers than foreign-born eastern groups. The eastern groups, he wrote, "were not as rough and ready as the Western miners." Louis M. Hacker and Benjamin Kendrick wrote that the I.W.W. "was an indigenous movement, growing out of a particular American situation, for it had its roots and flourished in the labor camps of the western country. . . ."[32]

Donald Barnes first questioned the validity of the frontier activism theory. In his study on the I.W.W.'s ideology, Barnes argued that references to conditions only begged the question of ideological conviction. While "anti-social emotions penetrated both the leadership and the rank and file of the I.W.W.," he wrote, "those anti-social convictions received expression in a radical ideology which in turn influenced the entire Wobbly movement. The use of industrial conditions alone, or a combination of these with psychological traits, to explain the movement and the devotion of its members presupposes a deterministic epistemology. . . ."[33]

Barnes' conclusion, however, did not spark an interpretive study calling into question the romanticized view of the western miners' role in the birth of the industrial union movement. In spite of Barnes' conclusion, the possibility of more complex sources of influences informing the I.W.W.'s emergence was not addressed. Melvyn Dubofsky, in his attempt at a definitive history, merely elaborated on the theory of frontier activism. His study presents the fullest argument for locating the I.W.W.'s emergence in indigenous labor activism resulting from mining conditions in the western part of the United States at the turn of the twentieth century.

In *We Shall Be All,* Dubofsky argued that the origins of the I.W.W. are best understood in terms of the responses of hard rock miners (who eventually formed the W.F.M.) to conditions in the area of the United States that stretched from "the northern Rockies to the Mexican border, and particularly in the states of Colorado, Idaho and Montana. Nowhere in the late nineteenth century," Dubofsky wrote, "were economic and social changes which produced reform and radicalism so rapid and unsettling as in the mining West." Industrial cities replaced boom camps, corporations displaced grubstaking prospectors, and a handicraft economy changed into one based on machine production.[34]

The western miners who confronted this evolving "urban industrial frontier," whether American or foreign-born, were "first generation
immigrant" to the new industrial environment. The western workers,
who would later form the I.W.W., "mirrored the perplexities and confusion, the strivings and ambitions of a generation compelled to contend
with a world it had never made."[35] Their radicalism responded to the
modernization and corporatization of western mining conditions, der-
iving directly from economic and social conditions. Changes in job
classification which diluted skills, company stores, saloons, and board-
ing houses which charged noncompetitive prices and business interests
that manipulated local, state, and federal authorities and police agencies pushed miners toward militant action.

As national corporations replaced local enterprise, local management lost authority to determine ultimate labor policy. Workers and
union negotiators were caught between local agents and home offices.
"This divorce between ownership and local management, this geogra-
phical gulf between worker and ultimate employer, led to violent
industrial conflicts. . . ." In the ten year period between 1894 and 1904,
Western miners struggled to build a new form of industrial organization
against opposition from their capitalist adversaries. Miners clashed in
battles with private armies marshalled by mine owners at Cripple Creek,
Leadville, Coeur d'Alenes, and Colorado City. "From the fires of these
ashes," Dubofsky asserts, "emerged the radicals who ultimately founded
the I.W.W."[36]

In his study Dubofsky found all the ideology and tactics which
came to represent the I.W.W.'s form of labor radicalism to have originated among frontier activists. The distinguishing traits of the I.W.W.,
Dubofsky asserts

> ...had been formed in the American West by 1903. The combina-
> tion of industrial unionism, solidarity, political nonpartisanship,
> direct action and syndicalism so characteristic of the I.W.W. had
> already been subscribed to by the W.F.M. and its offspring, the
> American Labor union.

Dubofsky supports his exaggerated emphasis on frontier activism with
the contention that "no professed anarchist or known syndicalist

received the letter [of invitation to the I.W.W.'s founding convention]." Evidence, he argues, that the document that contained the kernel of what later became the I.W.W.'s syndicalist ideology originated among frontier activists.[37]

Dubofsky's elaborate reiteration of the indigenous frontier activism theory to explain the I.W.W. labor radicalism was harshly criticized for its economic determinism. William Preston, in his review of the revival literature, argued that Dubofsky's use of frontier activism reduced the I.W.W. labor radicalism to a product of bad conditions. Such a "social sore" theory, Preston held, assumes that labor radicalism is presumably the product of unique conditions peculiar to a particular period. Radicalism, however, has been endemic to the uneven distribution of wealth throughout American history.

> It seems unreasonable [he wrote] to assert that:...the I.W.W. was the first generation to deal with industrialism or "a world it never made." Given the nature of capitalism, every generation...has faced problems of blocked mobility, economic exploitation, status anxiety and political powerlessness....Historians admit that neither the ideas or tactics of the I.W.W. were, in general, new ones. This suggests a continuity and in the protest against... [exploitative conditions].[38]

Vernon Jensen, whose work on the hard rock miners[39] has been indispensable to historians of the I.W.W., also found fault with Dubofsky's theory of frontier activism. "Dubofsky finds all of the ideology of the I.W.W. existent in the West before the I.W.W. appeared," Jensen wrote. "There was a more highly mixed and confused situation than Dubofsky sees." He frequently lumped "all the workers together, as though there were no differences between them. There were wide differences between localities and there were wide differences within localities.[40]

Critical of these shortcomings, Paul Buhle has argued that Dubofsky is "oblivious to the political context in which the I.W.W. grew and was crushed" and fails to convey a sense of the complex interrelationships between the I.W.W. and S.P. members.[41] Buhle's point can especially be seen in the conflicts within the S.P. and between the S.P. and ST.&L.A. over the role of party politics in the founding of the I.W.W.[42] More importantly, arguments locating the I.W.W.'s emergence in frontier activism have completely neglected the role of immigrant anarchist groups as well as native anarchists whose activism reflected complex ties to the European syndicalist movement (discussed more fully in chapter 4). This neglect, however, is not limited to I.W.W. scholarship, but permeates the whole of labor historiography, a condition which led Buhle to characterize anarchist influences within the American labor movement as a "hidden text."[43]

Immigrant anarchists played an important role in the diffusion of syndicalist ideas, influencing rank-and-file activists who become associated with the I.W.W.'s inception. The example of the Paterson anarchists significantly demonstrates the complexity of influences affecting the militant unionism of the W.F.M. and emphasizes the importance of an interpretation which highlights the interaction among immigrant, migrant, and native-born workers in the formation of the I.W.W. Moreover, the activities of native and immigrant anarchists must be seen as galvanizing the oppositional tensions within the socialist and trade union movements as well as contributing to the confluence of tendencies converging in the beginning of the twentieth century to form the industrial unionism of the I.W.W. It was the confluence of tendencies, rather than the efforts of a militant union isolated from the majority of the industrial labor force, of which immigrants and migrants accounted for nearly four-fifths, that launched the I.W.W.

The spread of European syndicalism, however, was not limited to immigrant anarchist groups, which underscores the ubiquitous nature of these influences in the American labor and political community at the turn of the twentieth century. Among the left wing of the S.P. were many revolutionary socialists who leaned toward a version of anarcho-syndicalism, while within the S.L.P. a Marxist version of syndicalism emerged. The former tendency is best represented by William E. Trautmann, the latter by Daniel DeLeon. Both came from immigrant backgrounds and played instrumental roles in the founding of the I.W.W., though they represent different relationships to the European syndicalist movement.

Born in New Zealand to German parents, Trautmann was active in the socialist and labor movement in Germany and Russia before immigrating to the United States late in 1890.[44] Settling in Ohio, he became an organizer for the B.W.U. Eventually, he was elected to the

Industrial Worker, October 10, 1912, p. 1.

union's General Executive Board and became editor of the union's rank-and-file paper, *Brauer Zeitung.* Between 1900 and 1905, Trautmann took on a central role in the founding of the I.W.W. and continually occupied key positions in the I.W.W.'s formative period. Early in 1905, he took the initiative in calling the meeting that led to the I.W.W. inaugural convention.[45]

   Combining his experiences with the labor movements in German, Russia, and America and the ideas he derived from European syndicalism, Trautmann formulated many of the basic ideas which later represented the political and economic philosophy of the I.W.W. A revolutionary socialist, Trautmann briefly acted as national committeeman for the S.P., representing Ohio before being expelled from the party for "treasonable conduct."[46] Trautmann is credited with being among the first to formulate an American version of revolutionary industrial unionism which incorporated aspects of European syndicalism. He corresponded with Emile Pouget, secretary of the C.G.T., receiving from him syndicalist literature.[47] Writing in the special Labor Day issue of the *American Labor Union Journal* of 1903, Trautmann discussed his developing ideas of industrial unionism:

> Socialists abroad, as well as here, perceive that the instruments for the management of the socialist republic, now in the process of formation, must be created, and they build the labor organizations according to this need. Who can judge how to regulate the required production of utilities in the various lines of industry better than those directly employed in a given industry? Industrial organizations are the forerunners of the society established on socialist foundations.[48]

Between 1903-1904, Trautmann wrote for the *Brauer Zeitung,* reporting and editorializing on issues galvanizing the European syndicalist movement. His articles and editorials discussed the inadequacy of the ballot, the general strike as a weapon in the class war, and syndicates as the bias for governing the socialist order. The power of the union movement Trautmann argued, did not lie in its ability to build electoral constituencies but in the union's potential to become the actual economic structures that would govern and administer the new socialist society. The union, not the party, was the vehicle of revolutionary change; the general strike, not the ballot, would be the means of proletarian emancipation. Becuase of his intense activity with the nascent industrial union movement, the General Executive Board of the B.W.U. removed Trautmann from his post as editor of the organization's journal early in 1905.[49]

Daniel DeLeon had both direct and indirect knowledge of the European syndicalist movement which he actively incorporated into his political philosophy in the period between 1900 and 1905. Born on the island of Curacao, Venezuela, in 1852, Deleon immigrated to the United States in 1874. Settling in New York City, he studied law and political science at Columbia University, receiving an L.L.B. in 1878. After practicing law for a short period in Texas, DeLeon returned to New York City and joined the Knights of Labor (K. of L.) in 1888. In 1890, he became a member of the Socialist Labor Party (S.L.P.) and editor of the party's organ, *The People,* in 1891. In 1895, he led a secessionist movement from the K. of L. and founded the Socialist Trade and Labor Alliance (S.T.&L.A.).[50]

Though he lagged behind other leading founders of the I.W.W. in expressing a form of industrial unionism that built on European syndicalism, DeLeon nevertheless introduced the American labor community to the ideas of the European syndicalist movement. Initially, DeLeon gained knowledge of the European syndicalist movement through his reading of the French proletarian magazines *La Petite Republique Socialiste, Le Socialiste* (L.E.), and *Le Mouvement Socialiste* (L.E.S.), which featured articles by such syndicalist theoreticians as Edouard Berth, George Yvetot, Emile Pouget, Fernand Pelloutier, and Victor Griffuelhes. Under DeLeon's editorship, reprints of articles from *L.M.S.* and *L.E.* appeared as early as July 2, 1899, in the *Weekly People;* and by 1903, news articles and commentaries by and about Spanish and Italian syndicalists began to appear in the *Daily People* as well. Through the organs of the S.L.P. and S.T.&L.A., DeLeon provided American socialists with direct knowledge of the broad outlines of the European syndicalist movement though reprints, articles, and commentaries.[51]

In 1904, DeLeon supported the revolutionary proletarian faction of the Italian syndicalist movement led by Antonio Labriola. At the time, Labriola was lauded by socialist intellectuals as one of the "two most important leaders of [Italian syndicalism]."[52] Deleon supported Labriola's early position in spite of Labriola's attack on parliamentary socialism as a "degeneration of the Socialist spirit." Later, however, Deleon would emphasize the fact that Labriola combined syndicalism with party activity: "Labriola belongs with the 'syndicalist' wing ... of the Socialist PARTY of Italy," he declared. "Labriola's position ...is [as] exactly that of the S.L.P. as two positions in two different countries can be."[53]

Though he identified himself with the revolutionary proletarian faction of the Italian syndicalist movement, DeLeon became increasingly critical of the direction of French syndicalism. Attending the Lille conference of the French socialist party and serving as a delegate to the Congress of the Second International in the summer of 1904, DeLeon was exposed to the controversy and debate concerning the strategy of the general strike as advocated by the revolutionary wing of the C.G.T. In

Amsterdam, he heard Jules Guesde's attack against the C.G.T.'s program. Guesde's criticism of the anti-political approach and concept of the general strike advanced by the anarcho-syndicalist element within the C.G.T. made a deep impression on DeLeon. In a report on his European experiences, DeLeon wrote that Guesde's argument provided conclusive proof that conceptions of the labor movement that denied its essentially political character were false. Following his direct contact with the French labor movement, DeLeon became increasingly critical of the growing opposition to all forms of political action within the C.G.T. and warned that the C.G.T. was becoming overrun by the anarchist element.[54]

Though Trautmann considered the S.L.P. and S.T. & L.A. precursors of industrial unionism.[55] he was also extremely critical of its mixture of politics and unionism. In the five-year period prior to the founding of the I.W.W., Trautmann maintained a syndicalist version of industrial unionism in which the union and not the party would constitute the actual agency governing and administering the new socialist society. Trautmann's idea conflicted with DeLeon's, who in this period was still struggling with the problem of how to prevent labor's electoral mandates from being "counted out" by "the agents of the capitalist class."[56] Disagreeing with Trautmann that the union should supplant the party, DeLeon advanced the idea that the unions, by their capacity to carry on production, represented the potential instrument through which labor's decision at the polls for socialism could be implemented. DeLeon never discussed industrial unionism in any of his speeches or writing until late in 1904, nor did he give unqualified endorsement to the concept of industrial unionism until the summer of 1905. In the May 1905 issue of the *Voice of Labor,* Trautmann wrote that the S.T. & L.A. was "a duodecimo edition of the K. of L. [Knights of Labor]. It has the same district alliances with the same intellectuals as leaders: the same local craft organizations and the same mixed locals [as well as] ;the centralized autocracy at headquarters. . . ." Its most fatal weakness, Trautmann concluded, "was the political union of the S.T. & L.A. with the S.L.P."

It may have been because of these political differences that DeLeon was not invited to the informal conference which met in the fall of 1904 to lay the ground work for the coming convention. DeLeon learned only indirectly of the plans to launch the new movement. While it is clear that no members of the S.L.P. or S.T.&L.A. were involved in the initial planning conference, it is questionable whether members of either organization received an invitation to participate even in the January conference that completed plans for the I.W.W.'s inaugural convention. In his explanation of how the S.L.P. became involved in the January conference, Henry Kuhn of the S.L.P. gave contradictory accounts. In his first account, S.L.P. member Frank Bohn received an invitation while in St. Louis, and "reported the matter to headquarters and was instructed to go ahead...." Later Kuhn wrote that Bohn "while on the road fell in with a group in Chicago which was about to issue a manifesto..." and through accident became a participant. The latter explanation is supported by Bohn: "While passing through Chicago," he explained, "I was invited to meet with this group and discuss the situation. This, after learning that the group was to meet as individuals, not as delegates, I agreed to do. . . . Not one member of the S.T.&L.A.," he later wrote, "had the slightest idea that the I.W.W. was to be launched until a few days before the conference."[57]

The letter of invitation to the January conference and the *Industrial Union Manifesto* drafted during this meeting, condemned the craft form of unionism, and electoral reformism, but reflected ambiguities regarding the positive policies that would lead to the revolutionary transformation of society. In the letter of invitation the authors expressed confidence "in the ability of the working class, if correctly organized, on both industrial and political lines, to take possession of and operate successfully the industries of the country." The letter went on to stress the belief "that working class political expression, through the Socialist ballot, in order to be sound, must have an economic counterpart in a labor organization built as the structure of Socialist society, embracing within itself the working class in approximately the same groups and departments and industries that the workers would assume in the working-class administration of the Co-Operative Commonwealth. . . ."[58] Although the invitation suggested that political ends would be gained through economic action, it did not address the role of the party. The *Manifesto* eliminated this ambiguity by asserting that the new movement "should be established as an economic organization of the working class without affiliation with any political party."[59] While clarifying that the politics the founders envisioned had nothing to do with political parties, the meaning and relationship of socialist politics to action on the industrial field was by no means clear at this point.

Among trade unionists and the left wing of the S.P. members, there was strong opposition to political affiliation. Convinced, through the experiences of the previous decade, that a political party could not fight against the capitalist class, this element conceived of the political phase of the socialist movement as serving an educational purpose. Deploring the trivial propaganda campaigns that emphasized "the politics of the day," they argued that agitational activities should be directed toward intrinsic connections between social and industrial problems through the development of labor agencies which would prepare workers for their role as reshapers of economic life.[60]

Many trade unionists and left-wing socialists supported the development of a militant and revolutionary industrial union movement that would unite all workers, nationally and internationally, into "One Big Union." William D. Haywood, who chaired the I.W.W.'s founding convention, but did not become a formal member of the I.W.W. until May of 1910,[61] was the strongest advocate of the "One Big Union" idea. Haywood, an active member of the S.P. until he was expelled in 1913 for his advocacy of anarcho-syndicalist tactics,[62] held that it was necessary to wage the class war primarily on the industrial field. Haywood's position had grown out of his experiences in the mining camps of the expanding West. Chief among the W.F.M. organizers, Haywood did not directly repudiate political action, but was hostile to electioneering campaigns as well as to attempts to gain gradual reform through existing governmental agencies. Haywood believed that only the workers themselves, through industrial unions, could take over control of industry from the capitalists. "One big unionists" favored the spontaneous initiative of rank-and-file militants but held that the centralized powers of capitalism could only be fought through an equally powerful working-class organization.[63]

Though some revolutionary socialists and anarchists differed with "one big unionists" on the issue of organizational conformity based on centralized authority, an issue which later divided the groups,[64] they were aligned on the primacy of direct industrial action as the most important form of revolutionary working-class activity. Since this alliance carried the threat of the party's dilution, the right and center wings of the S.P. did not want to see the new movement affiliate with the party. These political socialists wanted to see the movement adopt the German model in which the trade union movement was not affiliated to the party but accepted its leadership and was officered by party stalwarts.[65] The alliance between the left-wing socialists and anarchists, however, eroded the possibilities of such a role. Expressing concern over the alliance between left-wing socialists and anarchist trade unionists, a delegate at the convention observed that:

> We have the socialist who is so near the anarchist that he is beginning to think as the anarchist does, that action along the political lines is absolutely harmful instead of being useful.[66]

The importance of the alliance between revolutionary socialists and anarchists was apparent early in the I.W.W.'s formative stages and can be seen in the collaboration between William Trautmann and Thomas J. Hagerty, whose role in the founding of the I.W.W. will be discussed in chapter 3.

Shortly before the I.W.W.'s founding convention, Trautmann and Hagerty met with Eugene V. Debs to win his support for the new movement and discuss with him the meaning and implication of the nonaffiliation clause contained in the Industrial Union Manifesto.[67] In this meeting Trautmann and Hagerty outlined their reasoning for the necessity of the nonaffiliation clause. While they did not want to exclude political socialists from the movement, they felt a clause endorsing political affiliation, in addition to being objectionable to a large section of the movements supporters, would only draw attention to the existence of the rival socialist parties. While the nonaffiliation clause would be the basis for a new unity, it was also essential that the form of politics not make the mistake of combining "in the economic organization the functions of political parties necessary to exist until the political state, and political government, will be supplanted by agencies to be organized within the industrial organization of the working class." Following "a thorough explanation in which the labor history of France, Russia, Spain and Italy was thoroughly gone over," Trautmann reports in his "Brief History of the Industrial Union Manifesto," Debs finally agreed that "all those who stood for political action" could find "a common ground on the industrial field."[68]

In spite of their efforts not to combine in the economic organization the functions of a political party, a last-minute meeting with Daniel DeLeon effected a compromise on the political affiliation question. The result of this last-minute meeting would be debated until the clause was finally eliminated from the *Preamble* in 1908, when the convention refused to seat DeLeon as a delegate.[69] Arriving in Chicago two days before the convention, DeLeon met with Trautmann and Hagerty in the restaurant of the Belmont House. During this last-minute meeting, Hagerty showed DeLeon the original draft of the *Preamble* to the I.W.W.'s constitution. "No, that will not be acceptable to our delegation," DeLeon said after reading the document, "except that you insert the following clause: 'and on the political field, without any affiliation with any political party.' "Trautmann replied:

> Are you in agreement that this convention may be the basis for a unification of the present political parties now claiming to represent the Socialist movement? And yet, consider the circumstances, would it not be discretional to ignore this question now; did not the history of the American Railway Union set us an example not to mix things up and thereby confuse the workers, the element that alone will determine what actions will be necessary to fight the capitalist class every day, and until the overthrow of the social system is an accomplished fact.

"Very true," DeLeon responded, "but we must fight in the shadow when the sun burns too hot."[70] Whether Hagerty refused to insert the clause into his draft of the *Preamble* or not is a matter of controversy; the clause, however, appeared in the *Preamble* when discussion of it opened during the convention proceedings.[71]

During the I.W.W.'s founding convention, DeLeon effected a synthesis of the syndicalist notions he derived from American and European sources with the political Marxism held by S.T.&L.A. delegates and certain S.P. members against the anarcho-syndicalist and revolutionary socialist ideas expressed by such delegates as Trautmann,

Hagerty, and Lucy Parsons.[72] The ideology informing the I.W.W. conception of industrial solidarity did not reflect a single ideological position nor can its amalgam be explained entirely in terms of indigenous responses to industrial conditions. Informed by diverse and often contradictory sources of influence, the labor radicalism of the I.W.W. represented a complex expression of tendencies emerging out of the interaction between native and immigrant groups. The next chapters will examine in more depth the nature and extent to which the I.W.W. was influenced by native and immigrant anarchism and the relationship of this anarchism to the European syndicalist movement.

Industrial Worker, November 9, 1909, p. 1.

CHAPTER THREE

Anarchists at the Founding Convention

William D. Haywood, who chaired the I.W.W.'s inaugural convention, considered Haymarket the decisive event that shaped his convictions and commitment to labor radicalism. In his teens at the time of the Haymarket police riot, Haywood learned of the occurrence through newspapers and was deeply affected by what he read. He talked incessantly about the Haymarket affair with his friend Pat Reynolds, a member of the K. of L., from whom he had gained his first lessons about unionism. I kept "trying to fathom in my own mind the reasons for the explosion," Haywood wrote in his autobiography. "Were the strikers responsible? Why were the police in Haymarket Square?" Why were the authorities so set on hanging these men called anarchists? "The last words of August Spies," Haywood later remembered, "kept running through my mind: 'There will come a time when our silence will be more powerful than the voices you are strangling today.' It was a turning point in my life."[1]

Others attending the I.W.W.'s founding convention had participated in the eight-hour movement in the 1880's, which was the struggle
for an eight-hour work day. Some were in Chicago after the trial and saw
their brave comrades defy their executioners. During the convention
proceedings, these delegates articulated links between the Haymarket
anarchists and the form of industrial unionism being initiated at the
convention. Al Klemensic, who represented the Colorado Journeymen
Tailor's Union, powerfully invoked the memory of the Chicago anarchists in his speech to the delegates assembled in Brand Hall:

> You know that in this country there were industrial strikes begun
> in 1884 and 1885 and 1886, and you know what the result was....I
> have seen men hanged for the truth in this city, in this very place.
> (applause) Industrial unionism at that time had begun to shake
> capitalism to its very foundations, and the judges and plutocrats in
> this country decided to hang the men with the hope of hanging
> industrial unionism at the same time. But let me tell you that
> industrial unionism is here in this very city again to declare and
> demand its right. (applause) The voices that plutocracy thought to
> silence when it tried to hang unionism are heard again, and we are
> here today to recorganize the work they had started twenty years
> ago. (applause)[2]

Klemensic was referring to the "Chicago idea," which had developed
among native, German, French, and Bohemian sections of the International Working People's Association, also known as the Black International. The "Chicago idea," as outlined in the *Pittsburgh Manifesto,*
called for a free society in which the trade union represented the
formative cell. The new movement was intended to be a loose federation
of autonomous groups having as its connecting link an information
bureau located in Chicago. The program of the social revolutionaries
forming the Black International rejected all political parties, including
the necessity of a revolutionary party of the proletariat, and called for
direct action on the industrial field. The official organs of the "syndico-
anarchists" were the *Alarm,* an English language weekly, the *Arbeiter-
Zeitung,* a German paper published on week days, the *Verbote,* pub-

lished on Saturday, and the *Fackel,* published on Sunday.[3] The Metal Workers' Federation of America, organized in 1885, came closest to realizing the "Chicago idea," representing the earliest American expression of syndicalism.[4] Toward the end of the fifth day of the convention, Klemensic announced that a delegation would visit the graves of the Haymarket martyrs.[5]

The proceedings of the I.W.W.'s inaugural convention indicate that the participants were not only aware of the "Chicago idea" but were conscious of a continuity between their efforts and the struggles of the Chicago anarchists to initiate industrial unionism. Among the delegates attending the founding convention were also those who were aware of the European forerunners of industrial unionism. For some of these delegates, their original contact with the industrial union movement had begun in Europe. Moreover, the organizers of the convention had corresponded with and sent the letter of invitation to European syndicalist organizations, hoping that a delegate would be able to attend the convention. The importance of Haymarket, the role of delegates who had participated in the earlier eight-hour movement, and the contact with and awareness of the European syndicalist movement among the organizers who took the initiative in calling the convention have all been ignored or dismissed in the studies that have scrutinized the historical experience of the I.W.W.

The earliest interpretative studies concerning the relationship of revolutionary syndicalism to the industrial union movement made only cursory reference to the role played by anarchists in the confluence of tendencies that gave birth to the movement. This omission stemmed from the lack of a perspective locating anarchism within the context of the trade union movement and, more specifically from failure to recognize anarchism's relationship to the birth of the revolutionary syndicalism in American and Europe. It is, therefore, not surprising that the role of anarchism and the role played by anarchists in the founding of the I.W.W. is absent from narrative reconstructions of the I.W.W.'s formative period.

Brissenden, whose study provides the most thorough investigation of the I.W.W.'s formative period, considered the efforts of the Chicago anarchists to have been outweighed by the effects of the tragedy:

The labor movement lay stunned after its brief flirtation with
anarchy. The union men drew away from the anarchist agitators,
and taking their information from the capitalist press only, concluded that socialism and anarchism were the same thing, and
would, if tolerated, lead the movement to ruin and disaster.[6]

Serving, in his view, as an unquestionable setback to the labor and
socialist movements, the tragedy of the Chicago anarchists amounted to
little more than a peripheral forerunner of the I.W.W.'s form of industrial unionism. Brissenden concluded that "these riots (sic.) really gave
French unionists the idea of the general strike and thus helped to give
form, first, to modern French syndicalism, and second, both by relay
back to this side of the Atlantic and directly by its influence in this
country, to American syndicalism in the form of the I.W.W."[7]

Though aware of an anarchist presence at the I.W.W.'s founding
convention, Brissenden made no effort to search for continuities linking
these delegates to the eight-hour movement or to the European syndicalist movement. He merely identified the anarchists participating in
the I.W.W.'s inaugural convention as a small but constituent element
among the doctrinal types represented. He did not consider the efforts
of anarchists to be noteworthy until the I.W.W's third convention.[8] As a
consequence, subsequent accounts have neglected the role of both
native and immigrant anarchists in the beginning years of the I.W.W.

Historians rediscovering the I.W.W. in the 1950s and 1960s did
not question the meager role assigned by Brissenden and other historians to the contributions made by anarchists to the industrial union
movement. For the most part, these studies elaborated on the factional
disputes between reformist and doctrinaire elements in the S.P. and the
S.L.P., seeing in them the major determinants of the convention's
outcome. Joseph Conlin, in his interpretative study, argues unconvinc-
ingly that the anarchists present at the founding convention were merely
remnants of the Chicago group who exerted no real influence.[9]

The tendency within the current literature on the I.W.W. has,
therefore, been to deny or ignore the role played by anarchists present at
the founding convention by claiming their influence to be insignificant
or by arguing that anarchism was expressed through a formal group
representing a minority position incompatible with other political phil-
osophies. These assumptions regarding the influences of anarchism on

the founding of the I.W.W. not only ignored the impact of anarchists on the revolutionary industrial union movement, but also distorted the way in which syndicalist ideas entered the American labor movement.

Anarchists attending the I.W.W.'s founding convention represented a number of tendencies. Anarchists active within the Chicago area alone represented a range of sources of influences and relationships to the labor movement. Among the anarchists active in the Chicago area, Thomas J. Hagerty, Lucy Parsons, Jay Fox, and Josef Peukert attended the I.W.W.'s founding convention in an official capacity. Among anarchists active within the industrial union movement, Hagerty was a principal participant. He played an instrumental role in organizing the January conference that led to the I.W.W.'s founding convention, helped to draft the *Industrial Union Manifesto,* and authored the I.W.W.'s *Preamble.*

Hagerty's association with the reemerging industrial union movement began through his contact with the W.F.M. and the A.L.U. in New Mexico sometime around 1902. During the summer of 1902, he toured the mining camps of Colorado with Eugene V. Debs, recruiting members for the A.L.U. and the S.P. During 1903, Hagerty traveled throughout the country, lecturing under the auspices of the S.P.[10] His approach to socialism, however, soon became a source of increasing conflict to the dominant right wing of the party. Critical of the right wing's policy of gradualism, he spoke against their strategy of parliamentary reform and "boring from within" the A.FL. as effective methods of achieving the cooperative commonwealth.[11]

A speech to San Francisco socialists ended his brief career as a speaker for the S.P. In this speech, he denounced the Party's reformist tendencies and reliance on political action as a means of achieving emancipation of the working class. "We must have revolution," he is reported as having said, "peaceable if possible, but, to tell the truth, we care not how we get it." After the chairperson, whom Hagerty referred to as "a long-haired phrase peddler," broke his gavel attempting to bring the meeting to a close, angry socialists rushed the platform ending his speech. Outraged by the news of Hagerty's speech, Victor Berger wrote, "There is no room in our party . . . for Hagerty. [He] ought to do as anarchists do, and renounce all participation in politics."[12]

Hagerty's revolutionary attitude toward socialism had been formed through his contact with the Chicago anarchists, participation in the eight-hour movement, and through his reading of Benjamin

Tucker's semimonthly publication *Liberty*. In a letter to Joseph Labadie, dated March 1889, Hagerty wrote:

> I have been inactive in the cause since the murder of our brave comrades in Chicago. For one year prior to that sad event, I gave my entire time to collecting money to help defray the expenses of their trial, and to visiting the various trades Unions to create a favorable opinion and expression in their behalf. I was in New York for two months before their murder and devoted my spare time to aiding in their defense. My name having appeared in the papers at the time in connection with their case [broke] off negotiations which was pending between me and the Singer Sewing Machine Co. for the sale of a valuable invention. I was therefore left stranded in New York and had to borrow money to bring me here [i.e., San Francisco]. upon my return I was obliged to mortgage my property or home, and for a time felt dejected and careless.[13]

In his letter, Hagerty responded to Labadie's idea for the publication of a book or pamphlet containing several articles on the subject of anarchism. "I fully agree," Hagerty wrote, "that the time has arrived when the few men who understand and endorce the principles of Anarchy should step to the front and give reasons for their advocacy of a doctrine which is regarded with horrible forebodings of danger to society...."[14] Unsure as to whether he could meet with Labadie's request for an article on the subject, but prepared to affirm his anarchism publicly in spite of further repercussions, Hagerty wrote:

> I have little confidence in my ability to present my ideas of a true anarchistic condition of Society in a concise and plain a manner as the nature of your requirements might demand; as I have not had time to read any books bearing on the subject and would have to rely upon what little information I have received through the columns of "Liberty" as well as my own inherent knowledge of Justice and Liberty. yet I can promise you to do the very best that I can. I have no scruples that will stand in the way of my doing all that lays in my power to present our cause in its clearest light, and although it may bring great pecuniary and other losses to me

should I publically proclaim the faith that is within me, yet I always stand ready to make any sacrifice for a cause which I know to be right and just.[15]

Forming alliances with revolutionary socialists and trade unionists, Hagerty became one of the earliest advocates of industrial unionism. Writing for the *American Labor Union Journal* and later serving as editor of the *Voice of Labor,* Hagerty advocated a form of industrial unionism which drew on the ideas advanced by the Chicago anarchists and on knowledge he had gained about the European Syndicalist movement:

> The workers must so organize in proportion to capitalist concentrations in industry irrespective of trade or tool, that, when they shall have acquired a sufficient class conscious majority in every industry, they may be able to take over and collectively administer the machinery of production and distribution in the cooperative commonwealth.[16]

Hagerty later developed these ideas into a motion adopted during the January conference and incorporated into the *Industrial Union Manifesto,* the first document to announce publicly the coming convention.

It is, however, important to point out in referring to Hagerty's influences that his knowledge of the European syndicalist movement was not limited to the C.G.T. nor did he feel that the *Industrial Union Manifesto* which he helped to author, represented a brand new revolutionary code. In a number of his speeches to the delegation assembled in Brand Hall, Hagerty demonstrated broad knowledge of the European syndicalist movement:

> As much as we may wave the flag of American superiority and supremacy, I want to tell you that our continental fellow-workers, with whom we shall soon be in international, world-wide, revolutionary, economic relationship through this organization ... have had the experience we have not. They have already organized on these lines. Only last month in Spain a congress was held in Madrid which issued a manifesto somewhat longer than this

Manifesto; a manifesto summing up five years of experience in the experiment we are about to make....[17]

So that in spite of petty national lines, in spite of international division lines, the workers the world over are coming together on the grounds of their common working class interest....[18]

Though he drew from diverse traditions of labor radicalism, Hagerty consciously avoided invoking the language of Proundhon, Bakunin, Marx, or Engels and emphasized that the I.W.W.'s *Preamble* and *Constitution* be written in "...the plain, everyday language of the man in overalls."[19]

Among the industrial unionists participating in the January conference, Hagerty played a decisive role in generating a language that drew from these traditions but did not imitate them or invoke their authority. At this meeting he offered a motion, written into the *Industrial Union Manifesto,* which proclaimed that the new movement "be established as an economic organization of the working class without affiliation with any political party." Hagerty is responsible for the reintroduction of this conception of industrual unionism into the intellectual atmosphere of the time.[20]

Hagerty's original draft of the *Preamble* did not include a role for political parties, rather it emphasized the importance of the union as the center and foundation of revolutionary struggle. In it he wrote that between the working class and the employing class:

> ...a struggle must go on until all the workers come together on the industrial field, and take and hold that which they produce through an economic organization of the working class.

Hagerty's draft of the *Preamble* found strong support among left wing socialists and militant trade unionists. The *Preamble,* however, was altered before it reached the founding convention. In an eleventh-hour meeting with Hagerty and Trautmann, Daniel Deleon raised sharp disagreement to the *Preamble's* elimination of the role of the political party. DeLeon declared that the *Preamble* would be unacceptable to the S.T.&L.A. delegation unless the clause, "and on the political field without affiliation with any political party," was inserted. Given the rivalries between the two socialist parties and the need for a basis of unification between anarcho-syndicalist and political socialist versions of industrial unionism, the clause was accepted.[21]

Nevertheless a lengthy debate ensued over the meaning of the paragraph. The sentence which referred to the political field did not make clear for what purpose the workers were to unite. Moreover, since the workers were to gain all that they produced through an economic organization, politics seemed pointless. Defending his original intent, Hagerty argued that politics had nothing to do with political parties, that political ends could only be gained through economic action. Pointing to Russian workers currently engaged in politics through revolutionary strikes, he argued that the working class did not need a political party to gain its freedom. "The ballot box," Hagerty said, concluding his speech, "is simply a capitalist concession. Dropping pieces of paper into a hole in a box never did achieve emancipation for the working class, and to my mind never will."[22]

At the I.W.W.'s founding convention, Hagerty represented the Industrial Workers Club of Chicago.[23] No information concerning the ideology or activity of the club has survived. Among its members, however, was M.B. Quinn who had worked with Dyer D. Lum to create anarchist groups within the Knights of Labor.[24] Socialists were also among the members. However, from Hagerty's comments it appears that the club favored an anti-political position on the labor question. "The Industrial Workers Club," Hagerty told delegates in his speech on the preamble, "instructs me to oppose anything on this floor which puts this convention on record as in favor of a political party."[25]

The amended clause was ratified by the delegation but did not end the debate on the role of the political party in the industrial union movement. Discussion of politics within the I.W.W. locals raised the question of whether the working class should favor the S.P. or S.L.P. As locals included members of both organizations, discussions led to heated arguments. Workers primarily interested in the economic functions of the movement became impatient with both factions. Anarchists within these locals seized the opportunity afforded by such quarrels to point out the disruptive effects of politics.

Party leaders of the center and right wing of the S.P. began complaining that "active workers in the Socialist party all over the country have suddenly grown lukewarm in the efforts to build up a political organization and are enthusiastically proclaiming the advantages of industrialism...."[26] This coalition, which had been unanimous in its condemnation of the I.W.W. from the start, initiated a campaign of moving against left-wing S.P. members in the I.W.W. W. E. Trautmann, Secretary-Treasurer of the I.W.W., and Alfred S. Edwards, editor of the *Industrial Worker,* were both expelled from the party by their locals for "treasonable conduct."[27] Even Debs, who had lent support to the I.W.W. during its first year of existence, allowed his dues to lapse and his membership to expire. In a letter to William English Walling, Debs later explained his reasons for leaving the movement. "The I.W.W.," he wrote, "is an anarchist organization in all except name and this is the cause of all the trouble."[28]

Attacks by prominent political socialists aroused further resentments, driving many within the movement in the direction of opposition to political action. In the summer of 1906, I.W.W. local 85 of Chicago offered a resolution to amend the *Preamble.*

> Resolved, that in the opinion of this local the second paragraph of the Preamble to the Constitution should read: "Between these two classes a struggle must go on until the toilers come together on the industrial field, and take and hold that which they produce by their labor, through an economic organization, without affiliation with any political party."
>
> Our members do not agree with the idea of toilers coming together on any political field.[29]

Local 85's resolution led to an amendment to the *Preamble* at the I.W.W.'s second convention. In 1908, issues between the I.W.W. and the S.L.P., which split the movement into the Chicago and Detroit I.W.W.s, led to the final revision of the *Preamble.* The 1908 version of the controversial clause was completely re-written reflecting Hagerty's original intent:

> Between these two classes [working class and employing class] a struggle must go on until the workers of the world organize as a

class, take possession of the earth and the machinery of production and abolish the wage system.[30]

Commenting on the I.W.W.'s 1908 *Preamble,* Samuel Yellen was struck by its similarity to the *Pittsburgh Manifesto.* "In principle," he wrote, "the I.W.W. resembled the 'Chicago idea' anarchists of 1886, but advanced beyond them to syndicalism."[31] More than merely resembling the "Chicago Idea," the I.W.W.'s principles of industrial unionism resulted from the conscious effort of anarchists like Hagerty, who continued to affirm in the face of great adversity the principles which the Chicago anarchists gave their lives defending. The strength of Hagerty's contribution to the industrial union movement lies in the endurance of the original intent of the *Preamble* he authored and the courage of the I.W.W.'s rank-and-file to affirm its revolutionary principle.

In the years following the I.W.W.'s inaugural convention, Haymarket became the inspiration for songs, poems, and graphics which typically appeared in the November issue of the *Industrial Worker* and *Solidarity.* After I.W.W.s were martyred, Haymarket became intertwined with Wobblies who gave their lives in the struggle for industrial freedom. In a song entitled "November," Ralph Chaplin wrote:

> Red November, black November.
> Bleak November, black and red;
> Hallowed month of Labor's martyrs,
> Labor's heroes, Labor's dead.
> Labor's hope and wrath and sorrow—
> Red the promise, black the threat;
> Who are we not to remember?
> Who are we to forget!
>
> Black and red the colors blended,
> Black and red the pledge we made;
> Red, until the fight is ended,
> Black until the debt is paid.
> Wesley Everest and Al Parsons
> With Joe Hill and all the rest.
> Who are we not to remember?
> Who are we to dare forget![32]

At the founding convention, support for Hagerty's conception of industrial unionism came from other anarchists and revolutionary socialists. Chief among them was Lucy Parsons. Honored by a prominent seat on the platform, she made several speeches which defended the economic conception of industrial unionism. The daughter of Spanish and Indian parents, Parsons had been a strong advocate of anarchism, playing a critical role within the predominantly white male working-class movement in Chicago well in advance of the Haymarket police riot of 1886. More than the devoted assistant of her martyred husband, Albert Richard Parsons, she published newspapers, pamphlets, and books, traveled and lectured extensively, and led many demonstrations. Parsons concentrated her work among the unemployed and foreign-born, remaining active in the radical labor movement until her death in 1942.[33]

At the founding convention, Parsons did not consider herself the representative of a formal organization. "I entered my name," she told the delegates, "believing that I did not represent a mere body that met within the four walls of a hall, but that I represented that great body that has its face to the foremost corners of the earth." Parsons voiced her objection to the voting power of delegates being based on the numbers of workers affiliated with local, national, and international labor organizations.[34]

During the convention proceedings Parsons spoke in defense of Hagerty's important clause in the *Preamble* calling for workers to "take and hold" that which they produced by their labor. "My conception of taking possession," Parsons said, "is that of the general strike. The trouble with all strikes in the past has been that the workingmen . . . strike and go out and starve." She argued that the general strike did not mean abandonment of the workplace but entering into and taking possession of it. "My conception of the strike of the future is not to strike and go out and starve, but to strike and remain in and take possession of the necessary property of production."[35]

Parsons gave crucial support to Hagerty's "take and hold" idea elaborated in the final clause of the *Preamble*. The clause endorsing the idea of the general strike read as follows:

These sad conditions can be changed and the interests of the
working class upheld by an organization formed in such a way that
all of its members in any one industry, or in all industries, cease
work altogether whenever a strike or lockout is on in any department thereof, thus making an injury to one an injury to all.[36]

Support for this clause came also from William D. Haywood of the
W.F.M. who insisted that the *Preamble* endorse the general strike.[37]

Jay Fox, an Irish immigrant who had worked as a blacksmith and
carpenter, also attended the founding convention. Widely known
among labor leaders and anarchists, Fox had been wounded during the
Haymarket riot and had marched in the funeral train of the martyrs. An
active member of the Free Society group in Chicago, Fox worked on the
group's journal, *Free Society,* and collaborated with other anarchists,
such as Emma Goldman and Henry Addis, in making propaganda for
the cause.[38] Following the assassination of President McKinley, Chicago
police destroyed the Free Society's press and arrested Fox, along with
Abraham and Marie Isaak, their two children, Hippolyte Havel, and
other members of the Free Society group on charges of conspiracy to kill
the President. Emma Goldman left St. Louis after learning of the arrest of
her comrades. Authorities had connected her with the act and were
prepared to hold the Free Society group until her surrender. Soon after
her arrival in Chicago, Goldman was arrested and held in the Cook
County jail with her Chicago comrades. A day prior to Leon Czolgosz's
conviction, the Free Society group, including Fox, was released. Goldman was freed the next day. Thereafter, the biographical details available on Fox's life become rather sketchy. He did continue his agitational
activities through the Social Science League, a platform for radical
speakers which sponsored weekly meetings at the Masonic Temple in
Chicago, and did became involved with plans to replace Free Society's
defunct journal with the *Demonstrator,* an anarchist journal published
by the Home Colony.[39] He appeared at the I.W.W.'s founding convention as an individual delegate, but did not play a major role in the
proceedings.

In the summer of 1905, Fox reported on the I.W.W.'s founding convention and eventually became a regular contributor to the *Demonstrator,* concentrating on I.W.W. affairs. His association with the Puget Sound group, however, led to a split within the Chicago group. Fox had joined Parsons and other anarchists in organizing socials and picnics to raise money to launch a new anarchist weekly in Chicago. Disagreement developed when the Home Colony suggested that resources be combined with the Chicago group to continue publication of the *Demonstrator* with Fox as editor. Half the group supported the idea while the other half doubted the value of the "backwater" publication. Lucy Parsons, who favored a Chicago-based paper that focused on strikes and industrial conflict, demanded that the money collected over the summer be used to start a new paper. Fox refused and sent the money the group had collected to the Home Colony with a letter stating that plans for the new Chicago paper had been dropped. In spite of Fox's actions, Parsons was able to continue with her plans for the new weekly. The *Liberator* began publication in September of 1905, and became the first of the anarchist papers to affiliate with the I.W.W. An eye injury prevented Fox from leaving Chicago to begin work as editor of the *Demonstrator* as he had planned. In February of 1906, through the efforts of Al Klemensic, an I.W.W. department appeared on the front page of the *Demonstrator*.[40]

Josef Peukert, a Bohemian anarcho-communist, attended the I.W.W.'s founding convention. Peukert immigrated to the United States in 1890. He had fled Austria in 1884, amidst a wave of police repression against anarchist and revolutionary groups. Immigrating first to England, Peukert became involved with the International Anarchist Association and wrote for the German anarchist weekly, *Die Autonomie.* Arriving in New York, Peukert worked with adherents of the London "Autonomie" and edited a paper called the *Anarchist.* While in New York, Peukert began his association with Alexander Berkman and Emma Goldman, who both joined the "Autonomie group," in defiance of Johann Most who carried on an open feud with Peukert. Peukert eventually settled in Chicago, where he continued his activities within the trade union movement.[41] At the founding convention, Peukert represented the Chicago Debating Club. The Club engaged in propaganda activities, such as translating and publishing anarcho-communist and syndicalist tracts among which was "The Social General Strike," the influential work of the German anarchist Arnold Roller (Siegfried Nacht).[42]

The Spanish anarchist Florecio Bazora, about whom few bio-graphical details are available, attended the founding convention. He had been working with Emma Goldman, conducting anarchist meet-ings among the German and Russian residents of St. Louis.[43] A close associate of Ricardo Flores Magón, Bazora also contributed to the propa-ganda campaign of the Partido Liberal Mexicana (P.L.M.), helping the group to publish and distribute its newspaper, *Regeneración.*[44] Flores Magón attended the anarchist meetings organized by Goldman and Bazora, meetings which led him to a more open avowel of his anar-chism.[45] Bazora served as the initial contact between the P.L.M. and the I.W.W.,[46] beginning a relationship well in advance of the Cananea strike of 1906,[47] that would weather the defeats of the Liberal armies in northern Mexico and the imprisonment of Flores Magón. In the years between 1906 and 1914, hundreds of I.W.W.'s fought alongside the Magónistas against the Porfirio Diaz dictatorship. The I.W.W. continued its support of the P.L.M. after many socialists and trade unionists abandoned the Magonistas because of their explicit anarchist position.[48]

Although Emma Goldman did not attend the I.W.W.'s founding convention, she had carried on an active propaganda campaign in support of revolutionary syndicalism. Goldman first came into contact with the revolutionary syndicalist movement in 1900 while attending the Anarchist Congress in Paris. "On my return to the United States," Goldman said, "I immediately began to propagate syndicalist ideas, especially direct action and the general strike."[49] On her return from the Anarchist Congress, Goldman launched the first of her large agitational tours. Speaking on the European movement, she lectured from coast to coast in sixty cities over an eight-month period.[50] On the subject of syndicalism, Goldman wrote, "...in essence it is the economic expres-sion of anarchism. It represents the revolutionary philosophy of labor conceived and born in the actual struggle and experience of the workers themselves. . . . ."[51]

Goldman would come to have a complex relationship to the early I.W.W., much of which can only be inferred form the sketchy materials available on her life following her return from Paris.[52] In *Mother Earth* (M.E.), a monthly magazine she began publishing in March 1906, and which became a leading forum for the discussion of anarchist views on the controversial issues of the time, articles both

Final Sacrifice to Justice. *Tie Vapauteen*, January 1923, p. 30.

favorable to and critical of the I.W.W. appeared. In her ongoing column, "The Situation in America," Goldman described the I.W.W. as a recent attempt "to put the labor movement of America upon a more rational, progressive and revolutionary basis..." The I.W.W., she wrote,

> ...represents a great improvement upon the old method of trade organization. It was formed on the principle of uniting all branches of industry along the lines of their common solidarity.... They resolved to declare war against the existing economic institutions, aiming at the complete emancipation of labor from all forms of exploitation.

She, however, regretted that the new organization was not "preserving its singleheartedness and concentrating all its energy on the struggle with capitalism." The I.W.W.'s effectiveness, she felt, "has been considerably impaired by internal strife, jealousy, and legal litigation among themselves...." The "petty political machinations on the part of one of the wings of the socialist movement have further served to discredit the new organization."[53] These concerns prompted her to conclude:

> Our comrades, who have aided so actively in the organization and efforts of the I.W.W., will soon have to decide whether they shall remain, as members of the organization, a mere appendage of the S.L.P., or whether they should act independently, on their own initiative.[54]

Jean Speilman, a correspondent for *M.E.,* who had been present at the I.W.W. founding convention, disagreed with Goldman's observations concerning the direction of the new movement:

> The fact that there is internal strife in a labor organization does not necessarily mean the organization is "not preserving its single-heartedness and concentrating all its energies in the struggle with capitalism." It means simply that there are some elements within that organization which are trying to disrupt it; elements that are found everywhere where workingmen combine for mutual aid

and assistance. In every movement of this kind we find revolution-
ists and reactionaries, and when these forces clash, there must be a
split.

Spielman went on to discuss the I.W.W.'s strike activities and its recent
convention. He pointed out that the I.W.W. had met with many obstacles from the socialist and radical press, which had created many
misconceptions not only concerning its activities but also its composition. "It is not justified," he wrote "to call the I.W.W. an appendage of the
S.L.P."

> The fact that DeLeon is active [in the I.W.W.] does not mean the
> I.W.W. is a faction of the S.L.P. You might as well say that because
> of an anarchist's being active in the I.W.W., the latter is necessarily
> an anarchist organization. The I.W.W. is not as revolutionary as
> some anarchists think they should be—but we anarchists have not
> done much in that direction.

Spielman advised comrades to investigate the movement more closely,
and though not completely "imbued with anarchists' views," he concluded, the I.W.W. "is, nevertheless, revolutionary."[55]

In spite of criticism, Goldman and the circle of anarchists
connected with M.E. maintained contact with the I.W.W. and lent
support in crisis situations. The first issues of M.E., for example,
reported the arrests of Charles Moyer, William D. Haywood, and G.E.
Pettibone for the murder of former governor Steunenberg of Idaho and
appealed for action to prevent another judicial murder such as that of
1887. M.E. continued its coverage and appeals for support of the
W.F.M.'s officials until they were finally acquitted in August 1907.

Goldman, along with other anarchists connected through M.E.,
gave support to the I.W.W. in strike situations and during some of the
I.W.W.'s free-speech fights. During the San Diego free-speech fight of
1912, the most bitter and violent of the I.W.W.'s many free-speech fights,
Goldman joined forces with the I.W.W. Raising funds for the I.W.W. at
meetings, she also helped to organize a feeding station for victims of
vigilante violence at the I.W.W. headquarters in Los Angeles.[56]

Appreciative of Goldman's support and respectful of her powers as an orator, an I.W.W. who interviewed Goldman for an article in the *Industrial Worker* during the San Diego free-speech fights wrote:

A dozen women of Emma Goldman's type in the labor movement would give the movement a boost that would make it leap ahead with lightning speed. Unfortunately for our workmen today the working women are not as revolutionary and mostly have the absurd idea that by construing the workers' philosophy to mean nothing but a little reform they can do a whole lot of good. The socialist women in general are nothing more than a lot of geese, that confined themselves to cackling about uplifting the workers. . . . Not so with Emma Goldman, she stands by her guns through thick and thin, and goes with the police to jail with same defiance that she mounts the platform to speak to a hostile audience. . . .[57]

Few anarchists from the western and eastern part of the United States sent delegates to the founding convention. Anarchist groups in California, however, had already formed industrial union clubs, which were in many respects prototypes of the mixed local and became charter members following the convention. Mortimer Downing, a prominent member in the I.W.W.—active in the Ford and Shur case and later working as editor of the *Industrial Worker*,—joined the I.W.W. through one of these anarcho-syndicalist groups. Some of these groups were formed by Swedish and Russian lumberjacks and miners, many of whom had been members of the W.F.M. Others who organized these clubs, like George Speed, had been involved with the International Workingmen's Association. Speed organized an Industrial Workers Club in San Francisco, six months in advance of the I.W.W.'s founding convention.[58] P.L.M. members, after the strikes in Cananea and Rio Blanco, Mexico, formed Spanish-speaking locals in California and Arizona.[59]

Only one anarchist from the western states can be identified at the I.W.W.'s founding convention. Al Klemensic attended as a representative of the Colorado Journeymen Tailor's Union. A powerful spokes-

person for revolutionary industrial unionism, Klemensic emphasized
the futility of political action:

> All those who have been watching the movement in the different
> Socialist parties, Democratic party and Republican party, know of
> the corruption that has been going on in those places. Now, we
> know that it matters not what political party the workingman
> trusts in, he has been betrayed by every political party, and he is
> going to be betrayed by every political party in which he is going to
> trust. Therefore it was seen that there was a necessity for a new
> declaration of principles and a new reorganization of the labor
> forces. It was necessary for the workingman to see that his salva-
> tion lies in direct action, that is, in action directly to wrest from the
> capitalist the means of oppression and controlling his bread; and
> when he sees this he will take this if he can, either by violence, or
> through cooperation, or otherwise, according as the working peo-
> ple are able to organize themselves and find a means to solve this
> problem.[60]

Following the founding convention, Klemensic actively propagated the
I.W.W.'s form of industrial unionism within the anarchist community.
In the anarchist press, he wrote articles urging workers to join the I.W.W.
and reported on the progress of the industrial union movement. Klemensic's writings appeared in both the *Liberator* and the *Demonstrator*.

In addition to linking the I.W.W.'s developing form of industrial
unionism to the efforts of the Haymarket anarchists, speakers at the
convention discussed Bakunin, the activities of Russian anarchists and
revolutionaries, and the importance of French syndicalism.[61] Speaking
to the delegation concerning the I.W.W.'s intentions to promote a
worldwide organization of labor, W.E. Trautmann said:

> We are aware of the fact that...the followers of Bakunin...have in the
> last five years organized economic organizations on the class
> struggle that will eventually come under the head of the organiza-
> tion we are now going to form and with whom we can establish
> such relations as to bring the immigrants from foreign countries
> into the fold of industrial unions in this country.[62]

Little information exists on the I.W.W.'s initial contact with Slavic immigrants. However, through the efforts of Bill Shatoff, a Russian anarcho-syndicalist who immigrated to the United States in 1907, the I.W.W. gained many members of the Union of Russian Workers.[63] A jack-of-all-trades, Shatoff worked at various jobs—machinist, long-shoreman, and printer, and was on the staff of *Golos Truda,* the organ of the Union of Russian Workers of the United States and Canada. In both the Union of Russian Workers and the I.W.W., Shatoff took an active part, riding the rails from one end of the country to the other, working as an organizer and lecturer until his return to Russia in 1917.[64]

The Paterson anarchists, who had assisted the W.F.M. in union-forming activities, did not send an official delegate. It is probable that an observer attended but did not register as a delegate. *La Questione Sociale,* organ of the Paterson anarchist, announced in its August 5, 1905 issue that "the Chicago convention . . . was a partial anarchist victory." In September, Charles O. Sherman, first and last President of the I.W.W., and William E. Trautmann, Secretary-Treasurer, spoke to a packed and enthusiastic crowd at Helvetia Hall in Paterson on the merits of indus-trial unionism. Shortly after this meeting, sponsored by locals 8 and 20 of the Italian Silkworkers Union, A. Guabello, an anarchist affiliated with the "Right to Existence" group, led a strike against the Victory Silk Company. During the strike, which ended in a partial victory for the silk workers, the I.W.W. provided strike support. Throughout the winter months and into early spring of 1906, the I.W.W. continued in its support of the silk workers. On May Day, 1906, the Italian silk workers affiliated with the I.W.W. In its March 24th issue, the I.W.W.'s logo appeared on the masthead of *La Questione Sociale.*[65]

The influence of anarchism in the formation of the I.W.W. cannot be reduced to the work of a single individual, group or philo-sophy. More than mere remnants of the Chicago group of the 1880s, anarchists influencing the I.W.W.'s form of industrial unionism reflected a wide range of cultural and political experience. The ideas represented by immigrant anarchists attending the I.W.W.'s founding convention were rooted in the philosophy and activities of Bakunin and the libertarian socialists that founded the Anti-Authoritarian Interna-tional. Also attending the convention were anarchists whose original contact began among individualist anarchists who were born in the

United States. Some of these American anarchists drew from the experience of their European comrades. The foundations of American anarcho-syndicalism therefore was rooted in the combined efforts of native and immigrant social revolutionaries.

The activities and philosophy of anarchists, who struggled to build a relationship to the trade union movement, prefigured many of the principles and tactics eventually incorporated into the I.W.W.'s form of industrial unionism. Their activism defined a crucial part of the I.W.W.'s labor radicalism in the period before America's entry into World War I. The nature of the influence of anarchist principles and tactics on the industrial union movement was complex and ubiquitous. This view is substantiated by the emergence of anarchist groups whose ideas concerning industrial unionism paralleled those of the I.W.W. to such an extent that they affiliated without attending the inaugural convention. Those anarchists attending the founding convention affirmed a continuity with past attempts at building a revolutionary industrial union movement. Their presence was also an indication that labor radicalism needed to move beyond socialist or progressive politics, not because the movement lacked political ideas, but because political means no longer represented a viable path for labor radicalism to pursue.[66]

The French Unions are Infecting the Army with Anti-Militarist Propaganda

"Would You Kill Your Fathers, Brothers and Fellow Workers"

Industrial Worker, October 19, 1910, p. 1.

CHAPTER FOUR

The I.W.W. and the C.G.T.

I have argued that historical accounts of the I.W.W. have denied or trivialized the movement's early libertarian influences and relationship to European syndicalism. For the most part, these accounts reflect inadequate explanations of the origins and development of revolutionary syndicalism, its early impact on the American labor movement, and those who brought its belief system into the I.W.W. These omissions have particularly impacted historical perceptions regarding the nature and extent to which the I.W.W.'s principles of industrial solidarity were influenced by the C.G.T.'s (Confederation Generale du Travail, General Confederaion of Labor) form of syndicalism. This chapter, therefore, more fully elaborates on the I.W.W.'s relationship to French syndicalism. I will argue that the influences of the C.G.T. occur earlier and are more complex than existing narrative or interpretative accounts posit. I will show that the differences in theory, organizational forms, and strategy existing between the movements did not preclude mutual influence.

While the I.W.W. can not be considered an alien import but rather one that emerged from economic conditions and a particular cultural and political milieu indigenous to the United states, the founders did draw on the experience of French syndicalists in clarifying their objectives and strategy, as they did with other forms of labor radicalism that supported their developing conception of industrial unionism. In one of the few documents to survive the I.W.W.'s formative period, the important relationship of the C.G.T. to the birth of the I.W.W.'s form of industrial unionism is openly acknowledged. In a letter, dated April 10, 1905, W.E. Trautmann invited the officers and members of the C.G.T. to the Chicago convention intended to inaugurate the I.W.W. Trautmann concluded the invitation in the following manner:

> It is the desire of all those who have realized that the irrespressible class conflict in society demands adequate weapons and instruments to conduct the fight, to establish among such workers as adhere to the same principles such a unity of action, and effort similar to that now existing in France. . . .[1]

Emile Pouget, the anarcho-syndicalist associate secretary of the C.G.T., wrote in his reply that the great distance and expense made sending a delegate impossible. "But although we shall not be able actively to participate in that economic manifestation (manifestation of unionism), we are in full sympathy with you. . . ."[2]

While stressing "a unity of action and effort similar to that now existing in France," the I.W.W.'s early expression of solidarity with French syndicalists did not imply a relationship that was primarily structural or theoretical. The founders identified with the revolutionary activity of French syndicalism, acknowledging the fact that French syndicalists had given organized expression to a spirit, method, and aim emerging out of the self-activity of the industrial proletariat throughout the world. The I.W.W., in its expression of solidarity with French syndicalists, both indicated and affirmed the presence of a form of revolutionary activity that had transcended national boundaries. The worker intellectuals who played an instrumental role in the birth of the

I.W.W., like French syndicalists, considered their practice and sensibility the the result of experimentation. Their work was informed and shaped by conditions and diverse traditions of working-class struggle rather than by the authority of a single doctrine. The I.W.W. considered French syndicalism a particular manifestation of industrial unionism and referred to the C.G.T.'s form of syndicalism as industrial unionism.[3] In expressing solidarity with the C.G.T., the I.W.W. acknowledged the importance of French syndicalism to the rebirth of the industrial union movement, while maintaining a distinctive identity.

In acknowledging the importance of French syndicalism, the I.W.W. was not expressing interest in copying the C.G.T's form of syndicalism. Rather, the early Wobblies believed that they were in a position to learn from the experience of French syndicalists and improve on the contributions made by French syndicalists to revolutionary unionism. "The I.W.W. is in a position to profit from the mistakes and hardships of the French organization," proclaimed the *Industrial Worker* (*I.W.*) "and thus eliminate the useless waste of the past twenty years." In this editorial, the writer suggests that although some of the practices of the C.G.T. may be shortsighted, the position of the I.W.W. should not be one of criticism but of improvement "on the exactness with which it 'follows copy.' " The author emphasized the youth of the I.W.W., reminding the membership that the I.W.W. had not passed through the C.G.T.'s bitter school of experience. The writer concluded the editorial by encouraging I.W.W. agitators "to point to the truths learned by the C.G.T. in [its] weary years of effort."[4]

Since the I.W.W. did not imitate the specific organizational strategies emerging out of the European syndicalist movement, particularly those expressed by the C.G.T, early historians discounted the strength of European anarcho-syndicalist influences on the I.W.W. Louis Levine in his analysis of American syndicalism argued that contact between the movements represented a minor factor in the I.W.W.'s birth. Levine saw what he termed the "intellectual influence of France" to be outweighed by organizational differences between the movements. The points of agreement which later emerged between the C.G.T. and the I.W.W. he, therefore, considered to be self-evident and not worth dwelling upon. "The conception of the social role of the labor union, the idea of the 'general strike,' the emphasis on direct action as opposed to political action, the revolutionary spirit—these are elements common to both."[5] While nominal similarities existed in some of the terms employed, the I.W.W. made significant departures in its interpretations and application of these principles and tactics.

While early contact with French syndicalists and the uses made by the I.W.W. of the C.G.T.'s principles of revolutionary unionism indicate complex ideational interpenetration between the movements, Levine held that organizational and strategic differnces were of greater significance. Syndicalism emerged in France at a time when the syndicates were just beginning to grow, he pointed out. French syndicalists, unlike their American industrial unionist counterparts, found no established labor organizations to oppose them. French syndicalists, therefore, did not form separate organizations. The I.W.W., on the other hand, emerged as a separate organization and did not believe in the desirability of merging with the American Federation of Labor. The existence of sectionalism within the American Labor movement, he argued, made the movements differ so vastly that intellectual influences could only be considered of subordinate importance.[6] In relying solely on the criteria of organizational imitation, Levine's analysis not only trivialized contact between the movements but implied that structural differences precluded mutual influence.

Levine's analysis follows a major dispute within the I.W.W. over the application of one of the C.G.T.'s organizational strategies in America. Sent to represent the I.W.W. at the International Trade Union Secretariat convening in Budapest during the summer of 1911, William Z. Foster returned convinced that the I.W.W. needed to adopt the French syndicalist organizational strategy of "boring-from-within." In a letter which appeared in the *I.W.*, Foster pointed out that the I.W.W.'s membership was not growing as it should. He criticized the I.W.W. in light of the success of European syndicalists, particularly those in Britain and France, where "boring-from-within" was responsible for the capture of a huge number of socialists. Foster concluded his criticism in the following way:

> I am satisfied from my observations that the only way for the I.W.W. to have workers adopt and practice the principles of revolutionary unionism . . . is to give up its attempt to create a new

labor movement, turn itself into a propaganda league, get into the organized labor movement, and by building up better fighting machines within the old unions than those possessed by our reactionary enemies, revolutionize these unions even as our French Syndicalist fellow workers have so successfully done with theirs.[7]

Foster felt that it was a mistake to have the strong radical minority within the labor movement withdraw from the trade unions, leaving them in the hands of reactionaries.

Foster's letter sparked exchanges in *Solidarity* and the *I.W.* After allowing the debate to run across the pages of its journals, a column appeared entitled "Discussion Closed." In *Solidarity* the editor wrote:

Those who oppose it (boring-from-within), as a rule, base their opposition upon the experience gained in the "boring process" or upon critical study of the American labor movement. They bitterly resent the idea that they must necessarily follow the example of French syndicalists. And in fact, France seems to stand alone on the proposition, as the same resentment is shown toward Jorhaux' admonition to "join the conservative unions" on the part of revolutionary syndicalists in Germany, Sweden and other European countries.

[The I.W.W.'s] ... position is a flexible one, to this extent, it does not prevent any member from "boring in the craft unions" if he wishes to do so. But it commits our organization to a ceaseless warfare against all agencies and institutions of capitalism, on the one hand; and to the constructive task of supplanting capitalism on the other, by organizing THE UNION OF THE WORKING CLASS.

The editor concluded by expressed hope that "fellow worker Foster ... would abandon the idea when be became better acquainted with the American situation."[8] Foster, however, did not abandon the idea. Accusing the I.W.W. of dual unionism, Foster continued to agitate to change the I.W.W.'s organizational form and strategy. Under continued opposition to his idea that the I.W.W. imitate French syndicalism, Foster withdrew from the I.W.W. to found the short–lived Syndicalist League of North America in 1912.[9]

Joseph Ettor, an I.W.W. organizer who played a prominent role in the Lawrence Textile Strike of 1912, responded to the criticism from "boring-from-within" advocates. He held that the I.W.W.'s rejection of the strategy did not constitute dual unionism. Ettor argued that the I.W.W. had taken on the task of organizing immigrant and unskilled workers disfranchised from the trade union movement. The A.F. of L., he wrote, is:

> . . . a skilled workers' corporation, organized by and for the skilled, and controlled by and serving the economic interests of the skilled worker, against and at the actual expense of the unskilled and unorganized foreign and native workers alike.

Ettor concluded:

> We are not wasting our efforts by fighting the class struggle inside of capitalist institutions with a labor name. . . . We are developing and building a fighting machine in which only revolutionaries have anything to say as to "how" and "what."[10]

Ettor's argument against the charge of dual unionism called attention to the fact that the I.W.W.'s emergence and activities were not primarily a response to the existence of sectionalism. While industrial unionists deplored the fact that workers were not organized by trade unionists according to industry but as separate crafts, the critique of trade unionism went beyond the organizational weakness resulting from the structural limitations of craft unionism. The I.W.W.'s critique recognized the essential weakness of the economic base of craft unionism, which the I.W.W. argued was being eroded by technological development and industrial combinations:

> Social relations and groupings only reflect mechanical and industrial conditions. The *great facts* of present industry are the displacement of human skills by machines and the increasing of capitalist power through concentration in the possession of the tools with which wealth is produced and distributed.

Because of these facts trade divisions between laborers and competition among capitalists are alike disappearing. Class divisions grow even more fixed and class antagonisms move sharp. Trade divisions have been swallowed up in a common servitude of all workers to the machines that they tend. New machines, ever replacing less productive ones, wipe out whole trades and plunge new bodies of workers into the ever growing army of tradeless, hopeless unemployed.[11]

Machine technology was rapidly eliminating the property of the trade unionist and shifting the locus of revolutionary struggle:

Skilled labor is being qualitatively reduced to terms of unskilled labor. The crafts are tottering and the future of the proletariat is no longer in the hands of the aristocracy of labor but is being transformed at an ever increasing speed into those of the common labor masses.[12]

The I.W.W. saw the process of capitalist development as breaking down the dividing lines of the crafts, initiating a development that made the old form of organization of industry obsolete. The I.W.W., therefore, held that the unskilled laborer, excluded from the fold of craft unions yet ever increasing in numbers as the result of industrial and technological developments, was in the most strategic position in the labor struggle:

Since it (I.W.W.) is largely migratory in character and is used to the ebb and flow of demand, lack of employment does not have the same terrors for its members; it can manage without strike pay, and by frequent strikes of short duration can inflict a vast amount of damage upon the enemy without much suffering itself.[13]

French syndicalists, though their organizational structure and strategy differed from the I.W.W.'s, recognized the critical role of the unskilled laborer and developed methods to organize them.

The I.W.W.'s position on the debate within the C.G.T. on the strategy of "boring-from-within" did not preclude the acceptance and improvement of tactics pioneered by the C.G.T. An I.W.W. pamphlet, for example, lauded the C.G.T.'s effective organization of the unskilled worker, pointing out that the effective organization of these workers by French syndicalists had made the long strike obsolete:

> To win or lose in two weeks and go back with the organization intact is the aim of the leaders. The superiority of this method over the old fashioned long-fought struggle with the suffering of families and the expenditure of strike pay is obvious. Industrial conflicts tend to become shorter and sharper.[14]

The I.W.W.s not only lauded French strike strategy but sought to apply and interpret its lessons in particular strike situations and as a means of affirming the efficacy of its conception of industrial unionism.[15]

Brissenden however argued that no "direct contact" existed between the I.W.W., and the C.G.T. before 1908. He therefore concluded that the I.W.W.'s "relations with the French movement have not at any time been as close as is generally imagined."[16] The influence of French syndicalism on the I.W.W., he concluded, amounted to little more than a contagion of ideas that spread through personal contact and had little impact on the I.W.W.'s formal policy. While admitting that the I.W.W. did gain certain strike tactics from this contact, Brissenden held that they amounted to no more than "a foggy set of philosophical concepts about the 'General Strike' and the 'militant minority,' etc. . . ." Although the I.W.W.'s uses of these concepts were far from vague and were not intended to suggest unconditional acceptance of the C.G.T.'s program, Brissenden nevertheless asserted that "to this extent the I.W.W. represented a syndicalist union." However, he qualified this conclusion, embellishing on Levine's earlier findings:

> In structure [the I.W.W.] is a decentralized body (to the extent that it has a body to be decentralized), whereas the C.G.T. is decidedly centralized. In its attitude toward compatriot labor bodies it is at variance with the French Confederation. The French idea has taken more definite form in the United States in the shape of the Syndicalist League of North America.[17]

The structural emphasis of early accounts misrepresents the significance of the I.W.W.'s relationship to the C.G.T. Implicit in these early perspectives are the notions that the organizational structure of the C.G.T. formed the basis from which its syndicalist identity was drawn and that such organizational differences precluded ideological incorporation, thereby nullifying significant degrees of intellectual contact between the movements. The uses made by the I.W.W. of European anarcho-syndicalist beliefs, however, demonstrate that the activity, ideology, and symbols of revolutionary syndicalism, particularly those of the C.G.T., supplanted organizational correspondences as a source of influence and identification between the movements. Organizational differences between the movements in Europe and the United States did not initially serve to cancel mutual influences, but rather shaped the forms of syndicalist expressions entering the industrial union movement.

These complexities in the I.W.W.'s early relationship to the European syndicalism can especially be seen in the I.W.W.'s early discussion and use of the concept of the general strike. Initially, French syndicalists thought of the general strike as a legal, peaceful means of ushering in the social revolution. The general strike was conceived of as a "peaceful strike of folded arms" in which workers in many industries would simultaneously lay down their tools and leave. Such a strike could be decreed in advance, last a few days, paralyze the life of the country, reduce the ruling class to famine, and compel the government to capitulate to the workers' demand for social reconstruction.[18] Following the C.G.T.'s emergence, these ideas underwent some modification. At the Congress at Tours (1896), the following conception of the general strike was endorsed by the C.G.T.:

> The general strike cannot be decreed in advance; it will burst forth suddenly: a strike of railway men, for instance, if declared, will be the signal of the general strike. It will be the duty of militant working men, when the signal is given, to make their comrades in the syndicates leave their work. Those who continue work on that day will be compelled to quit.[19]

In the years prior to the I.W.W.'s founding convention, the C.G.T. made other changes in its conception of the general strike. All but the idea that the general strike would involve workers laying down their tools and leaving the factories changed. The Charter of Amiens, adopted at the C.G.T.'s 1906 convention, redefined the general strike as the final move in the class war. Rather than bursting forth in a spontaneous manner, such a work stoppage would require discipline and perfect coordination. French syndicalists came to conceive of the general strike not as an immediate possibility but as an action which would require years of effort and propaganda.[20]

These ideas had received earlier and fuller expression in Arnold Roller's well-known pamphlet on "The Social General Strike," translated and made available by the Chicago Debating Club in 1905. At the I.W.W.'s founding convention, the Industrial Workers Club of Chicago, which Hagerty represented, authored a resolution calling for the convention to adopt the "social general strike . . . as the final solution of the class struggle." The resolution argued that the social general strike represented "the most effective warfare [against] plutocratic capitalism" as well as a means of "inaugurat[ing] a universal democracy for the worker."[21]

Roller's pamphlet on the general strike represented the most complete elaboration of the history, theory, and application of the general strike available at the time. In his pamphlet, the German anarcho–syndicalist presented the general strike as an action in which all workers would lay down their tools at the same time to interrupt completely a country's production, stopping consumption and communication "for a time long enough to totally disorganize society." Following a period of propaganda, with proper organization and favorable conditions, labor unions would call for a general strike in all branches. The strike would begin with the complete disorganization of capitalist society and end with workers taking "possession through its labor unions of all the means of production, mines, houses, the land; in short, all the economic factors." Roller theorized that with proper organization a

> "...general strike [had] the most favorable prospects during a bad business cycle.... The crisis of overproduction is the best guarantee

for the success of the general strike, because the products on hand permit the satisfaction of all [the workers'] needs, before complete reorganization. Under such conditions the ruling class would be forced to yield to a reorganization of society. It is the passive obedience, the submission of the working people, upon which the power of the ruling class rests. . . . Their whole splendor and their wealth depend upon our work. If our obedience be discontinued, their power will be broken. Let us stop working for them and they will starve in spite of their money; and they must yield.[22]

In his pamphlet, Roller likened his idea of a social general strike to a poem written by Percy Bysshe Shelly. "What else can Shelly have thought," Roller asked, "in his splendid poem 'To the Men of England' when he wrote:

> Men of England, wherefore plough,
>> For the lord who lay low?
> Wherefore weave with toil and care
>> The rich robes your tyrants wear?
>
> Wherefore feed, and cloth and save,
>> From the cradle to the grave,
> The ungrateful drones would
>> Drain your sweat—nay, drink your blood?
>
> Wherefore, bees of England, forge
>> Many a weapon, chain and scourge,
> That these stingless drones may spoil
>> The forced produce of your soil?
>
> Have ye leisure, comfort, calm?
>> Shelter food, love's gentle balm?
> Or what is it ye buy so dear
>> With your pain and with your fear?
>
> The seed ye sow, another reaps;
>> The wealth ye find, another keeps;

> The robes ye weave, another wears;
> The arms ye forge, another bears.
>
> Sow seeds—but let no tyrant reap;
> Find wealth—let no imposter heap;
> Weave robes—let not the idle wear;
> Forge arms—in your defense to bear.[23]

"To the Men of England" was among the first poems and songs to appear on I.W.W. song cards, a small four-page brochure that sold for five cents a copy. These brochures contained such classic songs of revolt as "The Red Flag," "The Marseillaise," and "Hold the Fort." Song cards became a popular organizing tool during the I.W.W.'s early years and led to the publication of the I.W.W.'s *Little Red Song Book* in 1909. Organizers used these songs to awaken the class feeling of a larger solidarity, as a tool for education and dissemination of the ideas of industrial unionism and as a means to gather and hold crowds for I.W.W. speakers.[24]

A 1906 editorial on the general strike, however, while incorporating elements of French syndicalism, differed from the C.G.T. position in important ways. The editorial began by underscoring the critical role of industrial organization to the success of a general strike:

> We came nearer to a general strike in 1894 than at any other time in the history of the labor movement, and as everybody knows, that was far from being a *general* strike. Had all the great industries been operated at that time by workers industrially organized, instead of being in the impotent hands of workers organized in autonomous craft unions, the strike would have been general— and successful.

The editorial went on to harshly criticize the strategy of work stoppage as a means of effecting a general strike:

> A strike that separates the workers from the tools and stops production is a strike that can be settled with machine guns. . . .
> A strike that stops all work would be general. It would also

be a general calamity. If the working-class brain can devise no better way than a plunge into universal suspension of production and distribution, there is no hope for it.

To the conception of the general strike advanced by French syndicalists and elaborated on by Roller, the I.W.W. added the strategy of the "general lockout," in which workers would occupy the factories instead of leaving them:

> The general strike that will entail the least amount of suffering, that will not "paralyze the industrial life of the nation," but rather insure the continuance and uninterrupted progress of production, is a general lockout of all capitalist masters.

Though closer to the idea originally advanced by Hagerty and Parsons at the I.W.W. founding convention, the idea of the general lockout as elaborated in the editorial also included a role for political action. The lockout of the employing class would be followed by a takeover and possession of the machinery of government to legalize the holding of the factories, mills, mines, and workshops. The I.W.W., however, did not consider the advocacy of the general strike to be realistic at that stage of its development:

> We are now dealing with the immediate phenomena and conditions of the working-class struggle. Useless we are trying to deceive ourselves and hold out false hope to others, we will confront the facts squarely. The working class has neither a political or economic organization powerful enought to undertake a general strike.[25]

The I.W.W.'s elaboration of the tactical significance of the general strike first appears in connection with the trial of Moyer, Haywood, and Pettibone and will be addressed in the next chapter.

The theoretical and organizational differences that existed between the movements did not preclude incorporation in modified form, of ideas advanced by French syndicalists. In spite of the differences between the movements, the I.W.W. continued to affirm its solidarity with the C.G.T. In his report to the I.W.W.'s 1907 convention, General Secretary-Treasurer Trautmann emphasized that the "I.W.W. represented in even more advanced forms and tactics the same principles as espoused by the industrial unionists in France."[26] The *Industrial Union Bulletin* reported that the C.G.T. had endorsed the I.W.W.'s program of principles in advance of the I.W.W. third convention.[27] Early news articles in the I.W.W.'s official press suggested a deepening of fraternal ties between the movements. An article in *Solidarity,* for example, in reporting the recent activities of French syndicalists stated that: "The [General] confederation [of Labor] was organized 15 years ago. Its principles are substantially those of the I.W.W."[28] The *I.W.* celebrated the French postal workers' strike with an article entitled "Sunrise in France":

> Rise, crowned with Light; Industrial Union, rise!
> Exalt thy towering head and lift thine eyes!
> See hope its sparkling portals wide display
> And break upon thee in a flood of day!

"The news from our fellow workers in France," the articles continued, "is so welcomed that it is cause for widespread rejoicing among members of the same union here, the industrial union, Hurrah, Hurrah, Hurrah!"[29]

In addition to influencing the beliefs, principles, and tactics that led to the I.W.W.'s emergence and the development of its version of industrial solidarity, the influences of French syndicalism are especially apparent in the cultural forms developed by rank-and-file artists. As I will show in the next chapter, songs, poems, and graphics with explicit French syndicalist content appeared in the I.W.W.'s official literature and played an integral role in the development of the I.W.W.'s labor radicalism in the period before America's entry into World War I. These art forms further modified the meanings and applications of tactics derived from French syndicalists.

The complicated denials of the C.G.T.'s contribution to the emergence and development of the I.W.W. made by early historians were strengthened in Fred Thompson's official history of the I.W.W. Though an inhouse history of the I.W.W., Thompson's history differs markedly from the conventional "vanity" histories published by unions to flatter bureaucrats. Thompson took issue with Brissenden's ambiguous statements regarding the I.W.W.'s status as a syndicalist organization and presented an altogether different theory to account for the I.W.W.'s relationship to the C.G.T. Thompson argues that the identification of the I.W.W.'s form of industrial unionism with French anarcho-syndicalism occurred later than Brissenden suggests. Thompson argues that the identification of the I.W.W. with the C.G.T. began in the teens and derived from a mixture of right-wing quarrels in the S.P., sensational soapboxing, and the irresponsible and unofficial actions of the autonomous I.W.W. Publishing Bureau of Cleveland. Thompson argues that pamphlet literature containing French anarcho-syndicalist principles and tactics, though advertised and made available through the I.W.W. locals, never constituted official statements of the I.W.W.'s policy. The I.W.W. was not officially responsible for the views expressed in Arturo Giovannitti's translation of Emile Pouget's book *Sabotage,* or F. Charles's translation of E. Pataud and E. Pouget's *Syndicalism and the Cooperative Commonwealth.* Moreover, Thompson argues, pamphlets written by I.W.W. members which deal with French anarcho-syndicalist practices can not be considered official statements of policy since they were published through other presses.[30]

The official I.W.W. press, Thompson asserts, merely reported on the status of the French movement and promoted some of the pamphlet literature written by French anarcho-syndicalists on sabotage and the general strike. Thompson finds only one mention of syndicalist tactics in any official I.W.W. publication prior to 1912. He therefore concludes that this unofficial literature, some of which was made available through the autonomous I.W.W. Publishing Bureau, was responsible for the association of the I.W.W. with the C.G.T. form of syndicalism. This literature was primarily disseminated by soapboxers who:

> Found that talk of sabotage gave their audiences a thrill, and since dispensers [of official literature] were happy to send them along for sale on commission to all that would handle them, there was nothing to stop spielman, whether they were I.W.W. or not, from procuring these booklets, mounting a soapbox, talking about the I.W.W., talking up a collection, and selling the literature.[31]

In Thompson's view the I.W.W. merely printed news articles on the French syndicalist movement and advertised its pamphlet literature. While this contributed to the diffusion of French anarcho-syndicalist ideas and tactics, it was not synonymous with official advocacy on the part of the I.W.W. nor does it indicate that the I.W.W. was a syndicalist organization.

Although Thompson went overboard in his attempt to refute the efforts of earlier historians to pin the syndicalist label on the I.W.W., his conclusions regarding the I.W.W.'s official incorporation of the C.G.T's tactics at the level of formal policy is essentially correct. The I.W.W.'s official organizational policy eschewed advocacy of tactics, reasoning that "what may be revolutionary in one conflict may prove disastrous in another; what may bring temporary success now may turn into a defeat later. . . ."[32] The I.W.W. held that tactical success depended on the knowledge and initiative of the workers, not on its ability to advocate correct tactics. This is particularly evident in the I.W.W.'s first statements on the movement's methods and means:

> ...the capitalist class throughout the world, through their pliant tools, are watching every move of the proletarians, for fear that methods adopted successfully in the conflicts of one land may be copied in another; trembling because they would dread nothing more than to see the working class profit from the experience of all and thereby avoid the mistakes which doom others in their struggles. But knowledge is power; and to know the fighting methods applied by Industrial Unionists in every land the globe over . . . . is one of the essential requisites of those who struggle and strive to attain the quickest and best results in the war of the workers against the shirkers.[33]

The I.W.W., therefore, did not consider its use of knowledge derived from other revolutionary movements to be synonymous with official sanction or incorporation at the level of policy. The editor of *Solidarity,* for example, emphatically denied characterizations which sought to reduce the I.W.W.'s relationship with the European syndicalist movement to one of policy, simple imitation, or passive adoption:

Whatever terms or phrases we may borrow from the French or
other languages to denote our method cut no figure: the methods
[of the I.W.W.] conform to American conditions in relation to our
aim.[34]

Rather, the I.W.W.'s position on the practices of the C.G.T. and other
forms of European syndicalism indicates complex interpenetration
between its form of industrial solidarity and that advanced by European
anarcho-syndicalists. This fact is articulated by the I.W.W. editorial
position on the C.G.T. tactic of sabotage:

> Sabotage, though a new word, is as old as the labor movement. It is
> now assuming new and complex forms in relationship to that
> movement. We need not "advocate" it; we need only explain it.
> The organized worker will do the acting.[35]

In a letter to *Solidarity,* an I.W.W. who identifies himself as "the
Rambler," writes that sabotage:

> . . . is always an outcome of the class struggle in which the
> oppressed act directly rather than through representatives.
>   Sabotage is not a principle of the I.W.W., . . . it is a tactic the
> value of which will be determined by the workers who use it.[36]

The *I.W.* frequently asserted that, though in solidarity with
French syndicalists, this solidarity did not mean that the I.W.W. was a
syndicalist organization modeled after the C.G.T. In an article entitled
"Industrial Unionism Is Not Syndicalism," the editor emphasized the
iconoclastic nature of the I.W.W. philosophy of industrial unionism,
implying that its philosophy could best be described as a pluralism of
revolutionary tendencies:

> Industrial unionism accepts all of the syndicalist tactics that
> experience has shown to be available for present purposes. It
> stands for direct action, sabotage, anti-patriotism and the general
> strike. It out-socializes socialism by practicing internationalism
> instead of preaching it. The I.W.W. welcomes alike the American-

born and the Asiatic, although the latter is turned down by craft unionists and political socialists. From socialism, however, industrialism gets much basic thought while rejecting all ideas of state control or interference in industrial affairs. From anarchism it gains some useful tactics and vital principles but refuses to accept the individualism which is a preventative to solidarity.[37]

Although the use of organizational imitation and the corresponding concern with political formalism hardly capture the complexity of the I.W.W.'s relationship to the C.G.T. and have led to erroneous assumptions regarding the nature of the I.W.W.'s form of industrial solidarity, scholars rediscovering the I.W.W. in the fifties and sixties continued to invoke the legitimacy of these criteria in assessing the I.W.W.'s form of industrial unionism. For the most part these studies merely reiterate, elaborate, and emphasize the perspective on the I.W.W.'s relationship to the C.G.T. found in the early and official accounts of the I.W.W. Melvyn Dubofsky, as we have seen, finds all the ideology and tactics that came to represent the I.W.W.'s form of industrial unionism to have originated among frontier activists who formed the W.F.M. and A.L.U. According to Dubofsky, the syndicalism which entered the I.W.W formed in response to industrial conditions in the American West and had no intellectual basis in French or other form of European syndicalism. Like Brissenden, he asserts that the I.W.W. represented "the American variety of syndicalism." He considers the apparent complexity in the I.W.W.'s relationship to French syndicalism the result of "the fuzzy-mindedness of some Wobbly thinkers" and insists that "there was no incompatibility between industrial unionism and syndicalism." Dubofsky submits the I.W.W.'s use of syndicalist tactics to the same crude generalizations. "One might scarcely expect the typical Wobbly to comprehend the subtleties of nonviolent as compared to violent sabotage. Sabotage, after all, is a weapon of the disorganized, the defeated, the dejected, and, as such, it must have great appeal to workers drawn from the 'culture of poverty'."[38]

Philip Foner offered a slightly different interpretation in his account. He argues that the influence of French syndicalism occurred earlier than Brissenden believed. He cites an interview with William E. Trautmann to support his claim while ignoring the importance of

McKee's work on DeLeon and the early impact of libertarian and European sources of syndicalism on the American labor movement. Foner asserts that a reporter from the *Cincinnati Post* quoted Trautmann as explaining that the *Industrial Union Manifesto* was a reflection of the principles advanced by organized labor in continental Europe. He contends that Trautmann was quoted by this reporter as having said that this meant specifically the organization of labor under "revolutionary syndicalism."[39] Foner then leaps to the conclusion that "the theory of industrial unionism which the I.W.W. brought into sharp focus had no real intellectual basis in European syndicalism."[40] Rather, the I.W.W.'s form of industrual unionism developed out of the anti-political, anarcho-syndicalist tendency beginning to develop in America around 1880. Though he refers the reader to another volume of his history of the labor movement, Foner does not develop or elaborate on these links. Instead, he borrows from conclusions reached by Barnes, in his study of the I.W.W.'s ideology and organization, to insist that the basic nature of the I.W.W. was nevertheless that of a syndicalist organization.[41]

Joseph Conlin, in his interpretative study of the I.W.W. before World War I, disagrees. Critical of Foner's findings, he insists that the I.W.W. has been erroneously labeled syndicalist by both historians and critics. Drawing on Levine's discussion of the differences between the I.W.W. and the C.G.T., Conlin wrote:

> In the case of the Wobblies and syndicalism, the identification of the two has served to obscure historical perception of the I.W.W. Indeed, if the I.W.W. had had anything to do with it, the label would never have been fixed, for the union rarely acknowledged the term. Wobblies referred to themselves as revolutionary industrial unionists or industrial unionists or, simply industrialists. They often explicitly denied, sometimes with vehemence, any relationship with what they considered an essentially European movement.[42]

Here Conlin refers to the defensive posture toward associations with the European syndicalist movement that developed after the arrest of I.W.W. activists under the espionage and criminal syndicalist laws. An I.W.W. pamphlet, published during the government's attack on the movement, denied the exaggerated claim that the I.W.W. was a foreign import or by-product of French syndicalism:

> In the United States the word (syndicalism) is so lost in a maze of misunderstanding as to mean almost anything. . . . When the I.W.W. began to assume power in this country, the mongering apologists for the capitalist system attacked it most bitterly. To create a prejudice against it, they called it an importation—syndicalism from Europe. The name so attached itself to the organization that well-meaning "historians" have called the I.W.W. the syndicalist movement of America. The I.W.W. and the syndicalist movement of Europe differ widely in many respects. The I.W.W. is not a by-product of the syndicalist movement.[43]

As I have shown, the I.W.W.'s attitude toward the C.G.T. and other forms of European syndicalism is considerably more complex in the period before America's entry into World War I than Conlin's analysis suggests. The same is also true of the period during and after World War I. The I.W.W.'s use of syndicalist propaganda continued to appear in songs and graphics, not as statements of policy but as expressions of rank-and-file militancy. The "Harvest Song," for example, written by Ralph Chaplin in 1915 praises the French syndicalist tactic of sabotage:

> The ripening grain is waiting for us
> now,
> And they need us all in all the land.
> The guy who turns it into gold
> Is the hobo harvest hand.
> Get rich in a hurry—we're the ones
> you rob—
> And so we wear our sabots on the
> job.
>
> *Chorus:*
> The Wobbly is the boy to reap the
> harvest—

The one prepared to do it
    right.
The cockroaches and hogs who'd
    like to starve us,
    Will give us what we want or
    fade from sight.
The wooden shoe is the proper
    method
    To make them run their hold-up
    at a loss;
    Each sizzlook of a boss
    Gets "next" and come across;—
The Wobbly is the boy to reap the
    harvest!

The fields and jungles now are full
    of slaves,
    They are waiting to be put wise;
And the one big union is the way
    That all workers should organize.
Line them all up solid, union makes
    us strong;
And better hours and wages is our
    song.

Some day we'll take the good things
    of the earth
    That the parasites hoard and sell;
We'll keep our products for our-
    selves,
    And bosses can go to hell.
The earth is on the button that we
    Wobblies wear;
We'll turn the sab cat loose or get
    our share![44]

The song uses both the French syndicalist symbol of the wooden shoe and the I.W.W.'s modification of the symbol. The "sab cat" is a term of uncertain origins.[45] It first appeared in a poem published in *Solidarity* in 1913. Later, Wobblies extended the "sab cat" figure visually to illustrate striking on the job, direct action, the general strike, and sabotage, as agitation materials in support of Ford and Suhr clearly indicate.

Between the outbreak of and America's entry into World War I, the sab cat appeared in numerous cartoons, graphics and songs. In this period the sab cat changed visually from a tabby cat to a black cat, and its use was extended to "silent agitators," two-by-two-inch stickers printed in red and black.

FORD and SUHR INFORMATION

For leading a strike against their masters in the hop fields of California, Ford and Suhr were sentenced to life imprisonment.

Their case now comes up for appeal on Wednesday, June 24th.

The Masters' Law, through one of its courts, declared them guilty.

The Workers' Law, in the Union halls, declares them innocent.

The Masters' Law Said that they must remain in prison for life.

The Workers' Law Demands that they shall be set free, or no hops shall be picked in California.

If the masters' law is upheld by the Appellate Court,

Then Let The Masters' Law Pick The Hops

Solidarity, June 20, 1914, p. 3.

Analyses which limit their reading of the I.W.W.'s ideology of industrial solidarity to a single text, pamphlet literature, convention proceedings, etc., do not reflect the depth of Wobbly culture and contribute little to furthering an understanding of the I.W.W.'s use of European syndicalist beliefs and practices. On a formal ideological level, the I.W.W. offered explanations of European anarcho-syndicalist beliefs and principles as a means of interpreting, differentiating, and defining its form of industrial unionism. The I.W.W. also diffused and utilized for purposes of education the tactics advanced by European anarcho-syndicalists, leaving the question of their advocacy and application to the rank-and-file. The emergence of art forms which interpreted French syndicalist tactics were a consequence of the I.W.W's early relationship to the C.G.T. and indicate intricate correspondences between art and politics not always visible in the I.W.W.'s official policy. The I.W.W.'s relationship to European syndicalism, therefore, cannot be reduced to one of passively borrowing terms or simply imitating the practices of their European comrades. Although the I.W.W. officially recognized that their form of industrial solidarity "stood for direct action, sabotage, anti-patriotism and the general strike," the I.W.W. developed its own meanings for these terms and applied them to situations unique to American conditions.

In its most fundamental principles, the I.W.W. acknowledged and celebrated the workers' self-sufficiency, spirit of solidarity, and revolt against and resistance to injustice. The I.W.W.'s refusal to ally itself with parliamentary socialism, its repudiation of leaders or apotheosis of the collective membership, and its counteremphasis on drawing from a proletarian culture of struggle as a means of building a movement aimed at social transformation, defines its indigenous anti-political philosophy as well as its major link to European anarcho-syndicalism.

"Let one of these persistent, thought compelling designs do for you what a long argument oft times fails to accomplish," the ad for the stickerettes read. "Reach a thousand workers where only one was possible." Ads for these stickerettes or silent agitators, created by Ralph Chaplin, first appeared in the November 20, 1915 issue of *Solidarity*.[46]

WOWIE!

A final example from the *Industrial Pioneer,* September 1921, uses the sab cat to emphasize the futility of the government's efforts to supress the I.W.W.'s militancy.

Industrial Worker, March 23, 1911, p. 1.

CHAPTER FIVE

Art and Politics: Anarcho-Syndicalist Tactics in I.W.W. Art Forms

News articles on the C.G.T.'s activities, editorials and reprints of pamphlet literature by European syndicalists making propaganda for their interpretation of revolutionary unionism appear early in the I.W.W. official press. While not intended as statements of formal policy or admissions of unconditional acceptance of the C.G.T.'s program, this coverage nevertheless played a significant role in defining the I.W.W.'s philosophy of industrial solidarity. The I.W.W.'s early ideological uses of European anarcho-syndicalist beliefs and principles in this capacity also served as a means of interpreting, differentiating, and defining the I.W.W.'s form of industrial unionism. The early phase of the I.W.W.'s relationship to the C.G.T. was, therefore, characterized by expressions of solidarity with the principles of revolutionary unionism pioneered by French syndicalists, not its specific policies, methods, or organizational manifestations. For the most part, pamphlet literature advocating French syndicalist tactics was relegated to an unofficial status and published through non-I.W.W. presses. The relegation of pamphlet literature advocating specific tactics to unofficial status reflected the movement's pluralistic attitude toward revolutionary struggle, which was embodied in the I.W.W.'s belief that the determination of the appropriate means of struggle rested with the rank-and-file.

My discussion of the I.W.W.'s intellectual relationship to French syndicalism and the direct influence of immigrant anarcho-syndicalism and native forms of anarchism on the confluence of tendencies contributing to the I.W.W.'s emergence is not intended to suggest that the I.W.W. philosophy or form of industrial unionism was syndicalist or anarcho-syndicalist. One may find in the I.W.W. press of this period sufficient references to warrant a plethora of ideological labels. In elaborating on the presence of inherent and derived sources of influence neglected or thought to be insignificant by the I.W.W. scholars, my intention has been to establish the pluralistic nature of the I.W.W.'s philosophy of revolutionary unionism and the diverse cultural context out of which it developed. In representing a synthesis of the various traditions and forms of American and European labor radicalism that had expressed elements of revolutionary unionism, the I.W.W.'s philosophy of industrial solidarity initially suggested the possibility of the co-existence of opposing revolutionary tendencies within the labor movement under its umbrella.

The *Industrial Union Manifesto* reflected a desire not to mix party politics with unionism while not completely rejecting the fundamental principles of political socialism.[1] The synthesis between political Marxism, industrial unionism, and anarcho-syndicalism effected at the founding convention did not however end the factional fights. To many observers, it seemed that the I.W.W. was becoming a boxing ring for rival sects and individuals rather than a new trade union federation.[2] Antagonized by these factional fights on the role of politics in the new organization, the W.F.M. began leaving in 1906, formally breaking ties with the I.W.W. in 1907. The W.F.M.'s departure critically weakened the faction-torn organization, prompting predictions of the I.W.W.'s imminent demise. At the I.W.W.'s fourth convention, the bitter and disruptive controversy which had raged on the question of "political action" overshadowed all other issues. During the convention it became apparent that the I.W.W.'s administration was fatally divided. The 1908 convention marked the split in the I.W.W. between the doctrinaire group—supporters of the revolutionary Marxist tradition—and believers in political action and direct actionists—anarcho-syndicalists and nonpolitical industrial unionists. DeLeon and the "Socialist Laborites," or doctrinaire group, left the I.W.W. to form a rival I.W.W. in Detroit.[3]

The I.W.W.'s anti-political position had been an important part of the founders' critique of existing working-class organizations. The I.W.W.'s transition from a nonpolitical to an antipolitical position was hastened by the activities of anarchists and revolutionary socialists active within the I.W.W., the experiences of the European syndicalist movement, and the class collaboration of political socialists.

Industrial Worker, May 11, 1911, p. 1.

Anti-political cartoons, as well as other Wobbly art forms containing explicit European syndicalist content, affirm continuities in the I.W.W.'s struggle against the state and opposition to electoral politics. Since these expressions do not represent theoretical positions imposed through official policy, they reflect changes in the I.W.W.'s associational context resulting from the movement's increasing contact with and intervention into the lives and struggles of unskilled, migratory, and immigrant workers. These art forms, therefore, are important not only for the continuities they represent in the I.W.W.'s relationship to European syndicalism, but also for the way they express the I.W.W.'s belief in direct democracy and industrial autonomy locally and internationally.

I.W.W. graphics, poems, and songs indicate the incorporation of anarcho-syndicalist tactics not as official policy but as expressions of the iconoclastic culture and militancy of the rank-and-file Wobbly. Since these tendencies were part of the I.W.W.'s founding energies, their increased visibility within the movement indicates a developing continuity in the I.W.W.'s revolutionary pluralism. The I.W.W.'s antipolitical position had been an immanent part of the movement's original critique, which scorned the increasing powers of the state and federal government, the collaboration of the A.F.L. with the powerful business corporations represented by the National Civic Federation, and the ethnic and racial hostilities engendered by craft and party politics.

Worker intellectuals, rank-and-file cartoonists, poets, and song writers did not passively adopt the tactics advocated by French anarcho-syndicalists or other European syndicalists. In the art forms pioneered by Wobbly artists, the tactics of their European comrades are consciously transformed to interpret and apply the I.W.W.'s principles of industrial unionism in particular conflicts. In the forms initiated by worker artists the tactics of European syndicalists appear as approximate analogies intended to suggest different connotations and practices emerging out of the struggle of native and immigrant labor activists. In attaching their own meanings and symbols onto European anarcho-syndicalist tactics, I.W.W. worker artists played an important role in interpreting the I.W.W.'s ideology of industrial unionism.

While I.W.W. worker intellectuals had a major role in disseminating knowledge of the activities, principles, and tactics of European anarcho-syndicalists, worker artists went beyond formal political expressions to create a language and symbolism that made European anarcho-syndicalist ideology meaningful within the context of the workers' cultural and social alienation. Rank-and-file artists interpreted the contributions made by European syndicalists to revolutionary unionism and communicated their impact on the initiatives of rank-and-file I.W.W.s engaged in local struggles. This relationship between artistic expression and political ideology began well before 1912 and demonstrates the ubiquitous presence of anarcho-syndicalist beliefs within the workers' culture of struggle.[4]

The appearance of these art forms initially parallels the activities of French syndicalists. Following a strike among French postal workers that came close to becoming a general strike, an editorial in the *I.W.* articulated a renewed interest in the French anarcho-syndicalist application of the general strike:

> That a general suspension of work in one industry, let alone in all industries, can bring the employers to terms is well shown in the postal strike in France. This was a strike in one industry and in only one country. Society is so interlocked that the stoppage of one industry is like the breaking of one wheel in a clock; it paralyzes the rest of the industry.
>
> The general strike has also been called the general lockout of the employing class, the idea being that at the proper time the workers, being industrially organized, will simply take possession of the factories, the mines and the farms and tools of production and proceed to operate them for the sole benefit of the workers, thus locking out the employing class. . . . When the time comes, and there are many signs to show that it is nearer than many of us think, that the working class is so strongly organized, and industrially organized, that it is possible to suspend production either through the world at large, or over vast class districts, we will then be strong enough to act in defiance of the master—either by suspending production for a time or by continuing it for our good.[5]

Prior to the strike of French postal workers, interest in the general strike as a means of protesting legal repression in the Moyer, Haywood, Pettibone trial is suggested in a resolution at the I.W.W.'s second convention. Though defeated, the Committee on the Reports of Officers recommended that:

> ... a general lockout of the capitalist class is the method by which ... to emancipate our class. We believe that the general strike can be employed temporarily, as a means to wring concessions from the capitalist class from time to time. The committee believes that a protracted general strike would be no less than an insane act on the part of the working class.[6]

The general strike as a "temporary strategy to wring concessions from the capitalist class," however, does not appear in the I.W.W.'s literature until its efficacy had been demonstrated by the activity of French syndicalists. The editorial that followed news of the French postal workers' strike in the spring of 1909 represents the first instance in which the general strike is added to the I.W.W. tactics:

> The I.W.W. is the only organization for workers: we have the **partial** strike, **industrial** strike, **passive** strike, **irritant** strike, and the **general** strike.

The emergent tactical significance of the general strike was added to the I.W.W.'s list of methods with the following priviso:

> There is one thing that every member of the I.W.W., and working people generally, should always remember, and that is that success depends not necessarily on **blind following of rules,** without regard to circumstances and conditions, but success depends on **organization, discipline** and **courage.**[7]

Following the success of the French postal workers strike and the I.W.W.'s editorial, the first of the I.W.W.'s general strike poems to be written by a rank-and-file member was published in the *I.W.* H.T.K.'s poem, "To The Revolutionist," appears opposite an excerpt from Roller's pamphlet on "The Social General Strike." Several stanzas are quoted below:

For mighty are our members
  And strength that makes us bold;
And mightier than a cannon is
  The labor power we hold.
The mills, the mines, the factories,
  The transports and the farms
Are kept in motion only by
  Young giant labor's arm.

Lo! with strength and numbers
  Come interests that bind
Us into one great union—
  Skilled, trained and disciplined.
Industrially united and
  Class-conscious to the bone.
The workers of the world shall rise
  To take and hold their own.

Workers of the workd, unite!
  Wake slaves and organize!
None but the brave deserve the fair;
  None but the bold the prize;
And when we stand united, boys,
  We'll raise a mightly shout;
Then hold the tools of industry
  And lock the masters out.[8]

The French postal workers' strike also initiates the I.W.W.'s use
of the term *direct action*. While the tactic of direct action is implied in the
I.W.W. critique of party politics, the term was not invoked as a means of
naming the I.W.W.'s position against political action or in identifying
the I.W.W.'s methods of struggle until it appeared in connection with an
editorial on the strike. The editorial implied that the tactic of direct
action represented "actions that have real value for the worker." The
editorial suggests that this method of action involved workers throwing
off all dependence on everything but their organized force:

> On what does the power of the employer rest, if not on the
> traditional respect of law, custom and methods of society which
> are founded by the ruling class to enslave the minds and paralyze
> the courage of the workers?[9]

Though later used as part of the I.W.W. strategy to shift the scene of
conflict from the domain outside the factory to the place of employment, the term first appears in connection with the I.W.W.'s activities to
counter methods used by state, city and law enforcement officials to
undermine its struggle against private employment agencies.

In the depression years of 1907 and 1908, the fraudulent practices of employment agencies were the most pressing grievance encountered by I.W.W. organizers in their efforts to recruit the floating worker.
These agencies operated out of cities that served as gateways to the
mining, lumber, and agricultural industries in the western part of the
United States. The I.W.W.'s campaign against the "employment shark"
began in connection with efforts of western locals to organize the
thousands of transient workers roaming the region in search of jobs. The
I.W.W.'s first major offensive against the practices of employment agencies began late in 1908 in Missoula, Montana, and Spokane, Washington.[10]

The following cartoon shows the I.W.W. being coached in the
tactic of direct action by the working class.[11] The cartoon further
illustrates the I.W.W.'s sensitivity to rank-and-file initiative. It appears
in the center of an appeal to workers to join in the Spokane free-speech
fight. "Working men and women," the article asks, "shall the Revolutionary workers of America accept defeat from the notorious Pan Tan
political ring of Spokane, which is backed by the Washington Water
Power Co., the Weyerhauser lumber syndicate, and the Associated
Employment Agencies, when our fellow workers in Europe are whip-
ping their tyrannical National Governments to a standstill?" The article
discussed the successful struggles of French, Italian, and Spanish syndicalists to uphold their right of free speech and assembly. It went into
detail about the struggles of Italian workers in order to suggest parallels
with the I.W.W.'s struggle in Spokane:

A few years ago in Milan, Free Speech and Free Assembly were almost undreamed of. In order to attend a revolutionary meeting one had to hold a card in the organization conducting it; but the Italian workers, chafing at this restriction, declared war on the obnoxious regulation and flung their doors wide open to the public, which immediately thronged their halls. The authorities arrested the speakers as fast as they could mount the platform; but after four days of this, the jails in Milan were crowded to the limit; and still hundreds of speakers in sight. The authorities gave up in despair and their ordinance died a natural death. However, as usual, the authorities exercised strong censorship over speakers; and when one ventured to criticize the King or government, he was arrested for "lese majeste" and sent to the penitentiary for from ten to fifteen years. Flushed with victory the Italian workers declared war this law also and filled the jails with men charged with "lese majeste" for making disparaging remarks about the King. The Italian government took a hand in the matter and poured thousands of troops into Milan to check the disorder but it was of no avail. The whole working class of Italy rallied to the support of their struggling brothers in Milan and the King's very throne tottered. "Lese majeste" was sent to join its fellow, restricted assembly, in the museum of antiquities.[12]

In Spokane and other cities, employment sharks operating out of storefront agencies in the skid road districts used elaborate schemes to fleece migrant workers of their last dollars by sending them to nonexistent jobs or work from which they would be fired after their first pay.I.W.W. organizer Fred W. Haslewood describes the typical scheme used by employment sharks in their operation:

Over three thousand men were hired through employment sharks for one camp of the Somers Lumber Co. last winter to maintain a force of fifty men. As soon as a man worked long enough to pay the shark's fee, the hospital dollar, poll tax and a few other grafts, he was discharged to make room for more slaves, so that the fleecing

The I. W. W. Will Fight to Uphold the Rights of the Working Class.

Industrial Worker, February 19, 1910, p. 1.

process could continue. These different fees are then split, or cut up with the bosses. In most cases these fees consume the time of several days labor, when . . . discharged [workers were] paid with checks ranging from five cents and upward.[13]

I.W.W.s attempting to organize among ranch hands, lumber and construction workers, and miners victimized by shark operations were thwarted in their efforts by the lack of permanent work crews.

While organizing workers abused by shark operations, I.W.W.s began to systematically collect evidence of the hundreds of cases of workers cheated by these agencies. In the spring, summer, and fall of 1909, the I.W.W. shifted its tactic of recruiting workers on the job to a campaign against the agencies themselves. In the skid road districts of Missoula and Spokane, I.W.W.s began to hold street meetings in front of the employment agencies. Soapboxers would expose the extortionist practices of the sharks by naming time, place, amount, and names of workers who had been fleeced. I.W.W. soapboxers in Missoula called for a boycott of the agencies and demanded that companies hire through the union hall.[14]

Under pressure from the employment agencies, an ordinance prohibiting street speaking was passed in Missoula. There a handful of I.W.W. soapboxers defied the ordinance. Four of the six organizers in Missoula were arrested and sentenced to fifteen days in the county jail when they refused to obey the ordinance. The remaining organizers made an appeal to the *I.W.* for assistance. Their appeal, published in the September 1909 issue of the paper, invited all "who hate the tyrannical oppression of the police to go to Missoula" to help in the fight to restore the workers' right to free speech.[15]

A steady stream of I.W.W.s answered the call, beating their way by rail to Missoula, and were promptly arrested when they mounted soapboxes to speak in defiance of the ordinance. Offering no resistance to arrest, the soapboxers used the strategy of filling the jails as quickly as possible. The number of arrests eventually forced city officials to utilize the basement of the firehouse as a makeshift jail. With the city rapidly running out of room to house the free-speech fighters, its municipal administration clogged by arrested soapboxers demanding separate trials, and the cost of feeding the prisoners growing daily, the I.W.W.'s tactic forced the city to rescind the ordinance.[16]

In Spokane, I.W.W. soapboxers used songs, rapidly written and tailored to the situation, to expose and ridicule the employment sharks' operation. Many of these songs emerged spontaneously and later appeared in the *I.U.B., I.W., Solidarity,* or the I.W.W.'s *Little Red Song Book,* while others spread through word of mouth. These songs were used to generate a crowd for the speaker who would follow with detailed information on the agencies. "The Workers, So They Say," written by Richard Brazier as a parody of a popular tune, is typical of songs that sarcastically exposed a shark's operation. A portion of the song follows:

The workers, so they say,
Are getting skinned everyday
By fat employment sharks;
And it's really true,
But what are we to do?
Workers are such easy marks,
For they come into town
With a little stake;

And when they blow that in,
For a job their hearts do ache.
And so they buy a job
From some employment hog.
Whose office is across the way.

Chorus:
"That's an easy bunch of suckers," says the fat employment shark,
As he takes their coin and ships them far away.
"It is just like robbing blind men in an alleyway when its dark,
For I've sold that job already twice today.
There will be no job for them when they get off the train;
I'd like to bet their journey is in vain.
It's a shame to take their money
For it really, really gives me lots of pain."

When he gets off the train,
For a job he looks in vain,
But no job can he see,
So he says, "I'll wait
And ride back in a freight
To try and collect my fee."
But when he gets to town
And his money tries to get,
The grafter with a frown,
Says, "You'll get nothing here." You bet
He says, "Twenty-three for you,
From my office please skidoo,
Unless you want to buy another job.[17]

Other songs about employment sharks were written as parodies of the
Christian religious hymns used by the Salvation Army who frequently
occupied street corners in the same locality used by I.W.W. soapboxers.
The utilization of popular tunes and religious hymns as forms to carry a
language which simultaneously incorporated and subverted the popular theme or religious values from which they were derived represents a
unique feature of the I.W.W.'s songs in this period. The practice of using

derived symbolism is found in most of the I.W.W. art forms. Wobbilies drew freely from popular, classical, religious, and revolutionary literature, transforming their themes into forms that could be used as weapons in the class struggle.

In 1909 in the early months of the campaigns in these cities, the *I.W.* carried an editorial underscoring the urgency of the struggle against the employment agencies. The editorial emphasized that the private employment agencies needed to be abolished not only for their corrupt operations but because they impeded I.W.W. recruitment and fostered intolerable working conditions:

> By means of these go-betweens the bosses are able to pick out the most willing and ignorant slaves, those that are the hardest to organize. The fresh supply of help and the fight between the workers allows the boss to keep down the food supply, to increase the hours and furnish worse conditions of work.[18]

The editorial pointed to the success of the C.G.T. in its battle against the employment agencies in Paris as an encouraging sign to workers fighting to repeal the Spokane's gag law. "The industrial union in France," the author noted, "found it necessary to abolish all employment offices, and in the city of Paris it took just one day's work to persuade the government to quit business in favor of the unions."[19]

French syndicalists had coined the term *direct action* to refer to "actions by workers themselves without help of intermediaries." The precise meaning of the practice was intended to evolve through its applications in specific conditions. Although it was coined at the time of the C.G.T.'s emergence, Louis Levine, in his study of French syndicalism wrote that, "the agitation for the suppression of the employment agency appeared to all as a manifestation of the new theory of direct action."[20] Exasperated by the French government's failure to enact legislation to suppress the fraudulent practices of employment agencies, workers in the food-processing industry decided to take matters into their own hands. With the C.G.T.'s Bourses du Travail in Paris acting as a center of agitation, food-processing workers called for a demonstration against the employment agencies in Paris. The *Journal des Debates* reported that "a veritable riot took place" in which "police used their arms and many were wounded on both sides."[21]

Following this incident, the Confederal committee of the C.G.T. responded to the initiative of the food-processing workers by appointing a special committee to direct the struggle against the employment agencies. The strategy of the committee called for a wide agitation that would culminate in protest meetings on the same day in all industrial centers of France. On December 5, 1905, hundreds of meetings were held throughout France to protest the employment agencies and call for their abolition. In February of the following year, a law abolishing the employment agencies was finally adopted, after having failed to pass the Senate for many years. French syndicalists considered their agitation an illustration of the method of direct action and reported at their congress which met at Bourges:

> Under pressure from the workingmen the government, till then refractory to reform, capitulated. . . . Today it is an accomplished fact; wherever syndicalist action was exercised with perseverance and energy, the employment agencies have gone.[22]

The spectacle created in Spokane by I.W.W. soapboxers exposing and denouncing the practices of employment sharks in songs and speeches soon brought an ordinance prohibiting street speaking. Beginning in the winter months of 1909, a major battle ensued when soapboxers violated the ordinance in protest of the city's exemption of the Salvation Army from its ban. Following the pattern set in Missoula free-speech fights, I.W.W.s offered no resistence to arrest, filling the jail. When another facility had to be used as a lock up, city officials chose an unheated school to house unwanted violators. Arrested soapboxers were quickly sentenced to thirty days hard labor, forcing them to rethink the Missoula strategy.[23]

At first, imprisoned soapboxers refused to work for the city. Their resistance was met with beatings, torture, and a bread-and-water diet. In an attempt to break the solidarity of the free-speech fighters, prison guards formed slugging committees and routinely beat free-speech prisoners in the dark corridors behind the booking window. When soapboxers continued to refuse work, they were subjected to the "sweat box" treatment. Guards crammed them into a small cell and

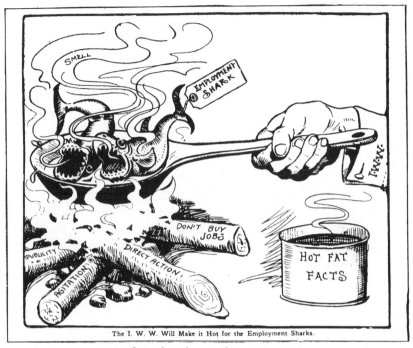

The I. W. W. Will Make it Hot for the Employment Sharks.

Industrial Worker, April 2, 1910, p. 1.

turned the steam up until the prisoners nearly suffocated. They were then moved to an ice-cold cell and beaten in their weakened state. Hospital reports show hundreds of prisoners treated for pneumonia, broken jaws and ribs, and blinded eyes.[24]

Prisoners formed a committee and later issued a report announcing their decision to change tactics. "We have adopted new tactics," the report published in the *I.W.* announced. "No more will we live on bread and water at the cost of two cents a day per man; but we will go on the chain gang and get three square meals a day at the cost of seventy-five cents a day per man." The committee reasoned that this change in tactics would do more damage to the city's treasury and cost the taxpayers an additional thousand dollars a day. Prisoners could further subvert the city's plan to profit from their labor by applying the tactic of passive resistance to the chain gang. "Don't think," the writer added, "that we will build the new Monroe bridge, we understand how to work too well to make any monument to free speech."[25]

Under the article was a short account of W.Z. Foster's experiences organizing the imprisoned free-speech fighters in Spokane. "I consider my experience in the Spokane jail as almost invaluable," Foster wrote, "through it I have learned a few of the possibilities of organization and 'direct action,' of the marvelous effectiveness of the passive resistance strike, in addition to learning many new wrinkles about law, police etc." Foster explained the meaning of direct action applied to the tactic of passive resistance:

> The effects of organization upon the work done on the rock pile was remarkable. . . . We simply went through the motions of working. For instance, two men chained together pounded for four days upon one rock when it accidentally broke. To break that small rock cost the city of Spokane about four dollars in food alone . . . besides the other expenses of guards etc..[26]

The tactic of passive resistance appears earlier in the I.W.W.'s literature than direct action. The tactic, also known as "passive action," was introduced in a series on the means and methods of industrial unionism, written by William E. Trautmann and published in the *I.U.B.* between 1907 and 1908. The series traces the origin of the term to an incident on an Austrian railroad in 1887. In moving freight trains, a railway employee was caught between two cars and badly mutilated. In disciplining the station master, railroad officials pointed to the fact that such accidents would not occur if rules and regulations were strictly followed. Officials issued a mandate by telegraph to station masters to enforce all regulations provided for by law. Noncompliance with the new mandate was cause for immediate discharge. As a consequence of strict compliance with regulations by station masters and their subordinates, the station where the accident had occurred became so blocked by passenger trains, switch engines, and freight cars that traffic from all directions was practically suspended. When called upon to explain the chaos in the yard, station masters could prove that they were simply obeying the company's instructions. "The workers," Trautmann wrote, "immediately realized the importance of such measures, and thus the station masters and higher officials unconsciously became the inventors of what is termed " 'passive action.' " Trautmann went on to report on the successful application of this tactic by European syndicalists.[27]

In the pamphlet version of Trautmann's series, a section on sabotage was added. The pamphlet suggested that the tactic be applied to avert situations in which workers forced to strike suffered the strong auxiliaries of the capitalists—police, militia and troops, injunction, and imprisonment—used against them. To avoid such defeats, the organized resistance within the work place could not be confined to passive action:

> Inferior goods are turned out by silent understanding of all workers in one shop or plant; time is taken up in getting tools prepared, and repair work attended to; in Harvey, Ill., where contractors of railway construction work announced a reduction of 50 cents per day for the Italian workers, the latter, having learned enough of the principles of industrial unionism, decided at once to cut their shovels half an inch, and work with these cut shovels, which they did; and, with the protestation, "Short pay, short shovels," they forced the contractors to restore the former wages.[28]

The cartoon on the following page appeared after the announcement of the tactical change made by Spokane free-speech fighters. "Industrial Organizational, Using Two Balls, Make a Clean Sweep Every Time," dramatizes the I.W.W. organizer using direct action to eliminate the obstacles set in the I.W.W.'s path.[29] The tactic of direct action and the threat of a general strike are pictured as a means of combating the state's use of courts, injunctions, bull pens, and the militia to restrict the I.W.W.'s activities. The cartoon suggests that the tactic used by European syndicalists in their struggle for industrial freedom is being successfully applied against methods used by government in collusion with big business to undermine the I.W.W.'s work of building revolutionary industrial unionism.

The large bow tie of the I.W.W. in the capitalist bowling alley makes reference to the overall brigade, who, dressed in red bow ties, black shirts, and blue denim overalls, rode the rails from Portland, Washington, to the I.W.W.'s fourth convention in Chicago. Along the

Industrial Organization, Using **These Two Balls**, Will Make a Clean Sweep Every Time.

Industrial Worker, April 9, 1910, p. 1.

way the brigade, dubbed the "I.W.W. Red Special," stopped in towns and hobo jungles to spread the I.W.W.'s message of industrial solidarity through songs and speeches. Representing the growing western membership, the native anarchist spirit of the overall brigade carried the I.W.W.'s fourth convention, expelling Daniel DeLeon and eliminating the political clause from the *Preamble*.[30] J.H. Walsh, who organized the brigade, was among the first I.W.W. organizers to recognize the importance of the struggle against the employment shark. The cartoon represents the merging of the indigenous anti-political philosophy of the western membership with anarcho-syndicalist tactics emerging out of the European syndicalist movement.

Following the publication of these cartoons and editorials on direct action, French anarcho-syndicalist tactics began to appear in the I.W.W. press with greater frequency.[31] Discussion of these tactics appeared in a news article that reported on a strike action by unorganized Jewish, Italian, Hungarian, and Bohemian garment workers employed by Lamm & Co. of Chicago. Invited by the plant's striking workers, who had walked out in protest of the company's treatment of women workers, I.W.W. organizers called a meeting to discuss various strategies whereby the garment workers could redress their grievances. *Solidarity* of June 4, 1910, reported that the strategy of a general strike was overriden by a garment worker who suggested "the method of sabotage." Workers in shops producing materials bound for Lamm & Co. had already sabotaged their work to such perfection that the company was beginning to feel financial losses. When negotiations between the firm and the striking workers effected a partial settlement of grievances, I.W.W. organizers argued that workers should temporarily accept the compromise and return to work. Following a lengthy discussion and vote, garment workers accepted the I.W.W.'s strategy of a temporary truce. The truce was based on an agreement that workers returning to their jobs would practice passive resistance as a means of interrupting the plant's operations until the employer complied with all of the demands that had led to the walkout.

In this report, the tactic of sabotage appeared for the first time in connection with the I.W.W.'s activities.[32] The report suggested that a tactic which relied on the collective action of all workers employed in the factory was a more effective form of action to continue a struggle in which the redress of a grievance was the object. More importantly, the tactic of passive resistance, beyond its tactical significance in the immediate situation, provided a vehicle for building solidarity among the workers struggling against the company's policies. Building solidarity was a principle inherent in all the tactics incorporated by the I.W.W. and was emphasized as the most salient precondition to building effective unionism.

This emphasis on building industrial unionism through worker initiative and solidarity was an important theme of cartoons and graphics in this period. Wobbly cartoonists, taking direct action as their subject, introduced other examples of direct action used by workers to redress grievances.

Industrial Worker, May 21, 1910, p. 1.

This cartoon, which appeared in the *I.W.* on May 21, 1910, dramatizes a strike action in Spokane by the cooks and waiters affiliated with the A.F.L.[33] The cartoon shows hotel and restaurant employees clobbering the Restaurant Employers' Association by walking off their jobs at the busiest time of the day in protest of thwarted contract negotiations. In the interview that accompanies the cartoon, a prominent member of the union explains that the workers found it necessary to circumvent the tactics and red tape of their organization:

> The A.F.L. had no time to say or do anything. . . . We had no time for red tape or usual procedures. . . . This time something had to be done—and we did it. It had got to a point where we had nothing to lose and a whole lot to gain.

The I.W.W. conducting the interview asked if the bakers had joined the strike action. The union member replied that they had not, adding that "they are going through the usual red tape of the organization." "Then why not throw out the leaders and organize industrially?," the interviewer asked.

> Lots easier said than done [the union representative answered]. The rank-and-file have the right instinct, but they are not good politicians and you know that politics play a large part in the convention. But we are waking up.[34]

The cartoon therefore pictures the I.W.W. organizer extending the club of industrial unionism, suggesting that without it the tactic of direct action has limited value.

European anarcho-syndicalist tactics were first used in the I.W.W.'s press as a means of dramatizing the importance of rank-and-file initiative in local struggles. The early appearance of European anarcho-syndicalist symbols in the I.W.W.'s art forms indicates the ubiquitous knowledge and application of proto-syndicalist principles and tactics among organized and unorganized workers. In the latter usage, art forms simultaneously criticized and affirmed the actions of organized workers who took initiative against the bureaucratic practices of craft unions. In identifying these actions as emergent patterns of revolutionary activity originating from the self-activity of workers engaged in struggle, I.W.W.s used European anarcho-syndicalist labels to connect these patterns of activity to the larger labor community both as a means of expressing solidarity with their European comrades and to indicate that their emergence confirmed the necessity of industrial unionism.

While the I.W.W.'s art forms exposed the limitations of craft unionism, the futility of political reform, and the hypocrisy inherent in the dominant values of civil society, they also actively shaped a conception of a workers' culture that would bring a brighter day in which workers directly administered to the needs of society (see cartoon and graphic on following pages). The effort to link art to revolutionary struggle, as a means of both disseminating political ideology and creating a worker's culture that challenged the definition of American life imposed by government and business elites, defined the major motif which emerged from the practice of Wobbly artists.

This culture was built on the initiative of rank-and-file workers and reflected their struggles, hopes, and aspirations. The labor radicalism of the I.W.W. was not rigidly drawn from a single ideological source nor can it be explained completely in terms of indigenous responses to industrial conditions. Informed by diverse, often contradictory, sources of influence, the I.W.W.'s labor radicalism formed a complex mixture of inherent and derived forms of knowledge and experience. An understanding of the I.W.W.'s revolutionary pluralism is essential to any assessment of the I.W.W. and defines an important dimension of its oppositional character as well as its status as a countermovement in the pre-World War I period.

WORKERS OF THE WORLD, UNITE!

Oh, it may be, oft meseemeth,
  In the days that yet shall be,
When no slave of gold abideth
  'Twixt the breadth of sea to sea.

    Oft when men and maids are merry,
      Ere the sunlight leaves the earth,
    And they bless the day beloved—
      All too short for all their mirth.

Some shall pause a while and ponder
  On the bitter days of old
Ere the toil and strife of battle
  Overthrew the curse of gold.

    Then, 'twixt lips of loved and lover,
      Solemn thoughts of us shall rise;
    We, who once were fools and dreamers,
      Then shall be the brave and wise.

      Life, or death—then who shall heed it—
      What we gain, or what we lose;
      Fair flies life amidst the struggle,
      And the Cause for each shall choose!
              William Morris.

This drawing entitled "The Brighter Day," appeared in the E. Pataud and E. Pouget pamphlet, "Syndicalism and the Co-Operative Commonwealth." While not an official publication of the I.W.W., it was distributed by I.W.W. locals in the pre-World War I period.

CHAPTER SIX

Wobbly Sensibility: Conclusions and Implications

My concern with calling into question the influences affecting the I.W.W.'s pre-World War I identity has been aimed at initiating a new perspective on the I.W.W.'s labor radicalism, one that departs from the conventional view of the I.W.W. in this period. To summarize the general outlines of my perspective, I have argued that the lack of consensus on the I.W.W.'s basic features derives from the narrow institutional perspective inherited from the economists who initiated the enterprise of labor historiography. Owing to their orientation, labor economists were uniformly insensitive to the cultural and social dynamics surrounding the birth and development of the I.W.W.

Labor economists analyzed the I.W.W. primarily through its convention proceedings, strike activity, and official literature. Little effort was made to document the social and cultural impact of the movement's activities nor were attempts made to interview the less visible, rank-and-file worker intellectuals and artists who formed the backbone of the movement and from which the movement's earliest anarcho-syndicalist tendencies developed. Labor economists directed their attention away from the I.W.W. as a social movement that mobilized oppositional political and cultural groups in order to create counterinstitutional formations that would serve the end of revolutionary reconstruction.

The concern of labor economists with mapping national-level events that lent an institutional semblance and formality to the I.W.W.'s ideology and activities has overshadowed the links forged by the I.W.W. between working-class culture, politics, and social formations. It has also drawn attention away from the fact that the I.W.W.'s agency and activity on the local level showed fluidity of form and function, and the movement's reliance on oral tradition and expressive arts formed a diffuse iconoclastic ideology. These important dimensions of the I.W.W.'s pre-World War I presence fell outside the pale of organizational history. Organizational accounts tacitly acknowledged the mixed local as a troublesome feature of the I.W.W.'s structural and organizational presence. The jungle, when not seen as a liability, was invoked as a romantic and colorful source of anecdote to fill out the dry details of strikes and convention proceedings.

Early narrative reconstruction of the I.W.W. reveals an overwhelming lack of information regarding the activities and way of life of the I.W.W.'s artists and worker intellectuals, the floaters and rebel tramps in the jungle, and the activities of the mixed locals when its members were not engaged in strikes or related conflicts. A number of consequences result from the neglect and lack of analysis of the I.W.W.'s social and cultural presence. Little has survived to provide a sense of the lived activity and culture of the Wobbly. Many of the foreign language newspapers that emerged out of the I.W.W.'s contact with immigrant activists can no longer be found or exist only in fragmentary form in archives and private collections scattered throughout the world. Biographical information on immigrant worker intellectuals and artists who wrote for these papers is equally difficult to come by. The more insidious consequences of this neglect is the difficulty of recovering elements from this culture that acted as catalysts and sources of influence shaping I.W.W. pre-World War I labor radicalism.

More recent studies of the I.W.W. have not confronted these problems or challenged this limited reading of the I.W.W.'s labor radicalism in any significant way.[1] The historical accounts of the I.W.W. in the fifties and sixties merely reexamined the narrative content of the early histories for factual flaws, embellishing and extending the interpretation of labor economists. My study contributes to a critique of this literature by focusing on the I.W.W.'s organizational form, ideology, tactics, and strategies within the context of its rank-and-file consciousness and culture. Rather than centering my study on the debate concerning the I.W.W.'s merits as a labor union, I have attempted to show the relationship of the I.W.W.'s early movement culture to the shaping of its conception of industrial unionism. My choice to emphasize the dynamics underlying the I.W.W.'s pre-World War I presence followed an analysis of the I.W.W.'s membership and activities prior to the outbreak of World War I. I found that the I.W.W.'s counterinstitutional presence had important consequences for the form of labor unionism it initiated in the pre–World War I period.

The I.W.W.'s concern with reaching the community of workers as a whole, irrespective of tool or trade, gave a broad context to its struggle against capital, initiating diverse activities that extended beyond the point of production. The I.W.W.'s status as a social movement proved more complex than the factors sociologists and historians typically ascribe to the birth of new organizations. I classified the I.W.W. as a countermovement for this reason and sought to demonstrate this dynamic quality of the I.W.W. presence. I drew attention to the oppositional nature of the I.W.W.'s agency, specifically its struggle against the state; the transitional quality of its form, as exemplified by the mixed local; and the iconoclastic content of its ideological expressions, which blended diverse traditions. I emphasized these features of the I.W.W.'s pre-World War I presence not only as evidence of the social, cultural, and political dimensions of the I.W.W. as a countermovement but also in order to draw attention to the development of a form of revolutionary pluralism that gave rise to a sensibility that superseded its ideological origins.

Underlying the I.W.W.'s activities in the pre-World War I period were efforts to derive from the diverse patterns of activity and sources of political and cultural influence emerging out of the international labor community an associational context that would augment concerted action among workers excluded from or in conflict with existing political and labor formations. The I.W.W.'s early years were, therefore, characterized by a constant interplay between activism and theoretical development in which the movement's original principles were tested, modified, redefined, or discarded.

In the period before the outbreak of World War I, the I.W.W. sought to occupy a terrain encompassing the revolutionary tendencies arising from the activities of fluctuating networks of labor, cultural, and political activists. Proto-syndicalist tactics, gained through contact with unorganized workers and anarchist and left-wing socialist ideologies articulated by rank-and-file members, were modified and integrated into the I.W.W.'s developing philosophy of industrial unionism. Syndicalist theory and culture, derived in part from this contact but also initiated by the I.W.W.'s rank-and-file membership, entered the I.W.W. through the art forms and unofficial literature of its membership. During this period of the I.W.W.'s development, new meanings and symbols derived from the amalgam of anarchism, syndicalism, and Marxism became attached to the I.W.W. philosophy of industrial unionism and were expressed through the movement's art forms far more than through official policy articulated in programmatic literature.

The I.W.W. acknowledged and celebrated the workers' self-sufficiency, spirit of solidarity, and revolt against and resistance to injustice. The I.W.W.'s refusal to ally itself with parliamentary socialism, its repudiation of leaders or apotheosis of the collective membership, and its counteremphasis on drawing from a proletarian culture of struggle as a means of building a movement aimed at social transformation, defines its indigenous anti-political philosophy as well as its major link to European anarcho-syndicalism.

The I.W.W. sought to consciously position itself between European forms of industrial unionism, particularly that of the anarcho-syndicalism wing of the C.G.T., and the evolving consciousness of its rank-and-file. Wobblies eschewed the authority of abstract doctrines, the rigidities inherent in formulas of action, and the limitations of formal organizational strategy. The I.W.W.'s reliance on rank-and-file initiative, rejection of the labor contract as a basis for its association with capital, and opposition to political ideology as a vehicle of working class solidarity, formed an associational context based on class feeling and drawn from rank-and-file initiative.

Appeals to class feeling rather than formal ideology is characterisitic of much of the Wobbly art forms and printed material that sought to define the I.W.W.'s form of industrial solidarity. This emphasis and appeal to class feeling is also evidenced in the poetry and songs which emerged from hobo culture and were appropriated by the I.W.W. An important part of the I.W.W.'s art forms concerns the expression of a class consciousness that lies outside of formal political ideology.

I.W.W.s focused anti-clerical propaganda against the dominant Protestant denominations as well as right-wing evangelists such as Billy Sunday, powerful regional religious groups such as the Mormons, and so called charity organizations like the Salvation Army. Franklin Rosemont has argued that there was no precise European anarcho-syndicalist anti-religious influences in I.W.W. anti-clerical art. Rather there seem to have been a kind of mutual exchange in which each recognized common problems and common approaches to solutions and, therefore, reinforced the other's efforts.[2]

Wobbly art forms were political because they opposed the non-proletarian elements of the dominant culture and implied syndicalist beliefs. Sharper syndicalist expressions that incorporated elements of French anarcho-syndicalism also appeared early on in the I.W.W. development. In the expressive art forms pioneered by Wobbly artists, the tactics of their European comrades were consciously transformed to interpret and apply the I.W.W.'s principles of industrial unionism in particular conflicts. In the art forms initiated by worker artists, the tactics of European syndicalists appeared as approximate analogies intended to suggest different connotations and practices emerging out of the struggle of native and immigrant labor activists. French syndicalist beliefs and symbols were grafted on to I.W.W. poems and graphic art in much the same way that the music of popular tunes were used to carry the class feeling and experience contained in the words of I.W.W. songs.

Underlying the I.W.W.'s philosophy of industrial unionism was a sensibility more than a doctrine or formal ideology. This sensibility, as opposed to ideological affiliation, gave passage to the social networks that defined its community. The major contours of Wobbly sensibility suggest the initiation of a complex departure from existing forms of

NO REAL CAUSE FOR DISBELIEF—JUST I. W. W. AGITATION

Political Freak: "Vote." (It will keep his mind from Industrial Organization.)
Labor Taker: "Crafts and Contracts." (He is an enemy of Industrial Organization.)
Sky Pilot: "Lay up treasures in Heaven." (The boss grabs everything in sight.)

Industrial Worker, June 11, 1910, p. 1.

labor organization and political radicalism. This departure can especially be seen in the I.W.W.'s attempts to create a common cultural
sphere whereby the various ethnic groups could be united on the basis
of shared sentiment. The I.W.W. affirmed the indigenous culture of its
members, and sought to utilize the diverse traditions of immigrant and
migratory culture as a means of galvanizing workers in new ways.

Wobblies replaced the institutional basis of unionism with a
conception of culture and community that was primary and constitu-
tive. They created and used cultural expressions as a means of unifying
workers and as a basis to move against the repressive social conditions
of industrial development that extended beyond the point of production. Cultural expressions such as songs, cartoons, and poetry became a
critical form and means of communication between the I.W.W. and its
members. While I.W.W. worker intellectuals had a major role in disseminating knowledge of the activities, principles, and tactics of industrial
unionism, worker artists went beyond formal political expressions to

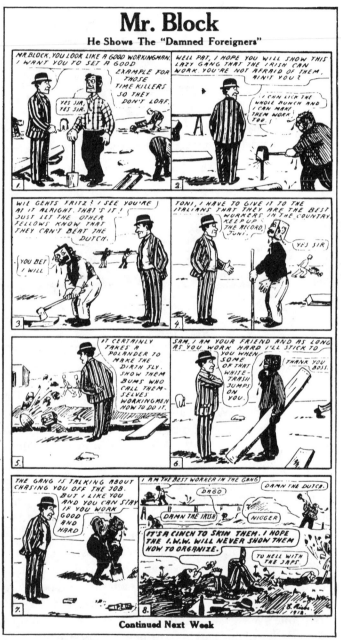

Industrial Worker, January 2, 1913, p. 4.

create a language and symbolism that made the I.W.W.'s principles meaningful within the context of the workers' cultural and social alienation. Rank-and-file artists not only interpreted the contributions made by their European comrades to the revolutionary union movement but also gave form to the lived experience and felt meaning of the rank-and-file, helping to activate and structure worker initiatives.

A number of important implications derive from my discussion of the I.W.W.'s pre-World War I labor radicalism. The ability of the I.W.W.'s form of industrial unionism to incorporate and oppose rather than pass by or accommodate emergent political ideologies defines the most neglected yet fundamental quality of the I.W.W.'s labor radicalism. The conception of industrial unionism initiated by I.W.W.s did not reflect a single ideological position, nor did it derive solely from indigenous responses to industrial conditions.

My analysis suggests that the consciousness of workers participating in the industrial union movement was shaped not only in relation to economic and political conditions, but in relation to the diverse cultural milieu that formed the community of unskilled migratory and immigrant workers. The cultural forms of expression such as songs, poems, and graphics which emerged out of the interaction between cosmopolitan and rural experience constituted a form of praxis. These forms not only enabled the I.W.W. to create a dynamic synthesis of political ideology but extended their critique of capitalism beyond the point of production, enabling the I.W.W. to carry its message of industrial solidarity beyond the confines of the factory gate. The I.W.W.'s art and cultural forms thus challenged the definition of American life imposed and diffused by government and business elites, while actively shaping a dynamic and revolutionary conception of workers' culture.

Notes

Introduction

1. Paul F. Brissenden, *The I.W.W.: A Study of American Syndicalism* New York.: Russell and Russel, 1957 [reprint, 2nd edition, 1920]), pp. 27-40. John Graham Brooks, *American Syndicalism: The I.W.W.* New York: Macmillian Co., 1913), pp. 62-72, and Andre Tridon, *The New Unionism* New York: B.W. Huebsch, 1913), pp. 93-100, also treat the I.W.W.'s forerunners. I cite Brissenden because his study incorporates their findings and forms the period's most comprehensive theory of the I.W.W.'s forerunners.

2. These studies are cited in my treatment of arguments locating the I.W.W.'s emergence in sources of western frontier activism; see chapter 2.

3. Melvyn Dubofsky, *We Shall Be All: A History of the I.W.W.* (Chicago: Quadrangle Books, 1969), pp. 19-35. See also Dubofsky'e earlier study: "The Origins of Western Working Class Radicalism," *Pacific Northwest Quarterly* LVIII (January 1966), pp. 131-154.

4. I consider the modern phase of America's cultural development to coincide with the "new immigration" which began around 1880. The best discussion of the sociological and anthropological contributions to the configurational hypothesis on the development of American culture is in Solomon Fishman, *The Disinherited of Art* (Berkeley: University of California Press, 1953), pp. 74-92. See also Herbert G. Gutman's essay, "Work, Culture and Society in Industrializing America, 1815-1919," *American Historical Review* 78(June 1973), pp. 531-587.

5. Fishman, *Disinherited,* p.99.

6. Fishman's work emphasizes the aesthetic dimensions of the nativist perspective on culture. For accounts that analyze the impact of nativism on social science and the Commons school of labor history, see Barbara Miller Solomon, *Ancestors and Immigrants* New York: John Wiley & Sons, 1956), pp. 123-151; Maurice Isserman, " 'God Bless Our American Institutions': The Labor History of John R. Commons," *Labor History* 17 (Summer 1976), pp. 309-328; John Higham, *Strangers in the Land Patterns of American Nativism 1860-1925* (New York: Atheneum, 1963). For analyses that explore the consequences of nativism on legislation against immigrant labor activists see William Preston Jr., *Aliens and Dissenters* (Cambridge :Harvard University Press, 1963); Robert Justin Goldstein, *Political Repression in Modern America 1870 to the Present* (Cambridge :Schenkman Publishing Co., 1978).

7. John S. Gambs, *The Decline of the I.W.W.* (New York: Russell & Russell, 1966 [reprint, Colombia University Press, 1932]), pp. 29-30. See also Eldridge Foster Dowell, *A History of the Criminal Syndicalist Legislation in the United States* (Balitomore :John Hopkins University press, 1939), pp. 13-44.

8. Ibid.

9. The principles of industrial solidarity are found in the I.W.W.'s *Preamble.* The *Preamble* changed several times before reaching its present form. It was amended from its original form following a meeting between Daniel DeLeon, William E. Trautmann, and Thomas J. Hagerty prior to the I.W.W.'s founding convention. Revised during the I.W.W.'s second convention and appeared in its amended form in the *Industrial Union Bulletin* of 9 March 1907. It was changed into its present form at the I.W.W.'s third convention. The 1907 and 1908 additions and deletions to the original *Preamble* are contained in Brissenden, *The I.W.W.,* pp. 351-352; he, however, does not date or discuss the 1907 changes. By far the most frequently printed of all the I.W.W.'s agitational and educational literature, the *Preamble* is typically appended to all official literature.

10. Social historians are beginning to study cultural influences in social movements. See, for example James R. Green, Grass Roots Socialism: Radical Movements in the Southwest 1895-1943 (Baton Rouge: Louisiana State University Press, 1978) Gareth Stedman Jones, *Languages of Class* (New York: Cambridge University Press, 1983); Lawrence Goodwyn, *The Populist Movement* (New York: Oxford University Press, 1978). Paul Buhle is one of the few historians to have studied immigrant activism within a cultural context; see, for

example, "Anarchism and American Labor," *International Labor and Working Class History* 23 (Spring 1983), pp. 21-34. Social movement literature has not yet reflected this direction in social history. Sociological studies typically draw from organizational history, use a functional model, and fails to address cultural influences. See Philip Selznick, "Foundations of the Theory of Organization," *American Sociological Review,* 13 (Feb. 1938), pp. 25-35; Sheldon Messinger, "Organizational Trasformation (sic.): A Case Study of a Declining Social Movement," American Sociological Review, 20(Feb. 1955), pp. 3-10; James W. Vander Zanden, "Resistance and Social Movements," *Social Forces,* 27(May 1959), pp. 312-315 (Vander Zanden is concerned with social movements that resist rather than promote social change); Roberta Ash and Mayer N. Zald, "Social Movement Organization: Growth, Decay and Change," *Social Forces,* 44(March 1966), pp. 327-341. Roberta Ash, *Social Movements In America* (Chicago: Markham Publishing Company, 1972) is the only sociological study to examine the I.W.W., but it reduces the I.W.W. to a movement whose strategy to organize the deroutinized and to create deroutinization failed to sustain or spread new ways of thinking or acting (pp. 163-167). Much of the conceptualization for my study was drawn from the work of Raymond Williams and James R. Green; see particularly William's *Marxism and Literature* (London: Oxford University Press, 1977), pp. 75-136 and Green's, "Culture, Politics and Workers Responses to Industrialization," *Radical America* 16 (Jan-Feb/March-April, 1982) pp. 101-128. It is from William's work that I derive the concept of oppositional culture and countermovement.

11. Archie Green's work on the I.W.W. represents an important exception; see "John Neuhaus: Wobbly Folklorist," *Journal of American Folklore* 73(July-Sept. 1960), pp. 189-217; "American Labor Lore," *Industrial Relations* 4(Feb. 1965), pp. 51-68. See also Steve Golin, "The Paterson Pageant: Success or Failure," *Socialist Review* 69(May-June 1983), pp. 45-78.

12. Peter DeShazo and Robert J. Halstead, "Los Wobblies Del Sur: The Industrial Workers of The World in Chile and Mexico" (unpublished manuscript, University of Wisconsin, 1974), pp. 1-57.

13. Michael R. Johnson, "The I.W.W. Prior to America's Entry Into World War I," *Science and Society,* XXIX(Winter 1965), pp. 91-95; Joseph R. Conlin, "Wobblies and Syndicalists," *Studies on the Left* 2(March-April 1966), pp. 81-91. See also the discussion between Robert L. Tyler and Melvyn Dubofsky in *Failure of a Dream? Essays in the History of American Socialism,* ed. by John H. M. Laslett and Seymour M. Lipset (New York: Anchor Books, 1974), pp. 286-299.

14. See my discussion in chapter 1.

15. Tom Connors, "The Industrial Union in Agriculture," in *Twenty Five Years of Industrial Unionism* (Chicago :I.W.W. Publishing Bureau, n.d.), p. 35.

16. Gambs, *The Decline of the I.W.W.,* p. 172.

17. W. Dirk Raat, *Revoltosos: Mexican Rebels in the United States, 1903-1923* (College Station: Texas A & M University Press, 1981), pp. 40-62. Ricardo Flores Magón was one of the most important anarchists in the Mexican revolutionary movement. Active at an early age against the dictorship of Profirio Diaz, he was forced to take refuge in the United States. In 1905 he founded the Partido Liberal Mexicano (Mexican Liberal Party) which organized two success-ful uprisings against Diaz. Members of the PLM were also known as Magónistas. For a good introduction to Ricardo Flores Magón and the PLM see: Ricardo Flores Magón, *Land and Liberty: Anarchist Influences in the Mexican Revolution* ed. by David Poole (United Kingdom: Cienfuesos Press, 1977).

18. Brissenden, *The I.W.W.,* pp. 315-316.

19. Robert A. Rosenstone, *Romantic Revolutionary, A Biography of John Reed* (New York: Alfred A. Knopf, 1975), pp. 117-132.

20. John Reed, "The I.W.W. in Court," in John Stuart (ed.), *The Education of John Reed* (New York: International Publishers, 1982), p. 181. Wobbly is a term of uncertain origins. It was used by both members and nonmembers to refer to a member of the I.W.W. Archie Green dates its usage around 1912 and is currently working on an essay that explores the etymology of the word. (Interview with Archie Green, San Francisco, CA, August 14, 1984.) The first printed reference to the term appears in *Regeneración,* April 27, 1912, and is reprinted in the *Industrial Worker,* "Wobbly 'Gene'," May 9, 1912, p.3. It is, however, likely that the word entered usage before appearing in print, (Corres-pondence with Archie Green, September-October, 1984.) Various accounts of the term's meaning can be found in Mortimer Downing's letter to the *Nation* (Sept. 5, 1923), p. 242; Peter Tamony, "The Wobblies," *Western Folklore* 30(Jan. 1971), pp. 49-54. The meaning of other terms used by I.W.W.s, migratory workers and hobos can be found in Green, "John Neuhaus," pp. 203-215; Joyce Kornbluh, *Rebel Voices: An I.W.W. Anthology* (Ann Arbor: University of Michigan Press, 1968), pp. 405-408.

21. Nels Anderson, *The Hobo: The Sociology of Homeless Men* (Chicago: University of Chicago Press, 1967 [reprint, University of Chicago, 1923]), pp. 16-18. See also Charles Ashleigh, "The Floater," *International Socialist Review* [ISR] XV(July 1914), pp. 34-39.

22. Anderson, *The Hobo,* p. 20.

23. Frank Thistlethwaite, "Migration From Overseas in the Nineteenth and Twentieth Centuries," in Herbert Moller (ed.), *Population Movements in Modern European History* (New York: Macmillian Co., 1964), pp. 78-79.

24. *Solidarity,* Nov. 21, 1914.

25. James Burkhart Gilbert, *Writers and Partisans: A History of Literary Radicalism In America* (New York: John Wiley and Sons, Inc., 1968), p. 14.

26. These songs can be found in Kornbluh, *Rebel Voices,* pp. 71, 77, 133.

27. Donald Barnes, "The Ideology of the Industrial Workers of the World: 1905-1921" (Ph.D. dissertation, Washington State University, 1962), p. 27.

28. Kenneth Allsop. *Hard Traveling: The Hobo and His History* (London: Hodderand and Stoughton, 1967), pp. 316-317.

29. Rexford G. Tugwell, "Casuals of the Woods," *Survey* 44(July 3, 1920), p. 472. See also Carleton Parker, *The Casual Laborer and Other Essays* (New York: Harcourt, Brace and Howe, 1920).

30. Researchers have demonstrated that the features alleged to characterize the culture of poverty are definitions of poverty itself, not of a distinct culture. See Hylan Lewis, "To Fulfill These Rights," in Lee Rainwater and Willian Yancy (eds.), *The Moynihan Report: The Politics of Controversy* (Cambridge: M.I.T. Press, 1967); Ulf Hannerz, *Southside: Inquires into Getto Culture and Community* (New York: Colombia University Press, 1969); Elliot Liebow, *Tally's Corner, A Study of Nego Streetcorner Men* (Boston: Little Brown, 1967); Charles A. Vallentine, *Culture and Poverty: Critique and Counterproposals* (Chicago: University of Chicago Press, 1968); Carol Stack, *All Our Kin* (New York: Harper & Row Publishers, 1974); William Preston, "Shall This Be all' Historians Versus William D. Haywood Et Al," *Labor* History 12 (Summer 1971), pp. 442-443; Larry Peterson, "The Intellectual World of the I.W.W.: An American Worker's Library in the First Half of the 20th Century," *History Workshop Journal* 22(Autumn 1986), pp. 153-172. Peterson's discussion of his grandfather's library contributes significantly to furthering our understanding of Wobbly culture.

31. Dubofsky, *We Shall Be All,* p. 148-151.

32. Letter from Richard Brazier to Joyce Kornbluh, November 8, 1963 I.W.W. Collection, The Archive of Labor History and Urban Affairs, Wayne State University). See also Harvey Swados' review of *Rebel Voices* in *Labor History* 6(Fall 1965)j, p. 256.

33. Stirling Bowen, "To an Unknown Proletarian," *Industrial Solidarity,* Jan. 21, 1922.

34. Letter from Archie Green to author, November 2, 1983. See also Archie Green, "Marcus Daly Enters Heaven," *Speculator* 1(Winter 1984), pp. 27-32.

35. Gibbs M. Smith, *Labor Martyr: Joe Hill,* (New York: Grosset & Dunlap, 1969), pp. 15-42.

36. Joe Hill, "The Rebel's Toast," *Solidarity,* June 27, 1914.

37. Fred Thompson, *The I.W.W.: Its First Fifty Years* (Chicago: I.W.W., 1955), pp. 81-82; Ernest Riebe, *Mr. Block: Twenty-Four I.W.W. Cartoons, edited by Franklin Rosemont (Chicago: Charles H. Kerr Publishing Co., 1984 [reprint, Block Publishing Co., 1913]), p. 6.*

Chapter 1

1. William E. Trautmann, "A Brief History of the Industrial Union Manifesto," *I.U.B.,* 15 February 1907. See also, Tatsuro Nomura, "Partisan Politics In and Around the I.W.W.: The Earliest Phase," *The Journal of the Faculty of Foreign Studies* 10(March 1977), pp. 86-139.

2. Brissenden, *The I.W.W.,* pp. 274-276.

3. For a discussion of the narrow institutional perspective of the Ely-Commons-Perlman tradition of labor historiography see Joseph R. Conlin (ed.), *At the Point of Production: The Local History of the I.W.W.* (Connecticut: Greenwood Press, 1981), pp. 4-6. While critical of the pitfalls of institutional history, Conlin's conception of local history does not offer an alternative perspective. The articles in his anthology merely examine the I.W.W. strike activities at a local level. For a more thorough analysis of the Ely-Commons-Perlman tradition see James R. Green, "L' historie de movement ouvrier et la gauche americaine," *Le Movement Social* 102(January - March 1979), pp. 9-40. Other useful studies include Maurice Isserman, "God Bless Our American Institutions; The Labor History of John R. Commons," *Labor History* 17(Summer 1976), pp. 310-328; Robert Zieger, "Workers and Scholars: Some Recent Trends in American Labor Historiography," *Labor History* 13 (Spring 1972), pp. 245-266; Thomas A. Kreuger, "American Labor Historiography, Old and New: A Review Essay," *Journal of Social History* 4(Spring 1971), pp. 377-385.

4. Compare accounts of the I.W.W.'s founding convention in *The Weekly People,* especially "Impressions of the Chicago Convention," July 22, 1905, in which the question of Hagerty's anarchism is discussed, with those appearing in *The International Socialist Review* (ISR), in which the I.W.W.'s contact with the C.G.T. is first mentioned by A.S. Simons, "Industrial Workers of the World," VI(August 1905), pp. 65-77. The early teens saw a rash of pamphlets and books concerning the I.W.W.'s relationship to the "new unionism" and syndicalism; the following are the most noteworthy examples of works written by activist intellectuals: Justus Ebert, *The Trial of a New Society* (Cleveland: I.W.W. Publishing Bureau, 1913); John Spargo, *Syndicalism, Industrial Unionism and Socialism* (New York: B.W. Huebsch, 1913); Andre Tridon, *The New Unionism* (New York: B.W. Huebsch, 1913); William E. Walling, *Progressivism and After* (New York: The Macmillan Co., 1914).

5. An exception to the typical coverage appeared in the *Cincinnati Post,* which gave a detailed account of the I.W.W.'s inaugural convention in an article entitled "To Supplant the A.F. OF L.," (January 9, 1905, p. 5,) which mentioned that the I.W.W. was "based on the same principles as organized labor in Continental Europe." The changes in press coverage and public opinion are documented in Brissenden, *The I.W.W.* pp. xiv–xxi, and John S. Gambs, *The Decline of The I.W.W.,* pp. 21–51.

6. For the best description and analysis of the reactions of the right and center wings of the S.P. to the I.W.W. see Ira Kipnis, *The American Socialist Movement 1897-1912* (New York: Columbia University press, 1952) pp. 164-198. Brissenden's account of the I.W.W. split with DeLeon remains the most complete; see his chapter on "The Coup of the 'Proletarian Rabble,' " in *The I.W.W.* For accounts critical of the I.W.W.'s position on political parties by left-wing socialists see Louis Fraina, "Syndicalism and Industrial Unionism," *ISR* XIV(July 1913), pp. 25-28; and Frank Bohn, "Is the I.W.W. to Grow?," *ISR* XII (July 1911) pp. 42-44.

7. By far the most interesting of the many articles written by supporters appeared in academic journals. Louis Levine's "The Development of Syndicalism in America," *Political Science Quarterly* 28(Sept. 1913), pp. 451-479, represents the best of the early attempts to come to grips with the complexities and subtleties between syndicalism and industrial unionism. O.D. Skelton's, "French Unionism Militant," *The Journal of Political Economy* 17(March 1909), pp. 125-143, is the best single source on the history and politics of the C.G.T. The *Industrial Worker* serialized Skelton's article, once beginning in May 1909 and again, due to numerous requests, in August 1910. Noteworthy examples

appearing in the radical press include Jean Spielman, "Are the I.W.W. Still Revolutionary?," *Mother Earth* 11(December 1907), pp. 457-460, and William E. Bohn, "The Industrial Workers of the World," *The Survey*, May 4, 1912, pp. 220-225.

8. See especially "Industrialism is Not Syndicalism," *Industrial Worker*, 9 January 1913.

9. Brissenden, *The I.W.W*, pp. 213-242; Eldridge F. Dowell, *A History of Criminal Syndicalist Legislation*, pp. 44-88; Gambs, *Decline of the I.W.W.*, pp. 21-52.

10. The I.W.W.'s defensive posture toward French syndicalism is evidenced in *Historical Catechism of American Unionism* (Chicago: Educational Bureau of the I.W.W., n.d.), p. 83. Songs and cartoons affirming the I.W.W.'s relationship to the movement continue to appear in *Solidarity* and the *Industrial Pioneer* in spite of official statements. (See chapters 4 and 5 which expand on the complexities of the I.W.W's relationship to French syndicalism.)

11. Fred. W. Thompson, The I.W.W.: Its First Fifty Years 1905-1955 (Chicago: I.W.W., 1955); Philip S. Foner, *History of the Labor Movement in the United States*, Vol. 4. *The Industrial Workers of the World 1905-1917* (New York: International Publishers, 1964); Joyce Kornbluh (ed.), *Rebel Voices: an I.W.W. Anthology* (Ann Arbor: The University of Michigan Press, 1964); Harvey O'Connor, *Revolution in Seattle* (Seattle: Left Bank Books, 1964); Foner (ed.), *The Letters of Joe Hill* (New York: Oak Publications, 1965); Foner, *The Case of Joe Hill,* (New York: International Publishers, 1965); Patrick Renshaw, *The Wobblies: The Story of Syndicalism in America* (New York: Doubleday & Company, Inc., 1967); Robert L. Tyler, *Rebels in the Woods: The I.W.W. in the Pacific Northwest* (Eugene: University of Oregon Books, 1967); Joseph R. Conlin, *Bread and Roses, Too: Studies of the Wobblies* (Connecticut: Greenwood Publishing Corporation, 1969); Conlin, *Big Bill Haywood and the Radical Union Movement* (New York: Syracuse University Press, 1969); Melvyn Dubofsky, *We Shall Be All: A History of the I.W.W.* (Chicago: Quadrangle Books, 1969); Gibbs M. Smith, *Joe Hill: Labor Martyr* (New York: Grosset & Dunlap, 1969).

12. Fred W. Thompson and Patrick Murfin, *The I.W.W.: Its First Seventy Years 1905-1975 (Chicago: I.W.W., 1976), p. 40.*

13. *Tyler, Rebels in the Woods, p. 215.*

14. Conlin, *Bread And Roses,* p. 82.

15. Foner, *I.W.W.*, pp. 23, 159-160.

16. William Preston, "Shall This Be All? Historians Versus William D. Haywood Et Al," *Labor History* 12(Summer 1971), p. 444.

17. Brissenden, *The I.W.W.,* pp. 349-350.

18. Ibid.

19. John G. Brooks, *American Syndicalism: The I.W.W.* (New York: The Macmillan Company, 1913), p. 175.

20. Donald M. Barnes, "The Ideology of the I.W.W.", p. 71. Thomas McEnroe, "I.W.W. Theories, Organization Problems and Appeals as Revealed in the Industrial Worker," (Ph.D. dissertation, University of Minnesota, 1960), p. 203, suggests but does not develop the idea that the I.W.W.'s union and revolutionary tasks were incompatable.

21. Daniel T. Rogers, "Tradition, Modernity and the American Industrial Worker: Reflection and Critique," *Journal of Interdisciplinary History,* 11(Spring 1977), pp. 652-655.

22. Preston, "Shall This Be All?," p. 440. See also Steward Bird, et al, "We Always Sang Those Wonderful Songs': Sophie Cohen, Joe Murphy and the I.W.W.," *Radical America* 19(1985), p. 58.

23. Paul Sebestyen [Sebastian] Transcript, "Oral History Interview on Akron's Rubber Strike and on General Ideological Background," by Roy Wortman, July 8, 1969, Joseph A. Labadie Papers, Labadie Collection, the University of Michigan Library.

24. Irving Abrams, Transcript of Interview by Frank Ninkovich, 1970, Book 17, p. 14, Labor Oral History Project, Roosevelt University, Chicago.

25. Ricardo Flores Magón, *Land and Liberty: Anarchist Influences in the Mexican Revolution, compiled and introduced by David Poole, (U.K.: Cienfuegos Press Ltd., 1977), p. 85.*

26. *Richard Brazier, "The Story of the I.W.W.'s 'Little Red Song Book,'"* *Labor History* 9(Winter 1968), pp. 91-92.

27. James Wilson, "Music: One of the Most Powerful Natural Forces," *Industrial Union Bulletin,* July 25, 1908.

28. Sinclair could be found walking a picket line with I.W.W.s in Tarrytown, N.Y., in protest of John D. Rockerfeller, Jr.'s role in the Ludlow Massacre—see John Graham, "Upton Sinclair and the Ludlow Massacre," *Colorado Quarterly* XXI(Summer 1972), pp. 55-67; or sharing a jail cell with

striking Wobblies in San Pedro—see his account of his experience with the
Marine Transport Workers in *Sing Jailbirds: A Drama in Four Acts* (Long Beach:
Published by the author, 1924), pp. 87-95.

29. Nels Anderson, *The Hobo: The Sociology of the Homeless Man* (Chicago: University of Chicago Press, 1967), p. 234.

30. Quoted in Barnes, "The Ideology of the I.W.W.," p. 83.

31. John Crow, "Ideology and Organization: A Case Study of the
Industrial Workers of the World," (M.A. Thesis, University of Chicago, 1958), p.
62.

32. Fred Thompson, Interview with writer, Dec. 14, 1983, Chicago.

33. James R. Green, "The Brotherhood of Timber Workers 1910-1913: A
Radical Response to Industrial Capitalism in the Southern U.S.A.," *Past and
Present* 60(August 1973), pp. 161-200.

34. Joseph R. Conlin (ed.), *At the Point of Production,* p. 24.

35. Proceedings, *Second I.W.W. Convention* (Chicago: I.W.W., 1906), p.
287; Barnes, "The Ideology of the I.W.W.," p. 77.

36. Leland W. Robinson, "Social Movement Organizations in Decline, A
Case Study of the I.W.W.," (Ph.D. dissertation, Northwestern University, 1973),
pp. 29-30.

37. Brissenden, *The I.W.W.,* p. 315.

38. John Reed, "The I.W.W. in Court," in *The Education of John Reed:
Selected Writings,* John Stuart (ed.), (New York: International Publishers, 1982),
p. 181.

39. Charles P. Lewarne, "The Aberdeen, Washington, Free-Speech Fight
of 1911-1912," *Pacific Northwest Quarterly* 66(Jan. 1975), p. 1. Most I.W.W.
accounts discuss the free-speech fights. See, for example, Brissenden, *The
I.W.W.,* pp. 262-266, 367; Dubofsky, *We shall Be All* 173-179; for accounts of
free-speech fights by participants, see Philip S. Foner, (ed.), *Fellow Workers and
Friends: I.W.W. Free-Speech Fights as Told by Participants* (Connecticut: Greenwood Press, 1981). There exists an extensive literature on individual free-
speech fights, see, for example, Ronald Gennini, "Industrial Workers Of the
World and Their Fresno Free-Speech Fight, 1910-1911," *California Historical
Quarterly* LII(Summer 1974), pp. 101-114; Robert W. Diehl, "To Speak or Not
To Speak: San Diego 1912" (M.A. Thesis, University of San Diego, 1976); Glen J.

Broyles, "The Spokane Free-Speech Fight, 1909-1910: A Study in I.W.W. Tactics." *Labor History* 19(Spring 1978), pp. 238-252; Robert L. Tyler, "The Everett Free-Speech Fight", *Pacific Northwest Review* 23 (February 1954), pp. 19-30.

40. Margaret Sanger, *My Fight For Birth Control* (New York: Farrar & Rinehart, 1931), p. 61; Meredith Tax, *The Rising of the Women* (New York: Monthly Review Press, 1980), pp. 156-163; Linda Gordon, *Woman's Body, Woman's Right: Birth Control In America* (New York: Penguin Books, 1976), p. 226. See also Ann Schofield, "Rebel Girls and Union Maids: The Woman Question in the Journals of The AFL and I.W.W., 1905-1920," *Feminist Studies*, 9 (Summer, 1983) pp. 335-358 for a comparison and analysis of sexism and paternalism in the AFL and I.W.W.

41. Most accounts of the I.W.W. do not mention in any detail the I.W.W.'s role in the Mexican revolution; see, for example, Renshaw, *The Wobblies,* pp. 288-290 or Foner, *The I.W.W. 1905-1917,* p. 188 (which deals with the I.W.W.'s complex relationship to the P.L.M. in a footnote). By far the best account of the I.W.W.'s relationship to the P.L.M. is in Dirk Raat, *Revoltosos,* pp. 40-62. See also Lowell L. Blaisdell, *The Desert Revolution, Baja California, 1911* (Madison: University of Wisconsin Press, 1962); Ethel Duffy Turner, *Revolution in Baja California: Ricardo Flores Magón's High Noon,* ed. and annotated by Rey Devis (Detroit: Blaine Ethridge Books, 1981).

42. Connors, "The Industrial Union in Agriculture," pp. 35-42. Connors dates the beginnings of the industrial union form advocated by the I.W.W. with the emergence of the Agricultural Workers Organization in 1915; Robinson, in his study, "Movement Organizations in Decline," pp. 29-32, notes a shift in the I.W.W.'s strategy occurring around 1916. "There was a feeling in 1916 that too much time and effort had been spent on soapboxing and glamorous free-speech fights, and relatively too little time spent on organizing stable, militant, radical unions." These sentiments led to changes in the organizational structure of the I.W.W. which were adopted by referendum early in 1917.

43. Herbert Blumer, "Collective Behavior," in Alfred M. Lee (ed.), *New Outline of the Principles of Sociology* (New York: Barnes and Noble, 1946), pp. 167-222.

44. Joseph R. Gusfield, "The Study of Social Movements," in David L. Shills (ed.), *International Encyclopedia of the Social Sciences* (The Macmillan Co. and the Free Press, 1968), p. 445.

45. William E. Trautmann, "Report of the General Secretary-Treasurer," *Proceedings, Second I.W.W. Convention* (Chicago: I.W.W., 1906), p. 3.

46. *Proceedings, The Founding Convention of the I.W.W.* (New York: Merit Publishers, 1969), pp. 247 & 229.

47. Don K. Mckee, "Daniel DeLeon: A Reappraisal," *Labor History* 1(Fall 1960), pp. 264-297.

48. Peter Carlson, Letter, May 8, 1983, to author, (quoted from Harry Burton, "I.W.W. Head Calls Syndicalism, Socialism in Working Clothes," *Boston Herald,* 12 July 1912.

49. Peter Carlson, *Roughneck: The Life and Times of Big Bill Haywood* (New York: W.W. Norton & Co., 1983), p. 146.

50. Ben H. Williams, "Syndicalism and Socialism," *Solidarity,* 27 April 1912.

51. "Are Tactics Revolutionary?," *Industrial Worker,* 16 May 1912.

52. Vincent St. John, *The I.W.W. Its History, Structure and Methods* (Cleveland: I.W.W. Pub. Bureau, 3rd ed., 1913), p. 17.

53. "About the Preamble," *Industrial Worker,* January 1906 p. 9.

54. *Industrial Worker,* 1 April 1909.

55. Brooks, *American Syndicalism,* p. 25.

56. *Industrial Worker,* "Revolution," 26 June 1913.

Chapter 2

1. Peter DeShazo and Robert J. Halstead, "Los Wobblies Del Sur", pp. 1-57. While their study does not focus on the I.W.W.'s early immigrant influence, it does discuss the I.W.W's internationalism and traces the development of some of the I.W.W. early foreign administrations.

2. Louis Levine, "The Development of Syndicalism in America," pp. 451-479.

3. William English Walling, "Industrialism vs. Syndicalism," *ISR* VII(March 1913), p. 666.

4. Robert Rives La Monte, "Industrial Unionism and Syndicalism," *New Review* 1(May 1913), pp. 527–529.

5. Bessy Beaty, "Syndicalism: Solidarity: Self-Sacrifice," *Solidarity,* Ocotober 17, 1914.

6. Levine, "The Development of Syndicalism in America," pp. 457-456.

7. Ralph Edwards Souers, "The Industrial Workers of the World" (M.A. thesis, University of Chicago, 1913), pp. 29-35. Souers acknowledges Franklin H. Giddens's introduction to Levine's monograph on French syndicalism for the theory informing his study.

8. Frank Thistlethwaite, "Migration From Overseas in the Nineteenth and Twentieth Centuries," pp. 78-79. See also Robert F. Foerster, *Italian Emigration of Our Time* (Cambridge, Harvard University Press, 1919).

9. G.D.H. Cole, *A History of the Socialist Movement:* Vol. III, Part II, *The Second International 1889-1914,* (London: Macmillan & Co. Ltd., 1956), pp. 796-797.

10. Al Gedicks, "The Social Origins of Radicalism Among Finnish Immigrants in Midwest Mining Communities," *Review of Radical Political Economy* 8(Fall 1976) pp. 1-31.

11. George W. Carey, "The Vessel, The Deed and The Idea: The Paterson Anarchists, 1895-1908", unpublished manuscript, pp. 248-286.

12. George W. Carey, "The Vessel, The Deed and the Idea: Anarchists in Paterson, 1895-1908," *Antipode* 10 & 11(1979), p. 56.

13. Carey, "Paterson Anarchists," pp. 252-259.

14. Ibid., p. 248.

15. Emma Goldman, "Johann Most," *American Mercury,* VII(June 1926), pp. 158-166; Paul Avrich, *The Haymarket Tradedy,* (New Jersey, Prinction University Press, 1984), pp. 61-63.

16. Avrich, *Haymarket Tragedy,* p. 64.

17. Ibid., pp. 71-74.

18. John R. Commons et al., *History of Labour in the United States,* vol. 2, (New York: Macmillian Co., 1918), p. 298.

19. Christian Corneissen, "Uber den Internationalen Syndikalismus," *Archiv fur Sozialwissenchaft* XXX(Jan. 1910); reprinted in the *Industrial Worker,* 18 June 1910, as "Origins of Syndicalism." See also Rudolf Rocker, *Anarcho-Syndicalism,* (London: Secker and Warburg Ltd., 1938), pp. 56-81.; Robert

Hunter, *Violence and the Labor Movement,* (New York: Macmillian Co., 1914), 154-193.

20. Quoted in Brissenden, *The I.W.W.,* p. 36.

21. Brissenden merely notes in passing that "all the main ideas of modern revolutionary syndicalism as exhibited by the I.W.W. may be found in the old International Workingmen's Association." Though admitting similarities between the I.W.W. and the program originally drafted by Michael Bakunin, he sees them as amounting to no more than slogans adopted by the I.W.W. (pp. 36-37). Likewise, Andre Tridone in *The New Unionism* (New York: B.W. Huebsch, 1913), pp. 93-94, mentions the I.W.P.A. in his treatment of the development of "new unionism" in the United States but fails to elaborate on its significance to the I.W.W.'s form of industrial unionism. In John Spargo's, *Syndicalism, Industrial Unionism and Socialism,* (New York: B.W. Huebsch, 1913), the International is discussed but no mention is made of the role of anarchism in the birth of the revolutionary syndicalist movement. By far the best contemporary account to deal with the many myths and misconceptions that impeded understanding of the revolutionary syndicalist movement is Bob Holton's *British Syndicalism 1900-1914, Myths and Realities,* (London: Pluto Press Ltd., 1976); see especially pp. 17-23, 200-212.

22. Quoted in Tridon, *New Unionism,* p. 17.

23. The complexities of the pattern of "cross fertilization" through which the theory of sabotage was developed is documented in Geoff Brown, *Sabotage: A Study of Industrial Conflict* (Great Britian: Spokesman Books, 1977), pp. 3-39; See also Emile Pouget, *Sabotage,* translated by Arturo M. Giovannitti (Chicago, Charles H. Kerr & Co., 1913), pp. 38-58.

24. Rudolf Rocker, *Johann Most: Das Leben eines Rebellen,* (Germany Verlag Detlev Auvermann, 1973), p. 394.

25. John Spargo, *Syndicalism, Industrial Unionism and Socialism* (New York: B.W. Huebsch, 1913); Andre Tridon, *The New Unionism* (New York: B.W. Heubsch, 1913).

26. Paul F. Brissenden, "The Launching of the Industrial Workers of the World," *University of California Publications in Economics* 4(Nov. 25, 1913), pp. 1-2.

27. Brissenden, *The I.W.W.,* p. 274.

28. Ibid., p. 41-42.

29. Drawing heavily from Robert Hunter, Brissenden wrote that the effect of "the famous Haymarket riots [sic.] in Chicago...was unquestionably to give the labor and socialist movement a serious set back." It did more to induce rank-and-file labor activists "to reject all association with revolutionary ideas than perhaps all other things put together" (pp. 39-41). For an excellent discussion of impact of Haymarket on the labor movement, see Avrich's discussion of the legacy of Haymarket in *Haymarket Tragedy,* pp. 428-436.

30. Brissenden, "The Launching of the I.W.W.", p. 2. In his later work, Brissenden further elaborates on the S.T. & L.A., concluding that the Alliance represented a revolutionary trade union rather than an industrial union (*The I.W.W.,* p. 49). This point is emphasized in Don K. McKee's ground breaking study, "Daniel DeLeon: A Reappraisal," in which he argues that DeLeon "never discussed industrial unionism until late in 1904 and did not give an unqualified endorsement until the middle of 1905" (p. 265).

31. Lillian Symes and Travers Clement, *Rebel America: The Story of Social Revolt in the United Statesw* (Boston: Beacon Press, 1972).

32. Virgil J. Vogel, "The Historians and the Industrial Workers of the World," Typescript, University of Chicago, June 8, 1955, pp. 14-15.

33. Barnes, "The Ideology of the I.W.W.," p. 198.

34. Dubofsky, *We Shall Be All,* p. 19; "Origins of Western Working Class Radicalism," *Labor History* 7(Spring 1966), p. 132.

35. Dubofsky, *We Shall Be all,* p. 5.

36. Ibid., pp. 19-35.

37. Ibid., pp. 73, 76-77.

38. Preston, "Shall This Be All?," pp. 437-438.

39. Vernon H. Jensen, *Heritage of Conflict; Labor Relations in the Non-Ferrous Metal Industry Up to 1930* (Ithaca: Cornell University Press, 1950).

40. Vernon Jensen and Melvyn Dubofsky, "The I.W.W.—An Exchange of Views," *Labor History* 11(Summer 1970), p. 356.

41. Paul Buhle, "The Wobblies in Perspective," *Monthly Review* (June 1970), p. 45.

42. See Nomura, "Partisian Politics"; Don K. McKee, "The Influence of Syndicalism Upon Daniel DeLeon," *The Historian* 20(May 1958), pp. 275-289; McKee, "DeLeon: A Reappraisal."

43. Paul Buhle, "Anarchism and American Labor," *International Labor and Working Class History* 23(Spring 1983), pp. 21-34.

44. Sally M. Miller, *The Radical Immigrant,* (New York: Twayne Publishers, Inc., 1974), p. 108.

45. Gary M. Fink et al, *Biographical Dictionary of American Labor Leaders,* (Westport, Connecticut: Greenwood Press, 1974), pp. 358-359.

46. Kipnis, *American Socialist Movement,* p. 195.

47. *Proceedings of the First Convention of the Industrial Workers of the World,* (New York: New York Labor News Co., 1905 [Merit Publishers, reprint 1969], pp. 289-290. See also Mckee, "The Influences of Syndicalism Upon DeLeon," pp. 284. The I.W.W.'s relationship to the C.G.T. will be discussed more fully in Chapter 5.

48. William E. Trautmann, "The United Brewery Workers and Industrial Organization," *American Labor Union Journal,* Sept. 3, 1903, pp. 15-16.

49. McKee, "DeLeon: A Reappraisal," p. 288; Kipnis, *American Socialist Movement,* p. 195.

50. Fink et al, *Biographical Dictionary of American Labor Leaders,* p. 75-76.

51. Mckee, *"Influence of Syndicalism Upon Deleon,"* p. 285-287.

52. Andre Tridon, *The New Unionism,* p. 156; John Spargo, *Syndicalism, Industrial Unionism and Syndicalism,* wrote, " . . . Labiola, whose position as the intellectual leader of Italian syndicalism is universally admitted, takes the view of the union as the unit of industrial and social administration held by Pouget, Sorel, Berth and other French leaders" (p. 27). It is, however, clear from Labriola's writings that he was not in agreement with the anarcho-syndicalist program of the C.G.T. of which Pouget was a major architect. Labriola's conception of syndicalism was Marxist in derivation [Tom Bottomore (ed., *A Dictionary of Marxist Thought* (London, Blackwell Publishers Ltd., 1983), p. 271)]. His idea that the unions might hire the capital of the capitalists, for a fixed return, using the capital cooperatively or through several cooperative bodies until the syndicates were strong enough to refuse return for the use of the capital, thereby forcing the capitalist to work while making use of "their indisputable directive and administrative capacity," (see Labiola's, *Riforme e Rivoluzione Sociale,* portions of which are quoted in Tridon, *New Unionism,* p. 157.) would have been considered reformist, at best, by the revolutionary wing

of the C.G.T. Such sloppy definitions and labels used by DeLeon and others to identify socialism with syndicalism were criticized by left-wing socialists. Louis Fraina, for example, wrote, following the publication of Tridon's and Spargo's accounts, that "many persons in adopting syndicalism have modified it to suit their convenience, with the consequence that pro-political industrialism is being preached in the name of Syndicalism. Industrial unionism is the application of socialist principles to economic organization, whereas syndicalism is anarchy unionized." ["Syndicalism and Industrial Unionism," *ISR*, XIV (1913-1914), p. 25.] Needless to say, Tridon and Spargo were also criticized in the anarchist press; see, for example, Hyppolyte Havel, "The New Unionism," *Mother Earth,* VII (Sept. 1913), pp. 213-218. In the teens, many versions of syndicalism coexisted, which underscores the fallacy of a "true" or "pure" syndicalism. This is not to suggest that there were no proponents of pure syndicalism. For an interesting analysis of a group that advocated a doctrinaire version of syndicalism, see Charlton J. Brandt, "Bringing *Real* Syndicalism to America: William Z. Foster and the Syndicalist League of North America, unpublished manuscript, 1983.

53. Mckee, "Influence of Syndicalism Upon Deleon," p. 288.

54. Daniel DeLeon, *Flashlights of the Amsterdam Congress,* (New York: New York Labor News Company, 1929), p. 99.

55. Trautmann, "Brief History of the Industrial Union Manifesto," *I.U.B.,* 22 February 1908.

56. Mckee, "Influence of Syndicalism Upon Deleon," p. 282-283.

57. Quoted in Nomura, "Partisian Politics," p. 92.

58. *Proceedings, First I.W.W. Convention, pp. 82-83.*

59. Ibid., p. 6.

60. Levine, *"Development of Syndicalism,"* pp. 464-465.

61. Thompson, (*First Fifty Years,* pp. 30-31) wrote that Haywood had "no connection with the I.W.W. other than as chairman of its first convention, and [following his acquittal on charges in connection with the murder of former Governor Steunenburg] went [on a] speaking tour for the Socialist Party, and in 1910 represented it at the International Socialist Congress in Copenhagen, toured Europe lecturing, and joined the I.W.W. upon his return to America in the fall of that year." Thompson's account of Haywood's role in the early I.W.W. is supported by William E. Trautmann. In "The power of Folded Arms

and Thinking Bayonets," *One Big Union Monthly* 1(Nov., 1937), p. 16, Trautmann wrote, "After his acquittal Haywood did not come near the I.W.W., ...he paid his dues to Joseph Ettor in Pittsburg on May 1, 1910."

62. Kipnis, *American Socialist Movement,* pp. 390-420.

63. Cole, *The Second International 1889-1914,* pp. 792-794.

64. Brissenden, *The I.W.W.,* pp. 299-319. See also Covington Hall, "Labor Struggles in the Deep South," Typescript, Joseph A. Labadie Papers, Labadie Collection, University of Michigan Library.

65. Cole, *The Second International 1889-1914,* p. 800; Bruno Ramirez, *When Workers Fight: The Politics of Industrial Relations in the Progressive Era 1898-1916* (West Port, Connecticut: Greenwood Press, 1978), pp. 194-211.

66. *Proceedings, First I.W.W. Convention,* p. 228.

67. Trautmann, "Brief History," *I.U.B.,* 8 August 1908.

68. Ibid.

69. Brissenden, *The I.W.W.,* p. 222-223.

70. Trautmann, "Brief History," *I.U.B.,* 8 August 1908.

71. Ibid. Trautmann, in his account, states that the clause was accepted by Hagerty who felt it was not made in "bad faith." For the argument that Hagerty refused to accept the addition of the clause, see Nomua, "Partisian Politics," p. 104.

72. McKee, "DeLeon: A Reappraisal," p. 292.

Chapter 3

1. William D. Haywood, *The Autobiography of Big Bill Haywood,* (New York: International Publishers, 1977 [reprint, International Publishers, 1929]), pp. 30-31.

2. *Proceedings, First I.W.W. Convention,* p. 128.

3. Anthony Bimba, *The History of the American Working Class* (New York: International Publisher, 1927), pp. 185-186; Samuel Yellen, *American Labor Struggles* (New York: Harcourt, Brace and Co., 1936), pp. 44-48; Avrich, *Haymarket Tragedy,* p. 73.

4. Richard T. Ely, *Recent American Socialism* (Baltimore: John Hopkins University, 1885), p. 31; Commons, *History of Labour,* Vol. II, pp. 297-298.

5. *Proceedings, First I.W.W. Convention* p. 216.

6. Brissenden, *The I.W.W.,* p. 39.

7. Ibid., p. 40.

8. Ibid., p. 109.

9. Joseph R. Conlin, *Bread and Roses,* p. 43.

10. Fink et al., *Bibliographic Dictionary,* p. 139.

11. Robert E. Doherty, "Thomas J. Hagerty, The Church, and Socialism," *Labor History,* 3(Winter 1963), pp. 51-53.

12. Quoted in Ibid., p. 51-52

13. Thomas J. Hagerty to Joseph A. Labadie, March 31, 1889, pp. 5-[6], Joseph A. Labadie Papers, Labadie Collection, University of Michigan Library.

14. Ibid., p. 1.

15. Ibid., pp. [2-3].

16. Thomas J. Hagerty, "Reasons for Industrial Unionism," *Voice of Labor,* March 1905, p. 8.

17. *Proceedings, First I.W.W. Convention,* p. 354-355.

18. Ibid., p. 570.

19. Ibid., p. 233.

20. Ibid., p. 86.

21. Trautmann, "Brief History," I.U.B. 8 August 1908. See chapter 2 for a more detailed discussion of this meeting and its significance.

22. *Proceedings, First I.W.W. Convention,* p. 152.

23. Ibid.

24. Ronald Creagh to writer, 16 May 1983.

25. *Proceedings, First I.W.W. Convention,* p. 152.

26. Quoted in Kipnis, *American Socialist Movement,* p. 194.

27. Idid., p. 197.

28. Quoted in Bernard J. Brommel, *Eugene V. Debs: Spokesman for Labor and Socialism* (Chicago: Charles H. Kerr Pub. Co, 1978), p. 144.

29. *I.W.,* July 1906, p. 4.

30. "The New Preamble," *I.U.B.,* 7 November 1908, p. 2.

31. Yellen, *American Labor Struggles,* p. 179.

32. "November," written in 1933, originally appeared as a song and was sung to the tune of "Love Divine," music by John Zundel; see John Neuhaus's unpublished collection of songs for the 30th edition of the I.W.W.'s song book, John Neuhaus Collection, Archie Green, San Francisco, CA. "November" also appears as a poem in *Songs of the Workers,* 34th ed., (Chicago: I.W.W., 1973), p. 57.

33. Carolyn Ashbaugh, *Lucy Parsons American Revolutionary* (Chicago: Charles H. Kerr Pub. Co., 1976), pp. 6-9.

34. *Proceedings, First I.W.W. Convention,* p. 56.

35. Ibid., p. 170.

36. Ibid., pp. 247-248.

37. McKee, "DeLeon: A Reappraisal," p. 283.

38. Hutchins Hapgood, *The Spirit of Labor* (New York: Duffield & Co., 1907), p. 186; Charles Pierce LeWarne, *Utopias On Pouget Sound 1885-1815* (Seattle: University of Washington Press, 1978), p. 208; Emma Goldman, *Living My Life* (New York: Garden City Publishing Co., Inc., 1934 [reprint, New York: Alfred A. Knopf, Inc., 1931]), p. 296.

39. LeWarne, *Utopias,* p. 206-207; Ashbaugh, *Lucy Parsons,* pp. 219-221; Alice Wexler *Emma Goldman: An Intimate Life,* (New York: Pantheon Books, 1984), pp. 106-107.

40. Ibid.

41. Goldman, *Living My Life,* pp. 74-75; Rocker, *Most,* pp. 339-341, 350-351; George Woodcock, *Anarchism: A History of Libertarian Ideas* (New York: Penguin Books, 1979 [reprint, Great Britian: Pelican Books, 1963]), p. 404. Very little biographical information concerning Peukert's activities is available. His autobiography, *Eninnerungen eines Proletariers ausrevolutionaren Arbeiterbewegung* (Berlin: Verlag Des Sozialistischen Bundes, 1913) chiefly concerns his feud with Johann Most.

42. Arnold Roller (Stephen Nact, [Siegfried Nacht]), *The Social General Strike* (Chicago: Debating Club No. 1, 1905), Joseph A. Labadie Papers, Labadie Collection, University of Michigan Library.

43. James D. Cockcroft, *Intellectual Precursors of the Mexican Revolution, 1900-1913* (Austin: University of Texas Press, 1968). pp. 119-121; Ellen Howell Myers, "The Mexican Liberal Party, 1903-1910," Ph.D. dissertation, University of Virginia, 1970, pp. 34-35.

44. Abad de Santillan, Diego, *Ricardo Flores Magón, el apostol de la revolucion social mexicana,* (Mexico City: Grupo Cultural "Ricardo Flores Magon," 1925), p. 16.

45. Barrera Fuentes, Florencio, *Historia de la revolución mexicana: La etapa precursora,* (Mexico City: Biblioteca del Institudeo de Estudios Historicos de la Revelucion Mexicana, 1955), p. 159; John M. Hart, *Anarchism and the Mexican Working Class, 1860-1931* (Austin, University of Texas Press, 1978), pp. 89-90.

46. Interview with Pietro Ferrua, 26 August 1984, Portland, Oregon.

47. Raat, *Revoltosos,* pp. 44-45. Raat found contact between Mexican miners and the W.F.M., who distributed I.W.W. newspapers and pamphlets in Spanish and English.

48. DeShazo and Halstead, "Los Wobblies Del Sur," p. 32; Raat, *Revoltosos,* pp. 60-61.

49. Goldman, *Living My Life,* pp. 406-407; Emma Goldman, "Syndicalism: Its Theory and Practice," *M.E.* VII(January, 1913), p. 375. There are large gaps in the archival materials available on Emma Goldman's life between 1900-1906.

50. Rocker, *Most,* p. 372.

51. Goldman, "Syndicalism," p. 376.

52. A thorough search through the material gathered from private collections, archives and government sources at The Emma Goldman Papers Project, Institute for the Study of Social Change, Berkeley, CA reveals critical gaps in the documentation on Goldman's activities in this period.

53. Emma Goldman, "The Situation In America," *M.E.,* II(October 1907), p. 323-324.

54. "Observations and Comments," *M.E.* II(October 1907), p. 229.

55. Jean Spielman, "Are the I.W.W. Still Revolutionary?" *M.E.* (Dec. 1907), pp. 457, 459-460.

56. Richard Drinnon, *Rebel in Paradise: A Bibliography of Emma Goldman* (Chicago: University of Chicago Press, 1961), p. 135.

57. Caroline Nelson, "Emma Goldman and Ben Reitman Tell of San Diego Experience," *I.W.*, 6 June 1912, p. 4.

58. Hyman Weintraub, "The I.W.W. in California," M.A. Thesis, University of California, Los Angeles, 1947, p. 18.

59. Very little information exists on the formation of Spanish-speaking locals in these areas. The early formation of Spanish-speaking locals in these states can, however, be inferred from a letter sent to *Solidarity* ("Help Madero's Victims," 24 February 1912, p. 4). F. Martinez Palomarez (Ferando Palomarez) wrote the letter following his arrest for violation of the neutrality laws. Prior to his arrest, Palomarez acted as joint secretray of I.W.W. locals 13(Los Angeles) and 174 (San Diego) and edited, with the help of Joseph Ettor, *Libertad y Trabajo,* a Spanish workers' weekly which succeeded *Revolución.* See also Myers, "The Mexican Liberal Party," pp. 253-254. Palomarez had been a participant in the Cananea and Rio Blanco strikes (Magón, *Land and Liberty,* p. 131). In his letter, Palomarez mentions the activities of the two I.W.W.s he was arrested with: R.A. Dorame, secretary of the Phoenix, Arizona I.W.W. Spanish-speaking local and editor of *La Union Industrial,* and Silvester Lomas, a member of the same branch.

60. *Proceedings, First I.W.W. Convention,* pp. 128-129.

61. Ibid., pp. 250-251, 287. I will treat the I.W.W.'s relationship to the C.G.T. in chapters 4 and 5.

62. Ibid., pp. 250-251.

63. Paul Avrich, *The Modern School Movement: Anarchism and Education in the United States* (Princeton: Princeton University Press, 1980), p. 120; Goldman, *Living My Life,* p. 595.

64. Paul Avrich, *The Russian Anarchists* (New York: W.W. Norton & Co., 1978), pp. 115, 137.

65. Carey, "The Paterson Anarchists," pp. 273-276.

66. Gabriel Kolko, "The Decline of American Labor Radicalism in the Twentieth Century," *Studies on the Left,* 6(September - October 1966), pp. 9-26.

Chapter 4

1. *Proceedings, First I.W.W. Convention,* p. 287; McKee, "The Influence of Syndicalism Upon DeLeon," p. 280.

2. *Proceedings, First I.W.W. Convention,* p. 290. In addition to the early correspondence between Trautmann and Pouget, the I.W.W.'s support of the C.G.T. extended to collaboration on French labor papers, most notably *La Vie Ouviere,* a bimonthly independent produced by a collective of revolutionary syndicalists and workers; see Larry Portis, *I.W.W. et syndicalisme Revolutionnarier aux Etats-Unis* (Paris: Edition Spartacus, 1985), pp. 79-81.

3. See, for example, "Report of General Secretary-Treasurer on the Work of the Organization," *I.U.B.,* 14 September 1907, p. 3; William E. Trautmann, "Industrial Unionism—Means and Methods—Active and Passive Action," *I.U.B.,* 29 February 1908, p. 3; "Industrial Unionism (Syndicalism) in its Economic Elucidation," *I.U.B.,* 20 June 1908; "The Employment Shark Must Go," *I.W.,* 25 March 1909, p. 3.

4. "The I.W.W. and the C.G.T.," *I.W.,* 2 November 1910, p. 2.

5. Levine, "The Development of Syndicalism in America," pp. 475-476.

6. Ibid.

7. William Z. Foster, "As To My Candidacy," *I.W.,* 2 November 1911, p. 2. See also Brandt, "Bringing *Real* Syndicalism to America," pp. 6-11.

8. *Solidarity,* 16 December 1911.

9. Brandt, "Bringing *Real* Syndicalism to America," pp. 15-22. See also William Z. Foster, *From Bryan To Stalin* (New York: International Publishers, 1937), pp. 58-72, for Foster's account on his role of forming the Syndicalist League of North America.

10. Joseph Ettor, "I.W.W. Versus A.F. of L.," *The New Review* 2(May, 1914), pp. 279 & 283. The most complete argument that the I.W.W. represented dual unionism is found in David J. Saposs, *Left Wing Unionism: A Study of Radical Policies and Tactics* (New York: International Publishers, 1926), pp. 122-163.

11. "Industrial Union Manifesto," in *Proceedings, First I.W.W. Convention, pp. 3-4.*

12. Austin Lewis, "Proletarian and Petit-Bourgeois," (Chicago: I.W.W. Publish Bureau, n.d.), p. 11. The ideas expressed in this pamphlet are part of an earlier book in which Lewis provides one of the most thorough explanations of the I.W.W.'s theory of industrial unionism. See his chapter, "What is a Union?," in *The Militant Proletariat* (Chicago: Charles H. Kerr & Co-coperative, 1911), pp. 99-152.

13. Lewis, "Proletarian and Petit-Bourgeois," p. 19.

14. Ibid.

15. See especially, William E. Trautmann, "Industrial Unionism—Means and Methods—Active and Passive Action," *I.U.B.*, 23 November 1907, 7 December 1907, 22 February 1908, and 29 February 1908. This series was later published as a pamphlet entitled, "Industrial Unionism. New Methods and New Forms." (Chicago: Charles H. Kerr Publishing & Co., 1909), 29 pp. The pamphlet, unlike the serial in the *I.U.B.*, contains a section on the French syndicalist tactic of sabotage and represents the first unofficial pamphlet written by an I.W.W. member to discuss the tactic. The publisher's note does indicate a difference between the serial and the pamphlet. It is, therefore, difficult to determine if the section was edited out of the series or whether it was added later.

16. Brissenden, *The I.W.W.*, p.274.

17. Ibid., pp. 275-276.

18. Louis Levine, *Syndicalism in France* (New York: Colombia University Press, 1914), pp. 65-68; Spargo, *Syndicalism, Industrial Unionism and Socialism*, pp. 104-106.

19. Levine, *Syndicalism in France*, p. 94.

20. David J. Saposs, *The Labor Movement in Post-War France* (New York: Colombia University Press, 1931), pp. 10-11; Levine *Syndicalism in France*, pp. 183-184.

21. *Proceedings, First I.W.W. Convention*, p. 184

22. Roller, "Social General Strike," pp. 16-17.

23. Ibid., pp. 17-18.

24. Brazier, "Story of the I.W.W.'s Little Red Song Book,' " p. 92.

25. "The General Strike," *I.W.*, July 1906, p. 9.

26. "Report of the General Secretary-Treasurer on the Work of the Organization," *I.U.B.*, 14 September 1907, p. [7].

27. "Le Syndicalism in France is Industrialism in America," *I.U.B.*, 13 June 1908, p. [2].

28. "European Movement," *Solidarity,* 15 January 1910, p.3.

29. "Sunrise in France," *I.W.*, 25 March 1910, p. 2.

30. Thompson, *The I.W.W.: Its First Fifty Years, pp. 80-87.*

31. *Ibid, p. 86.*

32. *William E. Trautmann, "Industrial Unionism Handbook No. 2, Means and Methods, Part 1—Old Methods," (Chicago: I.W.W., n.d.), p. 9. Ads for this pamphlet first appear in the I.U.B., 20 June 1908.*

33. Trautmann, "Industrial Unionism—Means and Methods—Active and Passive Action," *I.U.B.*, 29 February 1908, p. [3].

34. "Is the I.W.W. European?" *Solidarity,* 14 September 1912, p. 2.

35. "Two Views on Sabotage," *Solidarity,* 25 February 1912, p. 4.

36. Rambler, "Intellectuals and Tactics," *Solidarity,* 16 March 1912, p. 2.

37. "Industrial is Not Syndicalism," *I.W.*, 9 January 1913, p. 2.

38. Dubofsky, *We Shall Be All,* pp. 163 & 169; Preston, "Shall This Be All?" pp. 442-443.

39. Foner, *The I.W.W.*, p. 19. This writer could find no statement by Trautmann indicating that he meant specifically "revolutionary syndicalism" in referring to the principles of organized labor in Continental Europe when interviewed by the reporter from the *Cincinnati Post.* See Foner's source: *Cincinnati Post,* 9 January 1905. McKee is the first historian to refute Brissenden's contention that the I.W.W.'s contact with the C.G.T. occurred after 1908. See his study, "The Influence of Syndicalism on DeLeon," p. 280.

40. Foner, *The I.W.W.*, p. 23. Foner later argues that it is "incorrect to ignore the intellectual kinship that did exist between the I.W.W. and the European, particularly the French syndicalists." (p. 158.)

41. Ibid, p. 159.

42. Joseph R. Conlin, "The Wobblies: A Study of the Industrial Workers of the World Before World War I" (Ph.D. dissertation, University of Wisconsin,

1966), pp. 19-20; Conlin, *Bread and Roses,* p. 9. For his critique of Foner, see Conlin, "Wobblies and Syndicalists," pp. 81-91.

43. "Historical Catechism of American Unionism" (Chicago: Educational Bureau of the I.W.W., n.d.) p. 83.

44. Ralph Chaplin, "Harvest Song," *Solidarity,* 3 April 1915, p. 4. The song was written to the tune of "I Didn't Raise My Boy to Be a Soldier."

45. The best discussion of the "sab cat" is in Green, "John Neuhaus." Green however was unaware that the original sab cat is depicted as a tabby cat. He, therefore, elaborates on the symbolic meanings of the black cat which is considered to be synonymous with the sab cat. This association originates out of Ralph Chaplin testimony in *U.S. v. W.D. Haywood, et al.* During the trial, Chaplin explained that the black cat "was commonly used by the boys as representing the idea of sabotage. The idea being to frighten the employer by the mention of the name sabotage, or by putting a black cat somewhere around. You know if you saw a black cat go across your path you would think, if you were superstitious, you are going to have a little bad luck. The idea of sabotage is to use a little black cat on the boss." (*U.S. Vs. Haywood et al.,* Testimony of Ralp Chaplin, July 19, 1918, I.W.W. Collection, Box 112, Folder 7, pp. 7702 & 7711, Labor History Archive, Wayne State University.) The use of the black cat as a symbol of sabotage probably originates with the I.W.W.'s stickerettes or "silent agitators" as they became know in 1917; See Tony Bubka, "Time to Organize: The I.W.W. Stickerette," *American West* 5(Jan. 1968), pp. 21-22, 25-26. Chaplin relates his role in the drawing of the stickers in his autiobiography, *Wobbly: The Rough-and-Tumble Story of an American Radical,* (Chicago: University of Chicago Press, 1948), pp. 194-196, 205-207. My research indicates that the use of the sab cat to connote the I.W.W.'s interpretation of the French syndicalist tactic of sabotage begins in the teens. The sab cat appears in print in the form of an anonymous poem entitled "Our Masters' Brutus," *Solidarity,* 13 December 1913, p. 2. It is, however, likely that the term was used prior to its appearance in print.

46. The silent agitators are replicas made by Dick Ellington and Fred Rockerfeller in the late 1960s.

Chapter 5

1. Nomura, "Partisan Politics," pp. 86-139.

2. Daniel Guerin, *100 Years of Labor in the U.S.A.* (London: InkLink, 1979), pp. 76-79.

3. Brissenden, *The I.W.W.,* pp. 218-233, 243. In 1915, the Detroit faction changed its name to Workers International Industrial Union.

4. I have selected the period between 1909 and 1912 in order to establish the earliest phase and pattern accompanying the use of anarcho-syndicalist tactics by the I.W.W. Following 1912, European anarcho-syndicalist tactics appear in the I.W.W.'s press in art forms with greater frequency. Thompson, for example, in *The I.W.W.: Its First Fifty Years,* pp. 80-81, finds only one instance in which sabotage or direct action is mentioned in the I.W.W. press prior to 1912. His discussion, like that of Foner's (*The I.W.W. 1905-1917,* p. 160), does not address the earlier appearance of these tactics in art forms. Studies of I.W.W. art forms, for the most part, have limited their investigation to the I.W.W.'s songs. These studies have viewed the I.W.W.'s songs as forms of popular protest and have not commented on their importance as vehicles for carrying and expressing solidarity with European syndicalists. See Josh Dunson, "Songs of the American Labor Movement," *Mainstream* 15(August 1962), pp. 44-55; S. Serge Denisoff, "Songs of Persuasion: A Sociological Analysis of Urban Propaganda Songs," *Journal of American Folklore* 79(October-December 1966), pp. 581-589; Jerome L. Rodnitzky, "The Evolution of the American Protest Song," *Journal of Popular Culture,* 111(Summer 1969), pp. 35-45. An important exception is the work of Franklin Rosemont. See "A Short Treatise on Wobbly Cartoonists," in Joyce L. Kornbluh (ed.), *Rebel Voices: An I.W.W. Anthology* (Chicago: Charles H. Kerr Pub. Co., Revised Edition, 1988), pp. 424-443, for a superb analysis of the role of cartoons and humor in I.W.W. culture. While songs such as Joe Hill's "Casey Jones—The Union Scab" and Ta-Ra-Ra Boom De-ay," represent early sabotage songs (1912-1913), they appear after the incorporation of European syndicalist tactics in poetry and graphics. I have, therefore, selected these neglected art forms for their importance in establishing a pattern between artistic expression and political ideology which continued to develop in the I.W.W.'s later years. Two notable studies comment on French syndicalist influences in the period between 1912 and 1917. See Green, "John Neuhaus;" and Rosemont (ed.), "Mr. Block."

5. "The General Strike," *I.W.,* 10 June 1909, p. 2.

6. Brissenden, *The I.W.W.,* pp. 174-175.

7. "The General Strike," *I.W.,* 10 June 1909, p. 2.

8. *I.W.,* 19 August 1909, p. 3.

9. "Direct Action," I.W., 1 April 1909, p. 2.

10. Missoula and Spokane were the first of about thirty free-speech fights conducted by the I.W.W. Extensive coverage of the Missoula and Spokane free-speech fights can be found in the I.W. beginning in March 1909; see especially "Synopsis—Spokane Free-Speech Fight," 19 March 1910, p. 1.

11. I.W., 19 February 1910, p. 1.

12. Ibid.

13. Fred W. Haslewood, "Barbarous Spokane," I.S.R. X(Feb 1910), p. 711.

14. I.W., 19 March 1910, p. 1; Elizabeth Gurley Flynn, The Rebel Girl: An Autobiography (New York: International Pub., 1976 [third printing]), pp. 103-106; Foner, Fellow Workers and Friends, pp. 24-28; Kornbluh, Rebel Voices, pp. 94-98.

15. "Free Speech Battle; Fight or Be Choked," I.W., 30 September 1909.

16. Elizabeth Gurley Flynn, "Free Speech is Won in Missoula, Mont.," I.W., 20 October 1909, p. 1.

17. John Neuhaus, "I.W.W. Songs: Songs of the Workers on the Road, in the Jungles and in the Shops," suggested 30th edition, March 1958, John Neuhaus Collection, Archie Green, San Francisco, CA.

18. "The Employment Shark Must Go," I.W., 25 March 1909, p. 3.

19. Ibid.

20. Levine, Syndicalism in France, p. 170.

21. Ibid., p. 169.

22. Ibid., p. 170.

23. Kornbluh, Rebel Voices, p. 95.

24. Haslewood, "Barbarous Spokane," pp. 706-709; "Brutal Police," I.W., 12 February 1910. For an article that assesses the I.W.W.'s figures on injuries and conclusions concerning the success of the free-speech fight in Spokane, see Glen J. Broyles, "The Spokane Free-Speech Fight, 1909-1910: A Study in I.W.W. Tactics," Labor History, 19(Spring 1978), pp. 238-252.

25. "On To Spokane March First," I.W., 19 February 1910, p. 1.

26. Ibid.

27. Trautmann, "Industrial Unionism—Means and Methods," *I.U.B.*, 7 December 1907, p. 2. In a later pamphlet, Trautmann classified the practice of passive resistance as a form of indirect action whose aim was making "the job unprofitable for the master without [the workers'] leaving their place of employment." The tactic involved "the most minute observation of rules and the harassing of immediate functionaries of the employers of labor, by carrying out the orders with a complete suspension of [the workers'] own initiatve and ingenuity...' " The tactic was suggested as a means for curtailing the employer's power and control over the conditions of employment and as a method of establishing the workers' right to dictate the terms of production. Since the tactic stayed within the realm of what was legally mandated, Trautmann considered the tactic an indirect form of action. He was careful to point out, however, that the tactic was akin to and at times inoperative without sabotage, which implied "the withdrawal of efficiency from the work." ("Direct Action and Sabotage," [Pittsburg: Socialist News Co., 1912], pp. 20-26.) Passive resistance through the strict obedience of rule is later defined as a form of sabotage in Walker C. Smith's series on the tactic; see "Sabotage," *I.W.* 3 April 1913, p. 2.

28. Trautmann, "Industrial Unionism. New Methods and New Forms." pp. 24-25.

29. *I.W.*, 9 April 1910, p. 1.

30. Selig Perlman and Philip Taft, (ed.), *History of Labor in the United States, 1896-1932*, Vol. 4, (New York: August M. Kelley Pub., 1966 [reprint, Macmillian Co., 1935), p. 235.

31. See, for example, John Sandgren's translation of Arnold Roller's pamphlet on "Direct Action," *I.W.*, 23 April 1910.

32. On May 28, 1910, the *I.W.* printed an article entitled "How Sabotage Affects the Scizzor-Bills." Intended for the "floating-worker," the article began with a tongue-in-cheek warning: "Those who are 'honest' and believe in giving a 'fair days' work for a fair day's wages' should not read any more of this article... But those who believe in getting all they can and are not particularly concerned in seeing that the boss gets anything, are hereby authorized to read on." This article consisted of a discussion of the "ways and means to make the boss come through—how to get more of the goods." This "method of striking called 'Sabotage,' " the article went on to explain, "means in a general way GOING ON STRIKE WITHOUT STRIKING and has been proven by our Fellow Workers in France to be very effective." Citing examples of the practice in France and

describing the activities of Italian workers in Germany, the article concluded by encouraging those who had "fallen from Grace" with their employers "to try a little sabotage."

33. "Cooks and Waiters on Strike in Spokane," *I.W.*, 21 May 1910, p. 1.

34. Ibid.

Chapter 6

1. The only notable exceptions are the work of Archie Green, Rosemont, and Peterson cited in previous chapters.

2. Correspondence, Franklin Rosemont, September, 1988.

Bibliography

Manuscript Collections

Ann Arbor, Michigan. University of Michigan. Harlan Hatcher Library. Labadie
  Collection.
Organizational Papers and Pamphlets:
  Pre-World War I Anarchism
  I.W.W.
Personal Papers:
  George V. Carey
  Cassius V. Cook
  Mario Deciampis
  Eugene V. Debs
  Jay Fox
  Thomas J. Hagerty
  Agnis Inglis
  Joseph A. Labadie
  W. S. Van Valkenburgh

Berkeley, California. Institute for the Study of Social Change. Emma Goldman
  Papers Project. Government Surveillance and Internal Documents, 1907-
  1914.

_____. University of California. Bancroft Library.
Manuscript collections:
  Silvestre Terrazas
  Ethyl Duffy Turner
Personal Papers:
  Ricardo Flores Magón
  John Murray
  Fernando Palomarez

Boston, Massachusetts. Boston University. Mugar Memorial Library.
Personal Papers:
   Emma Goldman
   Almeda Sperry

————. Harvard University. Houghton Library. Joseph Ishill Collection

Chicago, Illinois. Roosevelt University. Murry Green Library. Labor Oral History Project.

Detroit, Michigan. Wayne State University. Walter P. Reuther Library. I.W.W. Collection.

Ithaca, New York. Cornell University. New York State School of Industrial and Labor Relations. Martin P. Catherwood Library. I.W.W. Collection.

Madison, Wisconsin. State Historical Society of Wisconsin.
Personal Papers:
   John R. Commons
   Richard T. Ely

Minneapolis, Minnesota. University of Minnesota. Immigration History Research Center. Italian American Collection.

New York, New York. New York University. Elmer Holmes Bobst Library.
   Tamiment Collection.
   I.W.W. Collection
   Anarchism (unclassified by collection)
   American Socialist Movement (unclassified by collection)

Saint Paul, Minnesota. Minnesota Historical Society.
Manscript Collections:
   Letters and Printed Materials Relating to the Non-Partisan League and Other Reform Organizations, 1905-1919
   Albert G. Wagner Papers

San Diego, California. Museum of San Diego. Research Archive. Junipero Serra Museum. I.W.W. Collection.

Tacoma, Washington. Washington State Historical Society. I.W.W. Collection.

Private Collections

Chicago, Illinois. Franklin Rosemont. I.W.W. Materials.

————. Fred W. Thompson. I.W.W. Materials.

Portland, Oregon. Pietro Ferrua. Materials on Mexican Liberal Party.

San Francisco, California. Archie Green. John Neuhaus Collection.

Journals and Newspapers

The Agitator. Home, WA, 1910-1912.
The American Labor Journal. Butte, MT, January, 1903-December, 1904.
Freedom. London, 1886-1927.
Industrial Pioneer. Chicago, 1921-1926
Industrial Union Bulletin. Chicago, March 2, 1907-March 6, 1909.
Industrial Syndicalist. London,
Industrial Worker. Joliet, IL; Spokane, WA; Seattle, WA, 1906-1916.
The International. San Diego, CA, 1914.
International Socialist Review. Chicago, 1905-1918.
Land and Liberty. Hayward, CA, 1914.
The Liberator. Chicago, 1905-1906.
The Liberator. New York, 1918-1924.
The Masses. New York, 1911-1917.
Miners' Magazine. Denver, 1905-1909.
Mother Earth. New York, 1906-1918.
New Review. New York, April, 1913-1915.
One Big Union Monthly. Chicago, 1919-1938.
The People. New York, 1891-1908.
Il Proletario. New York, 1899-1946.
Regeneración. San Antonio; St. Louis; Los Angeles, 1904-1914.
Revolt. New York, 1916.
The Social War. New York, 1913.
Solidarity. Chicago, December 18, 1909-1917.
The Syndicalist. London, monthly, 1912-_____.
Tie Vapauteen, Duluth, MN, 1919-1937.
The Toiler. Kansas City, MO, 1912-_____.
The Voice of Labor. Chicago, January, 1905-.
The Weekly People. New York, 1899-.
Why. Tacoma, WA, 1913-1914.

Books

Aaron, Daniel. *Writers on the Left. New York: Harcourt, Brace & World, 1961.*

Abrams, Philip. Historical Sociology. Ithaca: Cornell University Press, 1982.

Abád de Santillán, Diego. *Ricardo Flores Magón: apóstol de la revolución social mexicana.* Mexico: Grupo Cultural "Ricardo Flores Magón," 1925.

Adamic, Louis, *Dynamite: The Story of Class Violence in America.* New York: Viking Press, 1934.

Adams, Graham, Jr. *Age of Industrial Violence.* New York: Columbia University Press, 1966.

Allsop, Kenneth. *Hard Traveling: The Hobo and His History.* London: Hodder and Stoughton, 1967.

Anderson, Nels. *The Hobo: The Sociology of Homeless Men.* Chicago: University of Chicago Press, 1967.

Anderson, Rodney D. *Outcasts in Their Own Lands: Mexican Industrial Workers, 1906-1911.* DeKalb: Norther Illinois University Press, 1976.

Ameringer, Oscar. *If You Don't Weaken: The Autiobiography of Oscar Ameringer.* New York: H. Holt & Co., 1940.

Ash, Roberta. *Social Movements in America.* Chicago: Markham Publishing Co., 1972.

Ashbaugh, Carolyn. *Lucy Parsons American Revolutionary.* Chicago: Charles H. Kerr Publishing Co., 1967.

Avrich, Paul. *The Russian Anarchists.* New York: W.W. Norton & Co., 1967.

————. *An American Anarchist: The Life of Voltairine de Cleyre.* Princeton: Princeton University Press, 1978.

————. *The Modern School Movement: Anarchism and Education in the United States.* Princeton: Princeton University Press, 1980.

————. *The Haymarket Tragedy.* Princeton: Princeton University press, 1984.

Baldwin, Roger N., ed. *Kropotkin's Revolutionary Pamphlets.* New York: Dover Publications Inc., 1970.

Barrera Fuentes, Florencio. *Historia de la revolución mexicana: La etapa precursora.* 2d ed. Mexico City: Talleres Craficos de la Nacion, 1970.

Bell, Daniel. *Marxian Socialism in the United States.* Princeton: Princeton University Press, 1967.

Benello, George C., and Dimitrious Roussopoulos, eds. *The Case for Participatory Democracy.* New York: Grossman Publishers., 1971.

Berger, John. *The Moment of Cubism and Other Essays.* New York: Pantheon Books, 1969.

Bimba, Anthony. *The History of the American Working Class.* New York: International Publishers, 1927.

Blaisdell, Lowell L. *The Desert Revolution, Baja California, 1911.* Madison: University of Wisconsin Press, 1962.

Braunthal, Julius. History of the International, 1864-1914. London: Thomas Nelson and Sons Ltd., 1966.

Brissenden, Paul F. *The I.W.W.: A Study of American Syndicalism.* New York: Russell & Russell, Inc., 1957.

_____. *Launching of the Industrial Workers of the World.* University of California Publications in Economics, Vol. 4, No. 1. Berkeley: University of California Press, 1913.

Brommel, Bernard. *Eugene V. Debs: Spokeman of Labor and Socialism.* Chicago: Charles H. Kerr Publishing Co., 1978.

Brooks, John G. *The Social Unrest: Studies in Labor and Socialist Movements.* New York: Macmillan Co., 1903.

_____. *American Syndicalism: The I.W.W.* New York: Macmillan Co., 1913.

Boyle, James. *The Minimum Wage and Syndicalism.* Cincinnati: Stewart & Kidd Co., 1913.

Brody, David. *Workers in Industrial America.* New York: Oxford University Press, 1980.

Brown, Geoff. *Sabotage: A Study in Industrial Conflict.* Great Britian: Spokesman Books, 1977.

Carlson, Peter. *Roughneck: The Life and Times of Big Bill Haywood.* New York: W.W. Norton & Co., 1983.

Carr, E. H. *Michael Bakunin.* New York: Octagon Books, 1975.

Chaplin, Ralph. *When the Leaves Come Out and Other Rebel Verses.* Cleveland: Published by Author, 1917.

————. *Bars and Shadows: The Prison Poems of Ralph Chaplin*. Ridgewood: Nellie Seeds Nearing, 1922.

————. *Wobbly: The Rough-and-Tumble Story of an American Radical*. Chicago: University of Chicago Press, 1948.

Christie, Robert A. *Empire in Wood: A History of the Carpenters' Union*. New York: Cornell University, 1956.

Clark, Marjorie R. *Organized Labor in Mexico*. Chapel Hill: University of North Carolina Press, 1934.

————. *A History of the French Labor Movement (1910-1920)*. University of California Publications in Economics, Vol. 8. No. 1 Berkeley: University of California Press, 1920.

Coker, Francis W. *Recent Political Thought*. New York: D. Appleton Century Co., 1934.

Cole, George D.H. *The World of Labor*. London: G. Bell and Sons Ltd., 1919.

————. *A History of Socialist Thought*. 5 vols. London: Macmillan & Co. Ltd., 1956.

Commons, John R., and Associates. *History of Labour in the United States*. 4 Vols. New York: Macmillan Co. 1918.

Commons, John R., ed. *Trade Unionism and Labor Problems*. Boston: Ginn and Co., 1921.

Conlin, Joseph R. *Bread and Roses, Too: Studies of the Wobblies*. Connecticut: Greenwood Press, 1969.

————. *Big Bill Haywood and The Radical Union Movement*. New York: Syracuse University Press, 1969.

————, ed. *At the Point of Production: The Local History of the I.W.W.* Connecticut: Greenwood Press, 1981.

Corbin, David A. *Life, Work, and Rebellion in the Coal Fields*. Chicago: University of Illinois Press, 1981.

Cronin, James E., and Carmen Sirianni. *Work, Community, and Power: The Experience of Labor In Europe and America. 1900-1925*. Philadelphia: Temple University Press, 1983.

Crook, Wilfred H. *The General Strike: A Study of Labor's Tragic Weapon in Theory and Practice*. Chapel Hill: University of North Carolina Press, 1931.

David, Henry. The History of the Haymarket Affair: A Study in the American Social-Revolutionary and Labor Movements. 1936. Reprint. New York: Collier Books, 1963.

DeLeon, Daniel. Flashlights of the Amsterdam Congress. 1906. Reprint. New York: New York Labor News Co., 1929.

_____. Socialist Landmarks: Four Addresses; 2d. ed. Palto Alto: New York Labor News, 1977.

Destler, Chester McArthur. American Radicalism 1865-1901. 1946. Reprint. Chicago: Quadrangle Books, 1966.

Dolgoff, San, ed. Bakunin on Anarchy: Selected Works by the Activist-Founder of World Anarchism. New York: Vintage Books, 1971.

Dowell, Eldridge Foster. A History of Criminal Syndicalism Legislation in the United States. Baltimore: John Hopkins University press, 1939.

Drachkovitch, Milorad M., ed. The Revolutionary Internationals, 1864-1943. Standford: Stanford University Press, 1966.

Draper, Theordore. The Roots of American Communism. New York: Viking Press, 1957.

Drinnon, Richard. Rebel in Paradise: A Biography of Emma Goldman. Chicago: University of Chicago Press, 1961.

Dubofsky, Melvyn. We Shall Be All: A History of the I.W.W. Chicago: Quadrangle Books, 1969.

Dubois, Pierre. Sabotage in Industry. New York: Penguin Books, 1979.

Dulles, Foster Rhea. Labor in America. A History. 2d ed. New York: Thomas Y. Crowell Co., 1960.

Ebert, Justus. Trial of a New Society. Cleveland: I.W.W. Publishing Co., n.d.

Edwards, Owen Dudley, and Bernard Ransom, eds. James Connolly: Selected Political Writings. New York: Grove Press, Inc., 1974.

Egbert, Donald D., and Stow Persons, eds. Socialism and American Life. 2 vols. Princeton: Princeton University Press, 1972.

Ellis P. Berresford, ed. James Connolly: Selected Writings. New York: Monthly Monthly Review Press, 1973.

Eltzbacker, Paul. *Anarchism: Exponents of the Anarchist Philosophy.* Translated by Steven T. Byington, edited by James J. Martin. New York: Chip's Bookshop, Booksellers and Publishers, n.d.

Ely, Richard T. *The Labor Movement in America.* New York: William Heinemann, 1905.

Estey, James A. *Revolutionary Syndicalism.* London: P.S. King & Sons, 1913.

Falk, Candace. *Love, Anarchy and Emma Goldman.* New York: Holt, Rinehart & Winston, 1984.

Fernback, David, ed. *The First International and After: Karl Marx Political Writings.* Vol. 3. New York: Vintage Books, 1974.

Fishman, Solomon. *The Disinherited in Art: Writer and Background.* Berkeley: University of California Press, 1953.

Flynn, Elizabeth Gurley, *The Rebel Girl: An Autobiography.* 3d rev. ed. New York: International Publishers, 1973.

Foner, Philip S. *History of the Labor Movement in the United States: From the Founding of the American Federation of Labor to the Emergence of American Imperialism.* 4 Vols. New York: International Publishers, 1965.

————. *The Case of Joe Hill.* New York: International Publishers, 1965.

————, ed. *The Letters of Joe Hill.* New York: International Publishers, 1965.

————, ed. *Fellow Workers and Friends: I.W.W. Free-Speech Fights as Told by Participants.* Connecticut: Greenwood Press, 1981.

Foster, William Z. *From Bryan to Stalin.* New York: International Publishers, 1937.

————. *Pages From a Worker's Life.* New York: International Publishers, 1939.

Freeman, Joseph. *An American Testament: A Narrative of Rebels and Romantics.* New York: Farrar & Rhinehart, Inc., 1936.

Fried, Albert, ed. *Socialism in America: From the Shakers to the Third International—A Documentary History.* Garden City: Doubleday & Co., 1970.

Gambs, John S. *The Decline of the I.W.W.* 1932. Reprint. New York: Russell & Russell, 1966.

Gilbert, James Burkhart. *Writers and Partisans: A History of Literary Radicalism in America.* New York: John Wiley & Sons, Inc., 1968.

Ginger, Ray. *The Bending Cross: A Biography of Eugene Victor Debs.* New Brunswick: Rutgers University Press, 1949.

Goldberg, Harvey. *American Radicals: Some Problems and Personalities.* New York: Monthly Review Press, 1957.

Goldman, Emma. *Living My Life.* 2d ed. New York: Alfred A. Knoff, 1934.

_____, *Anarchism and Other Essays.* New York: Mother Earth Publishing Association, 1917.

Goldstein, Robert J. *Political Repression in Modern America.* Cambridge: Schenkman Publishing Co. Inc., 1978.

Goodrick, Carter, *The Miner's Freedom.* Boston: Marshall Jones Co., 1925.

Goodwin, Lawrence. *The Populist Moment: A Short History of the Agarian Revolt in America.* New York: Oxford University Press, 1978.

Gordon, Linda. *Birth Control in America: Woman's Body, Woman's Right.* 1976. Reprint. New York: Penguin Books, 1977.

Graham, Marcus, ed. *Anthology of Revolutionary Poetry.* New York: The Active Press, Inc., 1929.

Greaves, Desmond C. *The Life and Times of James Connolly.* New York: International Publishers, 1976.

Green, James R. *Grass-Roots Socialism: Radical Movements in the Southwest 1895-1943.* Baton Rouge: Louisiana State University Press, 1978.

_____. *The World of the Worker.* New York: Hill and Wang, 1980.

Greenway, John. *American Folksongs of Protest.* Philadelphia: University of Pennsylvania Press, 1953.

Guerin, Daniel. *Anarchism: From Theory to Practice.* New York: Monthly Review Press, 1970.

Gutman, Herbert G. *Work, Culture and Society in Industrializing America.* New York: Alfred A. Knopf, 1976.

Hapgood, Hutchins. *The Spirit of Labor.* New York: Duffield & Co., 1907.

_____. *A Victorian in the Modern World.* New York: Harcourt, Brace & Co., 1939.

Hart, John M. *Anarchism & The Mexican Working Class, 1860-1931.* Austin: University of Texas Press, 1978.

Lang, Lucy Robins. *Tomorrow is Beautiful.* 3d ed., with an introduction by William Green. New York: Macmillan Co., 1948.

Lasslet, John H.M. *Labor and the Left.* New York: Basic Books, 1970.

Lehning, Arthur, ed. Michael Bakunin Selected Writings. New York: Grove Press, Inc., 1973.

Lens, Sidney. *The Labor Wars: From the Molly Maguires to the Sit-downs,* Garden City, New York: Doubleday and Co., 1973.

Levine, Louis. *Syndicalism In France.* New York: Colombia University Press, 1914.

Le Warne, Charles Pierce. *Utopias on Puget Sound 1885-1915.* Seattle: University of Washington Press, 1978.

Lewis, Austin. *The Militant Proletariat.* Chicago: Charles H. Kerr & Co. Cooperative, 1911.

MacDonald, J. Ramsay. *Syndicalism: A Critical Examination.* London: Constable & Co., 1912.

Magón, Ricardo Flores. *Land and Liberty: Anarchist Influences in the Mexican Revolution.* Compiled and introduced by David Poole. United Kingdom: Cienfuegos Press, 1977.

Maximoff, G. P., ed. *The Political Philosophy of Bakunin: Scientific Anarchism.* Introduction by Rudolf Rocker, biographical sketch by Max Nettlau. 1953. Reprint. New York: The Free Press, 1964.

Mehring, Franz. *Karl Marx: The Story of His Life.* New York: Covici, Friede Publishers, 1935.

Miller, Martin A. *Kropotkin.* Chicago: Univeristy of Chicago Press, 1976.

Miller, Salley M. *The Radical Immigrant.* New York: Twayne Publishers, Inc., 1974.

Montgomery, David. *Workers Control in America.* New York: Cambridge University Press, 1979.

Moss, Bernard H. *The Origins of the French Labor Movement, 1830-1914: The Socialism of Skill Workers.* Berkeley: University of California Press, 1976.

Murray, Robert K. *Red Scare: A Study in National Hysteria, 1919-1920.* Minneapolis: University of Minnesota Press, 1955.

Haywood, William D. *The Autobiography of Big Bill Haywood.* New York: International Publishers, 1977 (1929).

Hicks, Gandville, *John Reed: The Making of a Revolutionary.* New York: Macmillan Co., 1936.

Higham, John. *Strangers in the Land: Patterns of American Nativism 1860-1925.* 1963. Reprint. New York: Atheneum, 1973.

Hillquit, Morris. *History of Socialism in the United States.* 5th rev. ed. New York: Russell & Russell, Inc., 1965.

————. *Loose Leaves From a Busy Life.* New York: Macmillan Co., 1934.

Hobsbawm, Eric. *Workers: Worlds of Labor.* New York: Pantheon Books, 1984.

Holton, Bob. *British Syndicalism 1900-1914.* London: Pluto Press Ltd., 1976.

Hoxie, Robert. *Trade Unionism in the United States.* New York: D. Appleton & Co., 1928.

Hunter, Robert. *Violence and the Labor Movement.* New York: Macmillan Co., 1914.

Industrial Workers of the World. *Proceedings of the First I.W.W. Convention.* 1905. Reprint. New York: Merit Publishers, 1969.

Jensen, Vernon H. *Heritage of Conflict: Labor Relations in the Nonferrous Metals Industry Up to 1930.* Ithaca: Cornell University Press, 1950.

Joll, James. *The Anarchists.* 2d ed. Cambridge: Harvard University Press, 1980.

Jones, Gareth Stedman. *Languages of Class: Studies of English Working Class History 1832-1982.* New York: Cambridge University Press, 1983.

Jones, Mary Harris. *The Autobiography of Mother Jones.* 1925. Reprint. Chicago: Charles H. Kerr & Co., 1972.

Kipnis, Ira. *The American Socialist Movement: 1897-1912.* New York: Colombia University Press, 1952.

Kornbluh, Joyce L., ed. *Rebel Voices: An I.W.W. Anthology.* Ann Arbor: University of Michigan Press, 1964.

Krimerman, Leonard I., and Lewis Perry, eds. *Patterns of Anarchy: A Collection of Writings on the Anarchist Tradition.* Garden City, New York: Doubleday & Co., 1966.

O'Connor, Harvey, *Revolution in Seattle*. New York: Monthly Review Press, 1964.

Parker, Carleton H. *The Casual Laborer and Other Essays*. New York: Harcourt, Brace & Howe, 1920.

Perlman, Mark. *Labor Union Theories in America*. New York: Row, Peterson & Co., 1958.

Perlman, Selig. *A Theory of the Labor Movement*. New York: Macmillan Co., 1928.

Pataud, E., and E. Pouget. *Syndicalism and the Cooperative Commonwealth*. Translated by Charlotte and Frederic Charles. Oxford: The New Industrial Publishing Co., 1913.

Peukert, Josef. *Erinnerungen eines Proletariers aus der revoluionaren Arbeiterbewegung*. Berlin: Verlag Des Sozialistischen Bundes, 1913.

Portis, Larry, *I.W.W. et syndicalism révolutionnaire aux Etats-Unis*. Paris: Edition Spattacus, 1985.

Pouget, Emile. *Sabotage*. Translated from the French and introduced by Arturo M. Giovannitti. Chicago: Charles H. Kerr & Co., 1913.

Preston, William Jr. *Aliens and Dissenters: Federal Suppression of Radicals 1903-1933*. Cambridge: Harvard University Press, 1963.

Quint, Howard H. *The Forging of American Socialism: Origins of the Modern Movement*. New York: Bobbs-Merrial Co., Inc., 1953.

Raat, W. Dirk. *Revoltosos: Mexico's Rebels in the United States, 1903-1923*. College Station: Texas A & M University Press, 1981.

Reichert, William O. *Partisans of Freedom: A Study in American Anarchism*. Bowling Green: Bowling Green University Popular Press, 1967.

Renshaw, Patrick. *The Wobblies: The Story of Syndicalism in the United States*. Garden City, New York: Doubleday & Co., 1967.

Ridley, R. R. *Revolutionary Syndicalism in France*. Cambridge, England: Cambridge University Press, 1970.

Rocker Rudolf. *Anarcho-Syndicalism*. London: Martin Secker and Warburg Ltd., 1938.

————. *Pioneers of American Freedom: Origins of Liberal and Radical Thought in America*. Translated by Arthur E. Briggs. Los Angeles: Rocker Publications Committee, 1949.

_____. *Johann Most: Das Leben eines Rebellen*. Germany: Verlag Detlev Auvermann KG, 1973.

Rosenstone, Robert. *Romantic Revolutionary: A Biography of John Reed*. New York: Alfred A. Knopf, 1975.

Russell, Bertrand. *Proposed Roads to Freedom: Socialism, Anarchism and Syndicalism*. New York: Henry Holt & Co., 1919.

Salvatore, Nick. *Eugene V. Debs: Citizen and Socialist*. Urbana: University of Illinois Press, 1982.

Saposs, David. *Left Wing Unionism: A Study of Radical Policies and Tactics*. New York: International Publishers, 1926.

Schuster, Eunice M. *Native American Anarchism: A Study of Left-Wing American Individualism*. Northampton, MA: Smith College, 1932.

Schroeder, Theordore. *Free Speech For Radicals*. Riverside, CT: Hillacre Bookhouse, 1916.

Seretan, L. Glenn. *Daniel DeLeon: The Odyssey of an American Marxist*. Cambridge, MA: Harvard University Press, 1979.

Shannon, David A. *The Socialist Party of America: A History*. New York: Macmillan Co., 1955.

Shulman, Alix Kates, ed. *Red Emma Speaks: Selected Writings and Speeches by Emma Goldman*. New York: Random House, 1972.

Smith, Gibbs M. *Labor Martyr: Joe Hill*. New York: Grosset & Dunlap, 1969.

Socialist Labor Party. *Daniel Deleon the Man and His Work: A Symposium*. New York: National Executive Committee, Socialist Labor Party, 1919.

Sombart, Werner. *Socialism and the Social Movement*. Translated by M. Epstein, 1909. Reprint. New York: August M. Kelley, 1968.

_____. *Why is There No Socialism in the United States?*. 1906 Reprint. White Plains, New York: M.E. Sharpe, Inc., 1976.

Sorel, Georges. *Reflections on Violance*. Translated by T.E. Hulme. 1915. Reprint. New York: Peter Smith, 1941.

Spargo, John. *Syndicalism, Industrial Unionism and Socialism*. New York: B. W. Huebsch, 1913.

Stavis, Barrie. *The Man Who Never Died: A Play About Joe Hill With Notes on Joe Hill and His Times*. New York: Have Press, 1954.

Symes, Lillian, and Clement Travers. *Rebel America: The Story of Social Revolt in United States*. New York: Harper, 1934.

Tannenbaum, Frank. *The Labor Movement: Its Conservative Functions and Social Consequences*. New York: G.P. Putnam's Sons, 1921.

Thomas, Brinley. *Migration and Economic Growth: A Study of Great Britian and the Atlantic Economy*. London: Cambridge University Press, 1954.

Thompson, Fred W. *The I.W.W.: Its First Fifty Years (1905-1955)*. Chicago: I.W.W., 1955.

Thompson, Fred W. and Patrick Murfin, *The I.W.W.: Its First Seventy Years 1905-1975*. Chicago: I.W.W., 1976.

Tridon, Andre. *The New Unionism*. New York: B.W. Huebsch, 1913.

Turner, Ethel Duggy. *Ricardo Flores Magón y el partido liberal mexicano*. Morelia, Michoancan: Editorial "Erandi," 1960.

————. *Revolution in Baja California: Ricardo Flores Magón's High Noon*. Edited and annotated by Rey Devis. Detroit: Blaine Ethridge Books, 1981.

Tyler, Robert L. *Rebels in the Woods: The I.W.W. in the Pacific Northwest*. Eugene: University of Oregon Books, 1967.

Walling, William English. *Progressivism—And After*. New York: Macmillan Co., 1914.

Williams, Raymond. *Marxism and Literature*. Oxford: Oxford University Press, 1977.

Woodcock, George. *Anarchism: A History of Libertarian Ideas and Movements*. 1962. Reprint. New York: Penguin Books, 1979.

————, ed. *The Anarchist Reader*. Atlantic Heights, New Jersey: Humanities Press, 1977.

Yellen, Samuel. *American Labor Struggles*. New York: Harcourt, Brace & Co., 1936.

Zinn, Howard. *The Politics of History*. Boston: Beacon Press, 1970.

Articles

Ashleigh, Charles. "The Floater." *International Socialist Review* (ISR) XV (July 1914): 34-38.

Avrich, Paul. "Bakunin and the United States." *International Review of Social History* 24 (1979): 320-40.

_____. "Kropotkin in America." *International Review of Social History* 25 (1980): 1-34.

Bailey, Samuel L. "The Italians and Organized Labor in the United States." *International Migration Review* 1 (Summer 1967): 56-66.

_____. "The Italians and the Development of Organized Labor in Argentina, Brazil, and the United States." *Journal of Social History* 2 (Winter 1969): 123-34.

Balch, Elizabeth. "Songs for Labor." *Survey* 31 (Jan. 3. 1914): 408-12, 422-28.

Baxandall, Rosalyn F. "Elizabeth Gurley Flynn: The Early Years." *Radical America* 8 (Jan.-Feb. 1975): 97-115.

Bohn, Frank. "Concerning the Chicago Manifesto." *ISR* 5 (March 1905): 585-89.

Brazier, Richard. "The Story of the I.W.W. 'Little Red Song Book.' " *Labor History* 9 (Winter 1968): 93-105.

Broyles, Glen J. "The Spokane Free Speech Fight, 1909-1910: A Study in I.W.W. Tactics." *Labor History* 19 (Spring 1978): 238-52.

Bruere, Robert W. "The Industrial Workers of the World." Harper's 137 (July 1918): 250-57.

Bubka, Tony. "Time to Organize: The I.W.W. Stickerette." American West 5 (Jan. 1968): 21-22, 25-26.

Buhle, Paul. "The Cycle of American Socialism." *Radical America* 1 (April 1967): 23-28.

_____. "New Perspectives on American Radicalism: An Historical Reassessment." *Radical America* 2 (July-August 1968): 46-58.

_____. "The Wobblies in Perspective." *Monthly Review* 22 (June 1970): 45-53.

_____. "The Poet Prophets: Revolutionary Artists in the U.S. from 1870 to 1930." In *Free Spirits: Annals of Insurgent Imagination,* edited by Paul Buhle et al., pp. 156-169. San Francisco: City Lights Books, 1982.

_____. "Anarchism and American Labor." *International Labor and Working Class History* 23 (Spring 1983): 21-34.

Calmer, Alan. "The Wobbly in American Literature." In *Proletarian Literature in the United States: An Anthology,* edited by Granville Hicks et al., pp. 340-349. New York: International Publishers, 1935.

Carey, George W. "The Vessel, the Deed, and the Idea: Anarchists in Paterson, 1895-1908." *Antipode* 10 & 11 (1979): 46-58.

Carter, David A. "The Industrial Workers of the World and the Rhetoric of Song." *Quarterly Journal of Speech* 66 (December 1980): 365-74.

Ciolli, Dominic T. "The 'Wop' in the Track Gang." *Immigrants in America Review* II (July 1916): 61-64.

Cleland, Hugh G. "The Effects of Radical Groups on the Labor Movement." *Pennsylvania History* XXVI (April 1959): 119-32.

Cletus, Daniel E. "In Defense of the Wheatland Wobblies: A Critical Analysis of the I.W.W. in California." *Labor History* 19 (Fall 1978): 485-509.

Colby, Elbridge. "Syndicalism in the Light of History." *Sewanee Review,* 22 (October 1914): 43-46.

Conlin, Joseph. "Wobblies and Syndicalists." *Studies on the Left* 6 (March-April 1966): 81-91.

————. "The I.W.W. and the Socialist Party." *Science and Society* XXXI (Winter 1967): 22-36.

————. "The Case of the Very American Militants." *American West* VI (March 1970): 4-10, 62.

Davis, Mike. "The Stop Watch and the Wooden Shoe: Scientific Management and the Industrial Workers of the World." *Radical America* 8 (January-February 1975): 69–95.

————. "Why the U.S. Working Class is Different." *New Left Review* 123 (September-October 1980): 3-44.

Dawson, Andrew. "The Paradox of Dynamic Technological Change and the Labor Aristocracy in the United States." *Labor History* 20 (Summer 1979): 325-51.

Debs, Eugene V. "The Industrial Convention." *ISR,* 6 (August 1, 1905): 85-86.

Destler, Chester McArthur. "Shall Red and Black Unite? An American Revolutionary Document of 1883." *Pacific Historical Review* 14 (December 1945): 434-51.

Doherty, Robert E. "Thomas J. Hagerty, The Church and Socialism." *Labor History* 3 (Winter 1962): 39-56.

Dubofsky, Melvyn. "The Origins of Western Working Class Radicalism, 1890-1905." *Labor History* 7 (Spring 1966): 131-54.

Ebner, Michael. "The Passaic Strike of 1912 and the Two I.W.W.'s" *Labor History* 2 (Fall 1970): 452-66.

Faler, Paul. "Working Class Historiography." *Radical America* 3 (March-April 1969): 56-68.

Fenton, Edwin. "Italians in the Labor Movement." *Pennsylvania History* XXVI (April 1959): 134-48.

_____. "Italians in the Stoneworkers' Union." *Labor History* 3 (Spring 1962): 188-207.

Ferrura, Pietro. "Sources of Study on the Mexican Revolution, II. The Archives of the U.S. District Court of Southern California." *Bulletin Centre International de Recherches sur l' Anarchisme* 31 (n.d.): 7-11.

Fine, Sidney. "Anarchism and the Assassination of McKinley." *The American Historical Review* 55 (July 1955): 777-99.

Foner, Eric. "Why is There No Socialism in the United States?" *History Workshop Journal* 17 (Spring 1984): 57-80.

Fraina, Louis C. "Syndicalism and Industrial Unionism." *ISR* 14 (July 1913): 25-28.

_____. "Daniel DeLeon." *New Review* 2 (July 1914): 390-99.

Genini, Ronald. "Industrial Workers of the World and Their Fresno Free Speech Fight 1910-1911." *California Historical Quarterly* LIII (Summer 1974): 101-14.

Genovese, Eugene. "Class, Culture, and Historical Process." *Dialectical Anthropology* 1 (1975): 71-79.

Goldman, Emma. "Syndicalism: Its Theory and Practice." *Mother Earth* VII (January and February 1913): 373-78 & 417-22.

Golin, Steve. "The Paterson Pageant: Success or Failure?" *Socialist Review* 69 (May - June 1983): 45-78.

Graham, John. "Upton Sinclair and the Ludlow Massacre." *Colorado Quarterly* XXI (Summer 1972): 55-67.

Graymont, Barbara. "Aspects of DeLeon." *Labor History* 15 (Fall 1974): 559-62.

Green Archie. "John Neuhaus: Wobbly Folklorist." *Journal of American Folklore* 73 (July - Sept. 1960): 189-217.

_____. "American Labor Lore: Its Meaning and Uses." *Industrial Relations* 14 (February 1965): 51-68.

_____. "The Workers in the Dawn: Labor Lore." In *Our Living Traditions: An Introduction to American Folklore,* edited by Tristam Potter Coffin, pp. 251-62. New York: Basic Books, Inc., 1968.

_____. "Industrial Lore: A Bibliographic-Semantic Query." In *Working Americans: Contemporary Approaches to Occupational Folklore,* edited by Robert H. Byington, pp. 71-102. Los Angeles: California Folklore Society, 1978.

_____. "Interpreting Folklore Ideologically." In *Handbook of American Folklore,* edited by Richard M. Dorson, pp. 351-58. Bloomington: Indiana University Press, 1983.

_____. "Marcus Daly Enters Heavan." *The Speculator* 1 (Winter 1984): 27–32.

Green, James R. "The Brotherhood of Timber Workers 1910-1913: A Radical Response to Industrial Capitalism in the Southern U.S.A." *Past and Present* 60 (August 1973): 161-200.

_____. "Comments on the Montgomery Paper." *Journal of Social History* 7 (Summer 1974): 530-35.

_____. "Populism, Socialism and the Promise of Democracy." *Radical History Review* 24 (Fall 1980): 7-40.

_____. "Culture, Politics and Workers' Responses to Industrialization in the U.S." *Radical America* 16 (January - February, March - April 1982): 101-28.

Hall, Stuart. "Marxism and Culture." *Radical Historical Review* 18 (Fall 1978): 5-14.

Haug, Charles J. "The Industrial Workers of the World in North Dakota, 1913-1917." *North Dakota Quarterly* 39 (Winter 1971): 85-102.

Haywood, William D. "The General Strike." *ISR* 11 (May 1911): 680-84.

_____. "Socialism the Hope of the Working Class." *ISR* 12 (February 1912): 461-71.

Hearn, Frank. "Remembrance and Critique: The Uses of the Past for Discrediting the Present and Anticipating the Future." *Politics and Society* 5 (1975): 201-27.

Henretta, James A. "Social History as Lived and Written." *American Historical Review* 84 (Dec. 1979): 1293-1333.

Haslewood, Fred W. "Barbarous Spokane." *ISR* 10 (February 1910): 705-13.

Hill, Mary A. "The Free Speech Fight at San Diego." *Survey* XXVII (May 4, 1912): 192-94.

Hodges, Leroy. "Immigrant Life in the Ore Region of Northern Minnesota." *Survey* XXVIII (September 7, 1912): 703-09.

Hoerder, Dirk. "Immigration and the Working Class: The Remigration Factor." *International Labor and Working Class History* 21 (Spring 1982): 28-41.

Holbrook, Steward H. "Wobbly Talk." *American Mercury* VII (Jan. 1926): 62-65.

Hoxie, Robert F. "Trade Unionism in the United States." *Journal of Political Economy* 22 (March 1914): 201-17.

Isserman, Maurice. " 'God Bless Our American Institutions:' The Labor History of John R. Commons." *Labor History* 17 (Summer 1976): 309–28.

Jensen, Vernon, and Melvyn Dubofsky. "The I.W.W.—An Exchange of Views." *Labor History* 11 (Summer 1970): 335-72.

Johnson, Michael R. "The I.W.W. and Wilsonian Democracy." *Science and Society* 28 (Summer 1964): 257-74.

_____. "Albert Parsons: An American Architect of Syndicalism. "*Midwest Quarterly* 9 (Autumn 1967): 195-206.

Kolko, Gabriel. "The Decline of American Radicalism in the Twentieth Century." *Studies on the Left* 6 (September - October 1966): 9-26.

Krueger, Thomas A. "American Labor Historiography, Old and New: A Review Essay." *Journal of Social History* 4 (Spring 1971): 277-85.

Levine, Louis. "The Standpoint of Syndicalism." *Annals of the American Academy* XLIV (November 1912): 114-18.

_____. "The Development of Syndicalism in America." *Political Science Quarterly* 28 (September 1913): 451-79.

Leinenweber, Charles. "The American Socialist Party and 'New' Immigrants." *Science and Society* 32 (Winter 1968): 1-25.

_____. "The Class and Ethnic Base of New York City Socialism: 1904-1915." *Labor History* 22 (Winter 1981): 31-56.

LeWarne, Charles. "On the Wobbly Train to Fresno." *Labor History* 14 (Spring 1973): 264-89.

Lynn, Kenneth S. "The Rebels of Greenwich Village." *Perspectives in American History* VIII (1974): 335-77.

Madison, Charles A. "The Insurgent I.W.W." *Labor and the Nation* 5 (July 1949): 35-38.

Martin, Vella. "Sabotage and Revolutionary Syndicalism." *ISR* 13 (July 1913): 53-54.

Miller, Grace L. "The I.W.W. Free Speech Fight: San Diego, 1912." *Southern California Quarterly* LIV (Fall 1972): 211-38.

Montgomery, David. "The Conventional Wisdom." *Labor History* 13 (winter 1972): 107-36.

_____. "The New Unionism and the Transformation of Workers' Consciousness in America: 1909-1922." *Journal of Social History* 7 (Summer 1974): 509-29.

_____. "Gutman's Nineteenth-Century America." *Labor History* 19 (Sum-mer 1978): 416-29.

_____. "To Study the People: The American Working Class." *Labor History* 21 (Fall 1980): 486-512.

McKee, Don K. "The Influence of Syndicalism Upon Daniel DeLeon." *The Historian* 20 (May 1958): 275-89.

_____. "Daniel DeLeon: A Reappraisal." *Labor History* 1 (Fall 1960): 264-97.

Nochlin, Linda, "The Paterson Strike Pageant of 1913." *Art in America,* 52 (May-June 1974): 64-68.

Nomura, Tatsuro. "Partisan Politics in and around the I.W.W.: The Earliest Phase." *The Journal of the Faculty of Foreign Studies* 10 (1977): 86-139.

Ozanne, Robert. "Trends in American Labor History." *Labor History* 21 (Fall 1980): 513-21.

Parker, Carlton. "The I.W.W." *Atlantic Monthly* 120 (Nov. 1917): 651-62.

Preston, William. "Shall This Be All? Historians Versus William D. Haywood Et Al." *Labor History* 12 (Summer 1971): 435-53.

Pernicone, Nunzio. "Italian Anarchism." In *Proceedings: Fifth Annual Conference,* pp. 1-29. New York: American Italian Historical Association, 1972.

Rawick, George. "Working Class Self-Activity." *Radical America* 3 (March-April 1969): 23-31.

Reichert, William O. "Toward a New Understanding of Anarchism." *Western Political Quarterly* 20 (Dec. 1967): 856-65.

Rodgers, Daniel T. "Tradition, Modernity and the American Industrial Worker: Reflections and Critique." *Journal of Interdisciplinary History* VII (Spring 1977): 655–81.

Schofield, Ann. "Rebel Girls and Union Maids: The Women Question in the Journals of the A.F.L. and I.W.W., 1905-1920." *Feminist Studies* 9 (Summer 1983): 336-58.

Shanks, Rosalie. "The I.W.W. Free Speech Movement San Diego, 1912." *Journal of San Diego History* XIX (Winter 1973): 25-33.

Shannon, David A. "The Socialist Party Before the First World War." *Mississippi Valley Historical Review* 38 (September 1951): 279-88.

Shulman, Alix Kates. "Dancing in the Revolution: Emma Goldman's Feminism." *Socialist Review* 62 (March-April 1982): 31-44.

Simons, A.M. "Industrial Workers of the World." *ISR* 6 (August 1905): 65-77.

Skelton, O.D. "French Unionism Militant." *Journal of Political Economy* 17 (March 1909): 125-43.

Soffer, Benson. "A Theory of Trade Union Development: The Role of the 'Autonomous' Workman." *Labor History* 1 (Spring 1960): 141-63.

Sombart, Werner. "Study of the Historical Development and Evolution of the American Proletariat." *ISR* 6 (September 1905): 129-36.

Stavis, Barrie. "Joe Hill: Poet/Organizer." *Folk Music* 1 (June 1964): 3-4, 38-50; 2 (August 1964): 27-29, 38-50.

Stevenson, James A. "Daniel DeLeon and European Socialism, 1890-1914." *Science and Society* XLIV (Summer 1980): 199-223.

Taft, Philip. "The I.W.W. in the Grain Belt." *Labor History* 1 (Winter 1960): 53-67.

———. "The I.W.W. and the West." *American Quarterly* 12 (Summer 1960): 175-87.

Thistlewaite, Frank. "Migration From Europe Overseas in the Nineteenth and Twentieth Century." In *Population Movements in Modern European History,* edited by Herbert Moller, pp. 73-92. New York: Macmillan Co., 1964.

Tobin, Eugene M. "Direct Action and Conscience: The 1913 Paterson Strike as an Example of the Relationship Between Labor Radicals and Liberals." *Labor History* 20 (Winter 1979): 73-88.

Tridon, Andre. "Syndicalism and 'Sabotage' and How They Originated." *The Square Deal* 10 (June 1912): 407-14.

———. "The Worker's Only Hope: Direct Action." *The Independent* LXXIV (January 1913): 79-83.

Tugwell, Rexford G. "The Casuals of the Woods." *Survey* 57 (July 3, 1920): 472-74.

Tyler, Robert L., "The Rise and Fall of American Radicalism: The I.W.W." *The Historian* XIX (Fall 1956): 48-64.

———. "The I.W.W. and the West." *American Quarterly* XII (Summer 1960): 174-87.

———. "The I.W.W. and the Brainworkers." *American Quarterly* XV (Spring 1960): 41-51.

Unger, Irwin. "The 'New Left' and American History: Some Recent Trends in United States Historiography." *American Historical Review* LXXII (July 1967): 1237-63.

Vann, Richard T. "The Rhetoric of Social History." *Journal of Social History* 10 (Winter 1976): 221-36.

Veblin, Thorstein. "An Unpublished Paper on the I.W.W." *Journal of Political Economy* 40 (December 1932): 796-807.

Walling, William English. "Industrialism vs Syndicalism." *ISR* 14 (July 1913): 666-67.

Weinstein, James. "Socialism's Hidden Heritage: Scholarship Reinforces Political Mythology." *Studies on the Left* 3 (Fall 1963): 89-108.

_____. "The I.W.W. and American Socialism." *Socialist Revolution* 1 (September-October 1970): 3-41.

Williams, Raymond. "Base and Superstructure in Marxist Cultural Theory." *New Left Review* (November-December 1973): 3-16.

Yarros, Victor S. "Philosophical Anarchism: Its Rise, Decline and Eclipse." *American Journal of Sociology* 41 (1936): 470-83.

Zelden, Theodore. "Social History and Total History." *Journal of Social History* 10 (Winter 1976): 237-45.

Zieger, Robert H. "Workers and Scholars: Recent Trends in American Labor Historiography." *Labor History* 13 (Spring 1972): 245-66.

Zerzan, John. "Understanding the Anti-Radicalism of the National Civic Federation." *International Review of Social History* 19 (1974): 194-210.

Doctoral Dissertations and Masters' Theses

Albro, Ward Sloan, "Ricardo Flores Magón and the Liberal Party: An Inquiry Into the Origins of the Mexican Revolution of 1910." Ph. D. dissertation, University of Arizon, 1967.

Barnes, Donald M. "The Ideology of the Industrial Workers of the World, 1905-1921." Ph. D. dissertation, University of Washington, 1962.

Buhle, Paul M. "Louis C. Fraina, 1892-1953." Master's thesis, University of Connecticut, 1968.

Christoph, James B. "Alexander Berkman and American Anarchism." Master's thesis, University of Minnesota, 1952.

Conlin, Joseph R. "The Wobblies: A Study of the Industrial Workers of the World Before World War 1." Ph.D. dissertation, University of Wisconsin, 1966.

Crow, John E. "Ideology and Organization: A Case Study of the Industrial Workers of the World." Master's thesis, University of Chicago, 1958.

Diehl, Robert Warren. "To Speak or Not to Speak: San Diego 1912." Master's thesis, University of San Diego, 1976.

Enberg, George B. "Labor in the Lake States Lumber Industry." Ph.D. dissertation, University of Minnesota, 1949.

Fenton, Edwin. "Immigrants and Unions A Case Study: Italians and American Labor, 1870-1920." Ph.D. dissertation, Harvard University, 1957.

Haller, Douglas M. "I.W.W. Cartoonist, Ernest Riebe: Originator of the 'Mr. Block' Series." Master's thesis, Wayne State University, 1982.

McEnroe, Thomas. "I.W.W. Theories, Organizational Problems and Appeals as Revealed in the *Industrial Worker*." Ph.D. dissertation, University of Minnesota, 1960.

Myers, Ellen Howell. "The Mexican Liberal Party, 1903-1910." Ph.D. dissertation, University of Virginia, 1970.

Perlin Terry M. "Anarchist-Communism in America, 1890-1914." Ph.D. dissertation, Brandeis University, 1970.

Robinson, Leland W. "Social Movement Organizations in Decline: A Case Study of the I.W.W.," Ph.D. dissertation, Northwestern University, 1973.

Schwantes, Carlos Arnaldo. "Left-Wing Unionism in the Pacific Northwest: A Comparative History of Organized Labor and Socialist Politics in Washington and British Colombia, 1885-1917." Ph.D. dissertation, University of Michigan, 1976.

Shaffer, Ralph Edwards. "Radicalism in California, 1869-1929." Ph.D. dissertation, University of California, Berkeley, 1962.

Souers, Ralph Edwards. "The Industrial Workers of the World." Masters thesis, University of Chicago, 1913.

Taylor, Kate Hanrahan. "A Crisis in Confidence: The San Diego Free-Speech Fight of 1912." Masters thesis, University of California, Los Angeles, 1966.

Van Tine, Warren R. "Ben H. Williams, Wobbly Editor." Masters thesis, Northern Illinois University, 1967.

Weintraub, Hyman. "The I.W.W. in California: 1905-1931." Masters thesis, University of California, Los Angeles, 1947.

Pamphlets and Leaflets

Brissenden, Paul F. *Justice and the I.W.W.* 3d ed. Chicago: I.W.W. General Defense Committee, n.d. 31 pp. (reprinted From *New York Call* of March 11, 1922).

Cannon James P. *The I.W.W.* New York: Pioneer Publishers, 1956. 31 pp.

Coal Mines and Coal Miners. Chicago: I.W.W. Educational Bureau, n.d. 108 pp.

Connolly, James. *Socialism Made Easy.* Chicago: Charles H. Kerr & Co., 1909. 61 pp.

————. *Craft Unionism—Why it Fails.* Chicago: I.W.W. Press, n.d. 46 pp.

Duff, Harvey, *The Silent Defenders, Courts and Capitalism in California.* Chicago: I.W.W. Press, n.d. 112 pp.

Ebert, Justus. *Is the I.W.W. Anti-Political?* Cleveland: I.W.W. Publishing Bureau, n.d. 2 pp.

Ettor, Joseph J. *Industrial Unionism, The Road to Freedom.* Chicago: I.W.W. Press [1913]. 31 pp.

Flynn, Elizabeth Gurley. *Sabotage: The Conscious Withdrawal of the Workers' Industrial Efficiency.* Chicago: I.W.W. Publishing Bureau, n.d. 31 pp.

Ford, Earl C., and William Z. Foster. *Syndicalism.* Chicago: W.Z. Foster, 1913. 47 pp.

Foster, William Z. *Insurgency or The Economic Power of the Middle Class.* Seattle WA: Trustee Printing Co., n.d. 14 pp.

George, Harrison. *The Truth About the I.W.W. Prisoners.* New York: ACLU, 1922, 47 pp.

Hansen, Nils H. *The Onward Sweep of the Machine Process.* Also contains: T. Glynn, "Industrial Efficiency and its Antidote," and Barbara Lily Frankenthal, "The Diesel Motor." Chicago: I.W.W. Publishing Bureau, [1917]. 32 pp.

Haywood, William D. *The General Strike.* Chicago: I.W.W. Publicity Bureau, n.d. 48 pp. (Address delivered in New York, March 16, 1911.)

Haywood, William D. and Frank Bohn. *Industrial Socialism.* Chicago: Charles H. Kerr & Co. Cooperative, 1911. 55 pp.

Herbe, Gustave. *Patriotism and the Worker.* New Castle, PA: I.W.W. Publicity Bureau, 1912. 32 pp.

Historical Catechism of American Unionism. Chicago: I.W.W., n.d. 95 pp.

The I.W.W. in Theory and Practice. 5th revised ed. Chicago: I.W.W., n.d. 124 pp.

The I.W.W. What It Is and What It Is Not. Chicago: I.W.W., n.d. 39 pp.

The Lumber Industry and Its Workers. 3d ed. Chicago: I.W.W. Workers Industrial Union No. 450, n.d. 91 pp.

Lewis, Austin. *Proletarian and Petit-Bourgeois.* Also contains: Charles Edward Russell, "What Comes of Playing the Game," and Scott Nearing, "Those Who Work and Those Who Own." Chicago: I.W.W. Publishing Bureau, n.d. 47 pp.

MacDonald, James Ramsey. *Syndicalism: A Critical Analysis.* London: Constable & Co., Ltd., 1912. 74 pp.

Nolan, Dean, and Fred Thompson. *Joe Hill I.W.W. Songwriter.* Chicago: I.W.W., 1979. 32 pp.

Oneal, James. *Sabotage or Socialism vs. Syndicalism.* St. Louis, MO: National Rip-Saw Publishing Co., [1912]. 32 pp.

Owen, William C. *The Mexican Revolution: Its Progress, Causes, Purpose and Probable Results.* Los Angeles: Regeneracion, [1912]. 16 pp.

―――. *Anarchism versus Socialism.* London: Freedom Press, 1922. 32 pp.

Perry, Grover H. *The Revolutionary I.W.W.* Also contains: Perry's "How Scabs Are Bred," and Ben H. Williams' "The Constructive Program of the I.W.W." Cleveland: I.W.W. Publishing Bureay, 1915. 24 pp.

Riebe, Ernest. *Twenty-four Cartoons of Mr. Block.* Minneapolis: Block Supply Co., 1913. 27 pp.

Roller, Arnold [Siegfried Nacht]. *The Social General Strike.* Chicago: Debating Club No. 1, June 1905. 32 pp.

Rowan, James. *The I.W.W. in the Lumber Industry.* Seattle, WA: Lumber Workers Industrial Union No. 500, n.d. 59 pp.

St. John, Vincent. *Industrial Unionism and the I.W.W.* New Castle, PA: I.W.W. Publishing Bureau, n.d. 15 pp.

―――. *Political Parties and the I.W.W.* Cleveland: I.W.W. Publishing Bureau, 1910. 2 pp.

―――. *The I.W.W.: Its History, Structure and Method.* Cleveland: I.W.W. Publishing Bureau, n.d. 31 pp.

Smith, Walker C. *Sabotage: Its History, Philosophy and Function.* Spokane, WA:, 1913. 32 pp.

Stavis, Barrie, and Frank Harmon, eds. *Songs of Joe Hill*. New York: Oak Publications, Inc., 1960. 46 pp.

The Story of the Ford Case. New York: American Civil Liberties Union, 1925. 11 pp.

Trautmann, William E. *Industrial Unionism. New Method and New Forms*. Chicago: Charles H. Kerr & Co., 1909. 29 pp.

————. *One Big Union: An Outline of a Possible Industrial Organization of the Working Class With Chart*. Chicago: Charles H. Kerr & Co., 1911. 31 pp.

————. *Direct Action and Sabotage*. Pittburg, PA: Socialist News Co., 1912. 39 pp.

————. *Industrial Unionism: The Hope of the Workers*. Pittsburg, PA: Socialist News Co., 1912. 64 pp.

————. *Industrial Unionism: Handbook No. 2. Means and Methods*. Chicago: I.W.W. Press, n.d. 32 pp.

————. *Why Strikes Are Lost: How to Win*. New Castle, PA: Solidarity Literature Bureau, n.d.

Twenty Five Years of Industrial Unionism. Chicago: I.W.W. Press, n.d. 79 pp.

A Union For All Railroad Workers. Chicago: I.W.W., n.d. 29 pp.

Veblen, Thorstein. *On the Nature and Uses of Sabotage*. New York: Dial Publishing Co., n.d. 21 pp.

Williams, Ben H. *Eleven Blind Leaders or "Practical Socialism" and Revolutionary Tactics from an I.W.W. Standpoint*. New Castle, PA: I.W.W. Publishing Bureau, n.d. 29 pp.

Woodruff, Abner E. *The Evolution of Industrial Democracy*. Chicago: I.W.W. Press, n.d. 45 pp.

Unpublished Manuscripts and Transcripts of Oral Testimony

Abrams, Irving. Untitled memoir. Chicago, n.d.

Carey, George W. "The Vessel, the Deed and the Idea. The Paterson Anarchists, 1895-1908." Typescript.

Hacker, Abbe. "The Anarchist Influence on the Industrial Workers of the World." Typescript, Verticle File, Labadie Collection, University of Michigan Library.

Montgomery, David. "Trade Union Practice and the Origins of Syndicalism in the United States." Paper read at the Sorbonne, 1969, Paris, France.

Ninkovich, Frank. "Interview With Irving Abrams." Transcript of oral history interview. Chicago: Roosevelt University, 1970.

Robinson, Cedric. "The First Attack is the Attack on Culture." Paper read at Afro-Latin Cultural Festival, 20 April 1975, at State University, New York, Binghamton. Mimeographed.

Trautmann, William E. "The Power of Folded Arms and Thinking Bayonets." Typescript. Detroit: Walter P. Reuther Library, Wayne State University, 1937.

Vogel, Virgil J. "The Historians and the Industrial Workers of the World." Term paper. Chicago: University of Chicago, 1955.

Williams, Ben H. "Saga of the One Big Union—American Labor in the Jungle." Detroit: Walter P. Reuther Library, Wayne State University, n.d.

Wisotsky, Isidore. "Such A Life." Typescript. New York: Tamiment Collection, Elmer Holmes Bobst Library.

Wortman, Roy. "Oral History Interview With Mr. Paul Sebestyen [Sebastian] on Akron's Rubber Strike and on General Ideological Background." Typescript, Verticle File, Labadie Collection, University of Michigan Library, 1970.

Interviews

Abrams, Esther. Chicago, December 13, 1983.

Avrich, Paul. New York, June 4, 1983.

Buhle, Paul. Providence, Rhode Island, October 25, 1983.

Cortez, Carlos. Chicago, December 16, 1983.

Creagh, Ronald. Cambridge, MA, Feb. 12, 1982.

Dolgoff, Sam and Esther. New York, June 3, 1983.

Falk, Candace. Berkeley, California, August 7 and 9, 1984.

Ferrua, Pietro. Portland, Oregon, July 25, 26, and 27, 1984.

Green, Archie. Cambridge, MA, March 29, 1983; San Francisco, August 13, 1984.

O'Connor, Harvey. Little Compton, R.I., February 4, 1983.

Preston, William. New York, December 11, 1983.

Rosemont, Franklin. Chicago, May 6 and 7, 1985.

Stavis, Barrie. New York, December 12, 1983.

Thompson, Fred. Chicago, December 13, 14, 15, and 16, 1983.

Thorne, Ahrne. New York, December 9, 1983.

Index

A

Abrams, Irving, 26, 28
Addis, Henry, 81
Agricultural Workers Organization,
See I.W.W.
Akron Ohio Rubber Strike, 26
Alarm, 70
American Federation of Labor
(A.F.L.), 96, 98; and the origin of
the I.W.W., 4; and the Cooks and
Waiters Union, 138–139
American Labor Union (A.L.U.), 2,
47, 56, 73, 110
American Labor Union Journal, 60, 75
Anarchism, 6, 21–22, 56, 58, 71,
146, 165; and formation of
I.W.W., 56, 58, 69–90; and In-
dustrial Unionism, 6, 70–73;
I.W.W.'s founding convention,
69–90; and I.W.P.A. 50–53. *See
also* anarcho-Syndicalism; "Right
to Existence" group
Anarchist, 82
Anarchist Congress, 83
Anarcho-Syndicalism, 29, 62, 94–95,
108, 113, 120, 122–123, 139, 144,
146; (*see also* European syndicalism; French syndicalism; G.G.T.);
American foundations, 49, 90;
origins of, 49–52; tactics of, 29,
129, 139. *See also* direct action;
general strike; sabotage
Anti-authoritarian International, 89

Anti-patriotism, 109, 114
Anti-militarist propaganda, 92
Anderson, Nels, 29
Arbeiter-Zeiting, 70
Ashleigh, Charles: *Rambling Kid,* 29

B

Bakunin, Michael, 50–52, 76, 88–89
Barnes, Donald, 55, 111
Bazora, Florecio, 83
Beard, Charles and Mary, 55
Beatty, Bessy, 46
Berger, Victor, 73, 121
Berkman, Alexander, 82
Berth, Edouard, 61
Black International. *See* I.W.P.A.
Blumer, Herbert, 35
Borah, Senator William E., 30
Bohn, Frank, 63
Bowen, Sterling, 13, 15
Brauer Zeitung, 59, 60
Brazier, Richard, 13, 28, 129
Brewery Workman's Union (B.W.U.),
54, 58, 60
Brissenden, Paul F., 2, 21; and the
Chicago anarchists, 71–72; impact
of C.G.T. on I.W.W., 20, 100, 107,
110; I.W.W. membership, 24–25;
origin of I.W.W., 1, 3–4, 53–54
Brooks, John G., 21, 25
Brotherhood of Timber Workers
(B.T.W.), 32
Buhle, Paul, 57–58

C

Carey, George, 49–50
Chaplin, Ralph, 79, 112, 115
Chicago Debating Club, 82, 102
"Chicago Idea," 51, 53, 70–72, 79
Clements, Travers, 54
Colorado Journeymen Tailor's
    Union, 70, 87
Confederation General du Travail
    (C.G.T.) Bourses du Travail, 131;
    Charter of Amiens, 102; Congress
    at Tours, 101; differences with
    I.W.W., 48, 95–100; and the
    general strike, 61–62; impact on
    I.W.W., 20, 24, 46, 53, 106,
    93–116, 119, 146, 153; struggle
    against employment agencies,
    131–132. *See also* French
    syndicalism
Conlin, Joseph, 24, 32–33, 72,
    111–112
Co-operative Commonwealth, 63,
    142
Cornelissen, Christian, 52
Craft Unionism, 25, 36, 98–99,
    139–140
Criminal syndicalism, 4, 22, 111
Crow, John, 31–33
Culture of Poverty, 10, 12, 157n.30
Czolgosz, Leon, 81

D

Daily People, 61
Dave, Victor, 53
Debs, Eugene V., 73, 78; and "In-
    dustrial Union Manifesto," 65–66

DeLeon, Daniel, 76, 111, 121, 137;
    and European syndicalism, 60,
    62; and I.W.W.'s "Preamble,"
    65–66; and January Conference,
    62–63; and S.L.P., 86: and
    S.T.L.A., 61–62
Demonstrator, 81–82, 88
Die Autonomie, 82
Direct Action, 23, 29, 40–41, 88, 95,
    109, 113–114, 118, 125–126,
    131–132, 134–138
Downing, Mortimer, 87
Dual Unionism, 98
Dubofsky, Melvyn, frontier activism
    and the I.W.W., 55–57, 110; and
    the "Culture of Poverty," 10, 12,
    157n. 30; and origins of I.W.W.,
    1–4
Dulles, Foster Rhea, 55
Duluth, Minnesota, 49

E

Ebert, Justus, 41
Edwards, Alfred S., 78
Eight-hour movement, 70–71
Employment sharks, 9, 126–134
Engles, Frederick, 76
Esteve, Pedro, 49–50
Ettor, Joseph, 98
European syndicalism, 2–3, 7,
    20–21, 29, 38, 45, 66–67, 93; and
    American Labor Movement 48;
    and DeLeon, 58–60, 66–67, 75;
    I.W.W.'s relationship to, 17,
    93–118, 121–122. *See also* C.G.T.;
    French syndicalism
Everest, Wesley, 79

F

Fackel, 70
First International, 52
Floaters, 8–9, 13, 144
Foster, William, Z., 96–97, 134
Foner, Philip, 24, 110
Ford and Shur case, 87, 113–114
Fox, Jay, 73; and *Demonstrator,* 81–82; and I.W.W. founding convention, 81
Free Society, 81
Free Society Group, 81
Free Speech Fights, see I.W.W.
Freiheit, 51, 53
French Syndicalism, 46, 61, 88, 123–124, 131, 160n. 10; boring-from-within debate, 96–100; culture of 106; symbols of, 15–16; and the IWW, 72, 93–118. *See also* C.G.T.

G

General Confederation of Labor. *See* C.G.T
General Lockout, 105
General Strike, 51, 60, 83, 95, 107, 123; and C.G.T. 100–102; and I.W.W. 80–81, 104–105, 109, 113–114, 123–124, 135–137
Gilbert, James B., 9
Goldman, Emma, 85, 173n. 52; and European syndicalism, 83; and Free Society group, 81; free speech fight, San Diego, 86–87; on General Strike, 83; and P.L.M., 83
Golos Truda, 89

Green, Archie, 156n.20
Green, James, 32–33
Griffuelhes, Victor, 61
Guabello, A., 89
Guesde, Jules, 62
Guillaume, James, 52
Gusfield, Joseph, 35–36

H

Hacker, Louis M., 55
Hagerty, Thomas J., and European syndicalism, 75–76; and general strike, 80, 105; and Haymarket martyrs, 74–75; and Industrial Unionism, 73–76; and "Industrial Union Manifesto," 65, 73, 75; and I.W.W.'s "Preamble," 37, 65–67, 73; and January Conference, 76
Haslewood, Fred W., 127
Havel, Hippolyte, 81
Haymarket, 54, 69, 80–81, 72, 74–75, 167n.29; and "Chicago Idea," 70–71; remembered by I.W.W.'s, 68, 79; in speeches at I.W.W. founding convention, 69–70, 88
Haywood, William D. (Big Bill), 26, 169n.61; and arrest in Steunenberg case, 86, 105, 123; and general strike, 81; and Haymarket affair, 69; and "One Big Union," 64; and syndicalism, 37–38
Hill, Joe, 10, 15–16, 79
Hobo, 8, 15, 28–29, 34, ballads 10; culture, 147; jungle, 137
Hobohemia, 29
Home colony, 82

I

Il Proletario, 44
Immigrant activism, 1–2, 67; and
    anarchistism, 81–87, 89–90;
    artists; 12–15, 21, 29, 144;
    intellectuals, 12–15, 21, 58–62,
    81; and European anarcho-
    syndicalism 48–53
Immigrant anarchists, 58, 72, 89. *See
    also* I.W.W.
Industrial Pioneer, 116
Industrial Union Bulletin (I.U.B.), 106,
    129, 134
Industrial strike, 124
Industrial Unionism: 6, 7, 38, 44, 54,
    56, 88–90, 111, 119–120, 122,
    131, 133, 135, 138–139, 145–147,
    151, 176n.12, 181n.27; American
    foundations, 70–72; and "Chicago
    Idea," 70–71, 79, 88; and C.G.T.
    100, 108–109; and I.W.W. 62,
    73–76, 88, 119; tactics of,
    109–110
Industrial Worker, 5, 11, 14, 27, 38,
    40, 68, 79, 87, 92, 95, 118, 121,
    128, 129, 133, 136, 138, 141, 148,
    149, 150
Industrial Workers Club of Chicago,
    77, 102
Industrial Workers of the World
    (I.W.W.), Agricultural Workers
    Organization, 163n.42; anti-politi-
    cal position of 121; (*see also* S.L.P.;
    S.P.; S.T.L.A.); constitution, 33–34,
    76; European influences on, 1, 7,
    20–21; (*see also* French syndical-
    ism; C.G.T.); industrial unionism;
    founding convention, 20–21, 57,
    59, 64–65, 69–90, 159n. 4; Free
    Speech Fights, 21–34, 86 162n.39,
    (Missoula) 128–132, (San Diego),
    86, (Spokane) 10, 24, 27,
    126–128, 134–135, 180n.10;
    General administration, 34; "In-
    dustrial Union Manifesto," 36, 63,
    65, 73, 75–76, 111, 120, 138; as
    labor union, 24–26, 31–36; *Little
    Red Songbook,* 28, 34, 104, 129;
    Local 85 of Chicago, 78; Mixed
    local, 7–8, 12, 33–34, 144–145;
    origins of, 1–4, 20–21, 53–67;
    overall brigade, 135; poetry 8, 9,
    13–15, 124–125; "Preamble," 36,
    66, 73, 76, 78, 80, 137, 154n.9;
    role of art forms, 6, 9, 15–17, 39,
    106, 114–115, 119–140; second
    convention, 34, 78; sexism and
    paternalism in, 163n.40; songs of,
    10, 15, 28, 39, 104, 112, 129;
    worker intellectuals and artists in,
    1, 13–14, 16, 21, 122–123, 144,
    147, 149–150. *See also* immigrant
    activism
International Anarchists Association,
    82
International Socialist Review, 46
International Trade Union
    Secretariat, 96
International Workingmen's Associa-
    tion, 87, 166n.21
International Working People's
    Association (Black International),
    50; and "Pittsburg Manifesto," 51,
    70, 79; and "Chicago Idea,"
    70–71, 79
Irritant strike, 124
Isaak, Marie, 81

Italian Socialist Party, 61
Italian Silkworkers Union, 89
Italian Syndicalism, 49–50, 168n.52

J

Jensen, Vernon, 57
Jorhaux, 97
Jungle, 8–9, 12–13, 28–29, 137, 144

K

Kendrick, Benjamin, 55
Klemensic, Al, 70, 82, 87–88
Knights of Labor, 2, 60–62, 69, 77
Kornbluh, Joyce, 13, 22
Kropotkin, Peter, 50
Kuhn, Henry, 63

L

LaMonte, Robert Rives, 46
La Questione Social, 49, 89
Labadie, Joseph, 74
Labriola, Antonio, 61, 168n.52
Lawrence Textile Strike, 37, 41, 98
Levine, Lewis, 46–47, 53, 95, 100,
  131
Liberator, The, (Chicago), 82, 88
Liberator, The, (New York), 8
Librera Socioligica, 50
Liberty, 74
Little Red Songbook. See I.W.W.
Lum, Dyer D., 77

M

Magón, Ricardo Flores, 28, 83, 84,
  156n.17

Magonistas, 7, 35, 83
Malatesta, Errico, 50
Marx, Karl, 76
Marxism, 120, 146; and industrial
  unionism, 6, 66
Masses, The, 8
McKee, 111
Merlino, Saverio, 50
Mexican Revolution, 7; I.W.W. in,
  35, 163n.41
Metal Worker's Federation of
  America, 71
Mr. Block, 150
Mixed local. *See* I.W.W.
Morris, William, 141
Most, Johann, 50–51, 53, 82
Mother Earth, 83, 85–86
Moyer, Charles, 86, 105, 123

N

Nacht, Siegfried. *See* Roller, Arnold
National Civic Federation, 122
Nativist perspective, 154n. 6
New Review, 46
New York Social Revolutionary
  Club, 51

O

One Big Union, 64
Owenites, 52
Overall Brigade. *See* I.W.W.

P

Paris Commune, 50
Parker, Carlton, 10
Parlimentary Socialism, 118, 146
Parsons, Albert, 51, 68, 79–80

Parsons, Lucy, 73; and I.W.W. found-
    ing convention, 67, 80; and
    general strike, 80–81, 105; and
    Liberator (Chicago), 82
Partial strike, 124
Partido Liberal Mexicana (P.L.M.),
    35, 83, 87
Passive resistance, 133–135, 138
Passive strike, 124
Paterson anarchists. See "Right to
    Existence" Group
Patoud, E., 107, 142
Pelloutier, Fernand, 53, 61
Pettibone, G.E., 86, 105, 123
Petit Republique Socialist, La, 61
Peukert, Joseph, 73, 82, 172n. 41
Pierrot, 53
"Pittsburg Manifesto," 51, 70, 79
Pouget, Emile, 53, 60–61, 94, 107,
    142
Preston, William, 24, 57
Proletarian cultural movement, 21
Proudhon, Pierre Joseph, 51, 76

Q

Quinn, M.B., 77

R

Reed, John; and mixed locals, 8
Reclus, Elisee, 50
Regeneratión, 83
Reynolds, Pat, 69
"Right To Existence" Group, 49, 58,
    89; Universita Populaire, 50
Roller, Arnold (Siegfried Nacht), 53,
    102; and "Social General Strike,"
    82, 124
Rosemont, Franklin, 147

S

Sab Cat, 23, 113–116, 178n.45
Sabotage, 16, 23, 29, 51, 107,
    109–110, 112–115, 135, 137,
    181n. 32. See also sab cat
St. John, Vincent, 38
Salvation Army, 130, 147
Sanger, Margaret, 35
Scab, 16
Sebestyen, Paul, 26
Second International, 61
Shatoff, Bill, 89
Shelly, Percy Bysshe, 103–104
Sherman, Charles O., 89
Silent agitators, 113, 115
Sinclair, Upton, 161n. 28; Jimmie
    Higgins, 29
Smith, Clarence, 36–37
"Social General Strike." See Arnold
    Roller
Social Science League, 81
Socialism, 22, 38, 46, 54
Socialist Labor Party (S.L.P.), 72; and
    DeLeon, 60–62; and factionalism,
    77–78; and I.W.W. founding con-
    vention, 72; and I.W.W.'s "Pre-
    amble," 37; and January
    Conference, 63; S.L.P. and I.W.W.
    84–86, 120–121
Socialist Party (S.P.), 107; and
    factionalism 77–78; and German
    model of trade union, 65; and
    I.W.W. founding convention, 52,
    72–73; and I.W.W.'s "Preamble,"
    37; left wing of 64–65
Socialist Trade and Labor Alliance
    (S.T. and L.A.), 54, 66, 76; and
    DeLeon, 61–62; and I.W.W. found-
    ing convention, 57; and January
    Conference, 63

Solidarity, 9, 23, 46, 79, 97, 108, 109, 113, 114, 115, 129, 137
Souers, Ralph E., 47–48, 53
Spanish speaking I.W.W. locals, 174n.59
Spargo, John, 53
Speed, George, 87
Speilman, Jean, 85
Spies, August, 51, 68–69
Sunday, Billy, 147
Symes, Lillian, 54
Syndicalism, 122, 146, 166n.21; American origins, 48–53, 70–71; European syndicalism, 2–3, 21, 29, 38, 45, 59–60, 66–67, 75; and First International, 52; and Emma Goldman, 83; and Industrial Unionism, 66; and I.W.W., 66–57. *See* also French syndicalism and C.G.T.
Syndicalist League of North America, 46, 98, 100

T

Thompson, Fred, 24, 32–33; impact of C.G.T. on I.W.W., 106–108
Tie Vapauteen, 31, 49, 84
Tramp, 9, 13, 28, 34, 144; anti-tramp bias 10, 12
Trautmann, William E., 65, 88–89, 106, 110–111, 181n.27; and European syndicalism, 59–60; expulsion from the S.P., 78; and I.W.W. founding convention 88, 94; and I.W.W. "Preamble," 65–66; and C.G.T., 94, 106; and industrial unionism, 60, 62; and passive resistance, 134–135; at second I.W.W. convention 36–37; and S.L.P. 58–60, 62, 66

Tridone, Andre, 53
Tucker, Benjamin, 73–74
Tugwell, Rexford, 10
Turner, John, 53
Tyler, Robert, 24

U

Union of Russian Workers, 89
United Mine Workers (U.M.W.), 50
Universita Populaire, 50

V

Verbote, 70
Voice of Labor, 62, 75

W

Walkout, 16
Walling, William English, 46, 78
Walsh, J.H., 137
Weekly People, 61
Western Federation of Miners (W.F.M.), 47, 54–58, 64, 73, 81, 86–87, 110; departure from I.W.W., 120; and Paterson anarchists, 89; role in origins of the I.W.W., 2–3
Wisconsin School of Labor Economics, 21
Wobbly, 8–9, 16, 29, 55, 79, 110–112, 122, 143, 146, 149; art forms, 122, 144; as artists, 14, 147; etymology of, 156n.20; and French syndicalists, 95; as homeless drifters, 12; in songs, 28, 112, 129; and syndicalism, 111; and syndicalist tactics, 110, 113
Woman Rebel, 35

Wooden Shoe (sabot), 15–16, 112

Y

Yellen, Samuel, 79
Yvetot, George, 5, 61

DATE DUE
